# A WOMAN
# OF DISTINCTION.

To Kitty —
you know this story
But

J. Hayden Hollingsworth
4/26/03

To order additional copies of this book, contact:
Xlibris Corporation
1-888-795-4274
www.Xlibris.com
Orders@Xlibris.com
16841

To Billy Hagan, grandson of Sallie Cocke,
without whose persistence this memoir
would not have been published

# CHAPTER I

As the train was crossing the Hudson river, Mammy Sophy had her nose pressed to the window. Although we had made the trip before, the fascination of the New York skyline still amazed her. The difference from Atlanta in the 1890s was striking. I watched her, wondering what must be going through her mind.

"Lawd da murcy, Miss Sallie," she said, not taking her eyes from the window, "Look at dat boat down yonder!" An ocean liner, longer than a city block, was edging toward its berth. How different that must have looked from the ship that brought Mammy's mother to Charleston, giving birth to Sophy on the way. Born on a slave trade ship from West Africa in the 1820s, freed by President Lincoln but choosing to remain in our family all of her seventy years, surviving the Civil War, the burning of Atlanta and the horrors of Reconstruction, it was hard to imagine all she had been through. What a life she had led! How could any of us have survived without Mammy and all those who stayed with my family, particularly right after the war!

And now we were on a month's holiday to New York to visit friends—Mrs. Patrick Calhoun, our hostess, among them. Mammy Sophy and I would bring news from "the sunny South," as Mrs. Calhoun referred to it in a somewhat deprecating way. I enjoyed spending time with ladies from Georgia who had moved to New York. It was pleasant to exchange stories of our current lives and how different they were, but we didn't spend much time discussing our younger, growing up years, which were difficult beyond belief. That we had all survived and through good fortune and marriage had re-established comfortable lives was a blessing we all shared. Since I was born in 1865, my first childhood memories were of the ruins of Atlanta. Knowing nothing of what the city had been before Sherman destroyed it I couldn't know how much had been lost but I did know we were more fortunate than most. Many had never recovered from the losses. These New York friends shared the same history as I, sisters of a sad time, but sisters who had moved on in different lives. Although we lived a thousand miles apart, in a sense we were still family. That's why these visits to New York were so pleasant.

One afternoon, shortly after our arrival, Mrs. Calhoun had one of her many luncheons where she entertained her friends. This particular time, I didn't know many of the women and they didn't seem particularly interested in knowing me. They were natives of New York, or so it seemed; not a Southerner in the bunch. I sat to the side and listened. Most of the conversation had to do with New York politics, a subject in which I had little interest and no knowledge. But then, I heard a name that caught my attention. Someone mentioned that Varina Davis seemed to be settling into her winter home in New York with ease. Since the death of her husband, Jefferson, the preceding year, her friends had been concerned about her.

"Varina Davis?" I asked. "She's living in New York now?"

Mrs. Calhoun looked at me impatiently. "Yes, Sally, she and her daughter, Winnie, live in an apartment not too far from here." Then she returned to the conversation.

"Do you suppose I could meet her?" I asked.

"Sally Johnson!" Mrs. Calhoun had persisted in always using my maiden name. "What on earth could you possibly have to say that would interest Mrs. Jefferson Davis?" she inquired. Everyone laughed at my impertinence. My hostess had an imperious manner that I was finding increasingly irritating, so I decided not to elaborate, but Mrs. Calhoun insisted. "Do tell us how you know such a famous woman."

"I would prefer Mrs. Davis tell you herself," I said, hoping to end my embarrassment.

Not to be denied, Mrs. Calhoun said, "Oh no, my dear. You tell us right now. After luncheon we shall call on Mrs. Davis and check up on your little story."

Whether the story was a spellbinder or they were intent on seeing me make a fool of myself, I couldn't say but they listened with great attention.

My mother, Mary Willis Cobb, and Varina Davis were great friends before the war when my uncle, Howell Cobb, was in Congress. Senator Davis had just married Varina Howell in 1845. They had a profound influence on my mother and her subsequent marriage. In fact, were it not for Varina Davis, it's not likely that I ever would have been born.

I gave a few details of what had happened to my mother, her flight to Washington and her subsequent failed romance, but I left them dangling. Having been roundly ignored by this group, I was enjoying having them in my control for a few minutes. After luncheon we took carriages across the park to Varina Davis' apartment.

As soon as we were seated and I was introduced, Mrs. Davis put her hands to her cheeks and said, "Sarah Cobb Johnson! You're Mary Willis Cobb's daughter? I can't believe it. She pulled a chair close to hers, asked Mrs. Calhoun to move aside and make room for me to sit next to her. We spent the rest of the afternoon recounting the events of the late 1840s and early 1850s. What I had said earlier was true: The turn of events that took my mother to Washington in 1848 changed her life and ultimately led to her marriage to my father. In looking back at my life, the stories my mother told me of those furious years before the Civil War, and how it changed her forever are vivid memories to this day.

If Little Howell had not died, maybe things would have been different for my mother. So many children died, mostly in the first year of their lives, that it shouldn't have been such a shock. Of course, who was to say how she would have reacted had he been her son, instead of her nephew? She wasn't even married at the time, let alone having suffered through the illness of one of her own children, so she was not really the one to speak. Then, of course, it depends on how the child dies—that's bound to have an effect on what happens. It would be a terrible burden even for the strongest of women. In this case, Mary Anne, Mary Willis' sister-in-law, was never a strong woman. She remembered when Mary Anne and Howell, my uncle, announced their engagement, Mary Anne took to her bed for a week, the emotional strain of it was just too much for her. Of course, they were both very young. Uncle Howell was only 19 in 1834 and had just graduated from the University of Georgia. My mother was only six years old when her brother married, but she remembered all that Mayon, as she was called, went through after the engagement was announced. If Mayon Lamar had been an only child, it might have been more understandable, but she had a younger brother, John, and he was about as normal as they come. He didn't have a nerve in his body when it came to things like that. It wasn't that he was insensitive; he was the gentlest, most sensitive man anyone ever met, so my mother told me, but he always had himself under control. Not Mayon—*everything* was a crisis to her. If it looked like rain when she'd planned a garden party, then you would think the end of the world was at hand.

Life had been easy for Mother so it was difficult for her to understand how Mayon felt when she and John lost their parents. That would be hard, she could imagine, although everyone knew people who have been through that and gone right on with their lives. Mother's family life was solid and loving. She and Uncle Howell were blessed by a rich and good life, with many faithful servants. The plantation was one of the largest in northeastern Georgia and it was well run, as were their holdings in Jefferson County in central Georgia. My grandparents were so good to Uncle Howell and Mother that it made them feel like nothing bad could ever happen. Of course, no one born in the 1820s lived very long without realizing that all sorts of terrible things could and did happen. It didn't matter whose family they were in, tragedy could come to anyone. But my mother never was frightened about things like that. Maybe that's the difference. Mayon was always frightened. It didn't matter if it was a thunder storm or somebody ill with yellow fever, she always expected the worst. Brother John helped her through hard times, particularly after their parents died. That's why she relied on him so much. She acted as though she couldn't draw a breath without John by her side. Mother thought after Mayon and Uncle Howell married, things would change. Being Mrs. Howell Cobb, a member of one of the most prominent families in Georgia, if not the whole South, everyone thought that would make her feel a little more secure, but it didn't.

All during the years of their marriage, Mayon had been frail and spent much of her time in bed. Uncle Howell was practicing law then, but in 1837 became interested in politics and was appointed solicitor general for northeast Georgia. He was strongly Unionist and had little interest in slavery, although the family had many servants on several plantations. Despite Mayon's illness, Howell became well known and was elected to Congress in 1842. He was 26 and my mother was 13. It was exciting to have a brother who knew the President! Mother said that he advanced very quickly in Congress because of his debating skills, his broad nationalist views, and his ability to avoid rancorous sectional debates. When Congressman Drumgoole of Virginia died in 1848, Uncle Howell was elected Democratic leader in Congress. But about that time Little Howell was born and things were never the same. Babies, even healthy ones, were always a worry back in those days. It's not much better now. Measles, whooping cough, chicken pox—all those things were happening all the time—but diphtheria, the pox, and infantile diarrhea—they were the terrible problems for children. Mother told me she had a hard time remembering when there wasn't some family that had just lost a child, or was getting ready to, from one of those dreadful diseases. Even strong children could be playing and looking just fine one day and in the ground before the week was out. But Little Howell never drew a well breath in his short life, so Mayon had double the worries of any other young mother. Mother was an old woman herself and had lived through the war and the death of so many people before she realized that sometimes death will not be denied, regardless of how hard you fight. She used to think that Mayon just about worried herself to

death over Little Howell and it was because of all that worry, that
fear Mayon had, that my mother's life got turned in a way she
would never have guessed. Even if she could have known what the
future held, it's hard to say she should have done things differently.
People don't get a lot of choices in life and, at eighteen, Mother
hadn't learned how important it was to know when a critical decision
comes along and to pay close attention.

John Lamar, Mayon's brother, was six months older than
Mother but they had known each other since they were children.
After Mayon and my uncle were married and came to visit in Athens,
John came around to the Cobb house a lot. Before Little Howell
was born, Mayon wouldn't go anywhere by herself. Her husband
would bring her to Athens, then, after a week or so, he would go
back to Washington. When Mayon was strong enough for travel,
John would have to ride the train back to Washington with her.
Sometimes my mother would go back with them. The trip from
Athens to Washington was a long one, and the trains sometimes
took several days, depending on the weather. That meant she and
John spent a lot of time together. Mayon didn't take a mammy
with her, so having Mother along was a big help to her. Travel tired
her out, as you can imagine, so while Mayon was resting, John and
Mother spent the long afternoons and evenings watching the
countryside slide by as they crept north. Sometimes they would
have to spend two nights on the way, stopping at hotels along the
railroad. Mrs. Cobb wanted Mother to take Aggie, one of the
servants, with her. She remembered the first time her mother
suggested it.

"Mary Willis, Aggie would be a big help, and that way you
won't have to worry about carrying the luggage. John will need
some help, and I know he would love to have Aggie along." Aggie
was the same age as Mother and had been with the family ever
since my grandfather, Colonel Cobb, bought her mother. Growing
up, they were more playmates than servant and mistress, but Mother
didn't want her to go on the trip with them. She felt that she was
responsible for Aggie even though she really wasn't. Mother
wouldn't have had any harm come to her for the world. Who knows

what could happen during the night when they were stopped in the hotel and Aggie was off looking for some place to sleep? She was a handsome colored girl and Mother knew how men were, especially when they're traveling. As it turned out, Aggie had plenty of trips to Washington and New York with Mary Willis, right up through the time she was a mammy herself and till she died just a year or two ago, but she didn't go on those first train rides.

During those visits my mother saw a style of life very different from the pleasant but simple life in Georgia. I remember Mother saying how she was surprised when she was told that Uncle Howell, as speaker of the house of representatives, was next in line to become President if something happened to the President and the Vice President. Of course, a lot of people were thinking of that, since that's how President Tyler came into office when President Harrison died. Tippecanoe and Tyler, too, turned out to be just John Tyler and only one month after the inauguration. President Harrison didn't wear a topcoat, caught pneumonia at the inauguration and was dead in a month. President Tyler decided not to run for re-election and James Polk became President. He was a democrat and had been speaker of the house before he moved to The White House. In 1849, when Uncle Howell was elected speaker, Mother, said it took 63 ballots before he finally was declared the winner. All the uncertainties of politics made Mayon nervous about living in Washington. Even before Little Howell was born, Mother said it was not unusual for Mayon to stay in her room for several weeks at a time, having servants or my mother bring her meals to her.

John wasn't always in Washington with Mother, but they enjoyed each other's company when they were together. John was very popular in Athens, as well as throughout the state. The Lamar family was even wealthier than the Cobb family and as a handsome, charming, a wonderful horseman, John was on everybody's guest list. When back in Athens, they would be at the same gala from time to time, but Mother was always with someone else. She watched him with all the belles and could tell any one of them could have been his. All he had to do was ask. She remembered being at a garden party in Savannah the year after Howell and

Mayon were married. She was with a terribly boring cotton merchant from Charleston. If he had ever been in a waltz figure before, her feet surely couldn't tell it. About halfway through the first set, her feet were about to fall off. Mother told him she would like a breath of air, so she walked out on the veranda, wondering how she would get through the weekend with this man who not only couldn't dance a step, but reeked of garlic. It was in May, a gorgeous night and the scent of magnolia and jasmine was filling the cool night air. Suddenly, there was John, standing beside her. He was having about as bad a time as she, so he said, but at least he could dance with whomever he pleased. When she mentioned that, he said, "You're the only one I want to dance with, Mary Willis." She was so surprised. She knew how she felt about him, but he had never said one word or even given her a look in all their time together that indicated he thought of her as anything other than Mayon's sister-in-law.

After that night, they saw each other frequently. She had never felt such a sense of contentment and excitement all mixed up together as when she was with him. To hear his carriage coming up the drive, his voice calling out for the stable boy to come get his horse made her catch her breath. And he seemed to feel the same way. He was so kind to the stable boy—he would bring sweet cane from his fields for him to eat. Most of the men who called were surly and rude to the servants, but John Lamar was never like that. Everyone loved to see him come. Even her mother and the Colonel enjoyed having him there, but they didn't realize that John and their daughter were in love. Somehow her parents thought that they were more like brother and sister, as if he had taken Howell's place in her life now that he was in Washington most of the time.

Then Little Howell was born and things began to change. Back in those days, it took a long time to get news from Washington. The telegraph that Howell was able to use in Washington was just in its early stages of development, and sometimes the family in Athens had trouble getting the messages. When Little Howell was born, Howell telegraphed that Mayon had had a son, but he wasn't strong. No one knew what that meant, but they knew it would be a burden on Mayon. Since she would have a long convalescence, they knew Mayon would need help. Howell had a lot of servants in Washington, but Aggie and my mother went along with John to help after Little Howell was born. John stayed several weeks and would come back every so often, but Aggie and Mother were there for three months. As soon as she saw the baby, Mother knew they were in for trouble. He didn't weigh more than four pounds when he was born, but that wasn't the worst part. It was his color. His little lips, his fingers and toes, were as blue as if they had been painted with pokeberry. Mayon didn't have any milk, but there were plenty of servants who had babies, so they had wet nurses around the house. Milk for the baby wasn't a problem. Getting him to nurse was. He would feed for a few minutes, then would be panting like a puppy on a hot day and wouldn't take any more. He would have to eat every hour or so just to get enough nourishment into him. That meant they had to have several different wet nurses. Mother never asked if their own babies were getting enough milk, but she suspected they were. Little Howell took such tiny bits, the mammies probably had enough to go around. The doctor said he was born with a weak heart but he might outgrow it. She'd never seen anything like that baby, but she knew he wasn't going to outgrow whatever was wrong with him.

Uncle Howell was busy in Congress all the time. The problems with the slavery issue were becoming more difficult by the month, and Mother could tell from the drawing room conversations he was having with his friends from congress things weren't going well. Women weren't included in those discussions, as if they didn't have sense enough to understand, but everyone understood things were getting worse. Mayon was in bed all the time. She was able to take very little responsibility for Little Howell, so Aggie and my mother really took care of him, except for the nursing. During that time, John and Mother were together in the evenings. In that big house, there were lots of servants, but her brother was at the capitol and Mayon was always in bed, Aggie and the wet nurses were looking after Little Howell, so they were left alone. She knew then, and John did too, that they wanted to be together always.

They talked about mentioning it to Howell, and then, of course, John would have to ask the Colonel, but everyone was so distracted about the problems with Mayon and Little Howell, to say nothing of the troubled times in the government, they thought it better to wait until a quieter, more peaceful time. They didn't know then such a time would never come. Not in their lifetime together.

When Little Howell was almost a year old when he began to get worse. He'd never been able to roll over in his crib or even hold his head up. He reminded Mother of a blue rag doll that didn't have enough stuffing. She didn't think he ever gained more than a few pounds in the eleven months he lived. Mayon had been caring for him as best she could, but everyone knew the servants had been doing most of it. When they let the family in Athens know the end was near, Mother went back to Washington to help any way she could. In the last week, the baby didn't take any milk, no matter how often it was offered to him. The doctor came and sat with him for a while, but said his heart was weak as a person a hundred years old. The tonics he had been given never seemed to help, and now he couldn't even swallow those.

Mayon knew what was coming. Mother supposed she had always known but had been hoping that somehow he would get stronger. Mayon spent most of her time in her room, but every day she would come into the nursery and stand by Little Howell's crib. Her eyes were flat and expressionless. She rarely spoke to whoever was in the room. She knew what they would say if she asked a question: "He's just the same, Ma'am." So she didn't ask. The night he died, my mother and her brother sat with him. Aggie sat over in the corner with her hands folded and clamped between her knees as if she was trying to hold on to his life for him. She had worked so hard to help, but, of course, she couldn't do anything. Right at the last as his tiny jaw hung slack, his head, not as big as your fist, pulling to the side whenever he took a breath. They could see his color darkening, like a lamp being slowly turned down. His breathing was faltering and the intervals became further and further apart until finally there was a little sigh—the last breath leaving and no more coming in.

"Lawd! Have mercy!" Aggie moaned. Neither of them said anything. Uncle Howell just reached over and patted his sister on the knee then walked into Mayon's room to tell her. There was no crying, no moaning, just an awful quiet. It was so still Mother said she could hear her own heart beating.

Not long after that, John and Mother began to talk about marriage. They had waited until things had settled down after Little Howell's death. John went to Washington to talk to Uncle Howell before he even said anything to Mother's parents. They thought with Mayon's having been so weakened by all she had been through they should ask Uncle Howell first how he felt about it. She had thought he would be pleased, but he wasn't. He said that it wouldn't be fair to ask Mayon to give up her brother so soon after she had lost her son. When John got back to Athens, Mother and the rest of the family were surprised. She hadn't thought that marrying John would be taking him away from Mayon. She had a husband of her own. John and my mother loved each other, and they both loved Mayon. Everyone was sad over what had happened to her, but they didn't see any reason that the rest of them should give up their lives, too. John felt the same way and they had even told a few of their friends that we were going to be married. Certainly, neither of them thought the Colonel and Sarah Cobb would have any objections. They knew what a fine man John Lamar was.

The rumors were flying, and although everyone was surprised that John Lamar, such a fine catch, would be marrying Mary Willis Cobb, everyone was delighted. Everyone except John's sister and my uncle. The doctors in Washington had told Uncle Howell that the shock of their marriage might be the death of Mayon; Mother hardly thought that was true, but she knew it would have to be faced.

Mother's parents told her one afternoon they would like to speak to her in the downstairs drawing room. She knew what it was about: Howell had sent them the news. As she was standing in the foyer, she could hear Ben, one of the slaves, working out in the flower garden. He didn't know what was going on in the house, but she could hear him singing:

> " 'Tain't no use to run from trubble
> 'Tain't no use—'taint no use!
> Eve done bit de apple—Adam done bit it too
> And out fell de worm dat's bitin' on you.
> 'Taint no use to run from trubble."

That didn't sound like a wedding song she wanted to sing. She could hear the Colonel talking to my grandmother. "Sarah," he said, "I'm convinced the doctors have exaggerated Mayon's condition, but I think it's wise that this engagement end. A family mixup could ruin Howell's career in Washington. No statesman can give his full attention to affairs of the country with anxiety at home. Serenity is of more importance at this stage of history than romance."

Before her mother could reply, Mother stepped into the drawing room. My grandmother was seated in her big wingback chair, her Bible in her hand. The Colonel stood behind her with his hand on her shoulder.

"Mother!" she said, as she walked to her.

"How long have you been standing there, Mary Willis?" she asked.

She ignored the question and stood in front of both of them. "I came to tell you that I am breaking off the engagement to John. I have sent him a message," she told them. Years later, my mother told me she was not sure why she spoke with such assurance. That may have been what her mind was thinking, but her heart was telling her something very different. Somehow she had made up her mind what she would do.

The Colonel looked shocked. I suppose he thought he would have to issue an order that she was expected to follow. His life in command had not deserted him. Instead of that, he looked at my mother with his eyes filling with tears and said, "My child, I . . . ."

She held up my hand and stopped him. "I could never be happy if I thought I had caused Mayon's death. So the engagement is over." She turned and started from the room.

"Wait! Mary Willis," Sarah called, "Don't go." But she kept right on walking, calling over her shoulder, "Please, Mother! I would like to be alone." In later years, she wondered if she had not left the room, if she had not followed the family wishes without so much as a dissenting word, how different things might have been. She doesn't have an answer, even after all this time, but had she not taken that course, then I would never have been born. I would be somebody else.

John Lamar was furious. He hadn't gotten back from Washington when all this happened, and not even talking with him about it had been a terrible thing to do to him. I supposed the strain of Little Howell had taken a toll on Mother, too, although she didn't realize it at the time. John was sure her family had forced her into the decision. They didn't—at least not consciously. She loved them so much. She was proud of Uncle Howell and what he had accomplished. It was certainly possible that he might run for the presidency some day. They still remembered all the family problems Andrew Jackson brought to the White House with his wife's death even before he took office. Jackson was elected in '28, the year my mother was born, but she remembered hearing about it when she was a little girl. When John got back to Athens, he was mad enough to fight a duel with somebody—anybody— about it, but he knew that wouldn't solve anything.

Poor Uncle Howell! He was desperate. His wife was in the midst of another nervous breakdown and he'd been told by doctors he trusted that she was close to death. Mother knew her brother loved her, but he didn't want to lose Mayon. He came home to Athens with a compromise. He suggested that my mother move to Washington and John stay in Georgia, but the engagement be left intact. He was confident that the separation would reassure Mayon and that, on her recovery, she might give her blessing to the marriage. Uncle Howell probably believed that, but in her heart Mother didn't think that Mayon would ever be the same. She had been a semi-invalid before all this happened and to think that she would rally to a state she had never known seemed ludicrous. Just as the family was having this discussion, John walked into the room. He stopped short, looking at Uncle Howell, and asked Mother, "What are they asking you to do now, Mary Willis?"

Uncle Howell walked over to him, knowing how angry John was, and put his hand on John's shoulder. Mother thought John might knock it off and who knows what might have happened then. Duels were still quite common, although John, himself, had not been insulted, a challenge could have certainly been issued.

"I want Mary Willis to go to Washington, John, as my hostess. As speaker of the house, I'm required to do a great amount of entertaining and Mayon, of course, is not able to help with that. Mary Willis will have a chance to meet many of the great statesmen of our time, and she will be a wonderful help to me. Mayon will be so grateful, I'm sure she will endorse your marriage in the future."

John thought about that for a moment. "Yes," he said very slowly, "Mary Willis may go to Washington with you, but as my wife. We will give you joint service."

Howell turned to his sister, a helpless look in his eyes. She took his hand in one of hers and John's in the other. "John will agree, brother Howell, when he really considers how little a few months' separation will mean to us in comparison to the danger our marriage might bring to his sister."

John stood there for a moment then raised her hand very slowly to his lips. So it was decided, much more quickly than she might have imagined, that Mother would move to Washington to live with Uncle Howell and Mayon. She had a week to get her things together, and again Aggie would go with her. No thought was given to the disruption their plans might have in the lives of the servants. They weren't called "slaves," although that's certainly what they were. The Cobb house in Athens was one of many mansions in that fine old university town. The number of servants varied from time to time because those who were visiting brought their own servants with them. There were twenty-three guest rooms in the main house, while all the servants lived in a small village on the back side of the property. It was in no way unusual for guests to remain for several months, particularly in the winter. Moving in and out of our house was something that was always happening. When guests would arrive, there would be a train of carriages pulling up in the circular drive, the servants wagon coming along behind. Mother's absence in the home would hardly be noticed by the servants, there was so much for them to do with all the guests and family that were always trooping through, but she knew that her mother and the Colonel would miss her terribly, as she would them.

During the week of packing, John came by several times, although he didn't have much to say. She wondered if he would truly wait. Half the belles in Georgia had their sights set on him and although the ones Mother knew said they were sad she was having to leave, she knew, deep down, they couldn't wait to have another chance with handsome John Lamar.

The train trip to Washington was by way of Marthasville, recently renamed Atlanta by the Western & Atlantic Railroad. They had made up that name and put it up on their station. It stuck and soon Marthasville became a thing of the past—just as her life in Georgia seemed about to become nothing more than a memory. Little could she have imagined what Atlanta would look like 17 years later when she became my mother. Aggie was excited about the train trip, about going to Washington and seeing the President, "Prezzerdint Poke," as she called him. She seemed to think they were all going to live in the same house, but it was a great adventure for her under any circumstance. It was hot and the windows let in more cinders and smoke than cool air. Keeping clean and neat was an impossibility. As Mother sat there in her many petticoats trying to make the best of an uncomfortable situation, she thought about what she might be losing. John was the light of her life, but if that were *really* so, why had she given in so easily to the demand that she break the engagement. It made her wonder if she had been as committed to him as she should have been, or was it just the romance of marrying a handsome and wealthy young man? If that were true, then maybe the time in

Washington would be a good thing. It would give them both a chance to re-evaluate the thoughts of their marriage.

Washington was nothing like the city it would become. There were very few hotels, most of the roads were no better than those of Marthasville, but around the center of the city life was different. Elegant boarding houses accommodated the members of Congress. While carriages were in abundance, most of the travel to and from the capitol was on foot. Everyone seemed to know each other and that surprised Mother. In Athens, of course, everyone in town was an acquaintance, but that was a lot smaller than Washington. She was pleased to find so much congeniality in the neighborhood around Uncle Howell's boarding house. Senator and Mrs. Jefferson Davis of Mississippi lived next door, and just across the street, Senator Henry S. Foote, also from Mississippi, lived with his family. Everyone went out of their way to make Mother feel welcome. Mayon's condition was well known and everyone seemed relieved that her husband would have someone to help him with his social duties. Aggie moved into the servants' quarters on the lot between their house and the Davis' house. She immediately fit right in with the large staff that worked in both homes. Sometimes it was hard to tell whose servants were whose, since they seemed to go back and forth from one house to the other, depending on what was happening in their homes. Aggie was always there when Mother needed her. I can't imagine what she would have done without her, just as I can't imagine my life without Mammy Sophy. Mrs. Davis—Varina, she told Mother to call her, was especially cordial to her. She knew my Mother had no experience in Washington etiquette and she gently led her through the intricacies of how to seat guests in the proper order in the dining room, how menus should be constructed for different types of dinners, choosing the right food for special visitors, things that a Washington hostess knew to be important, but Mother had no background to guide her. Varina would suggest which cooks she should use for particular meals since some were more skilled than others in the preparation of certain dishes. Varina's husband, Jefferson, was an inspiring-looking man. He had been in the war with Mexico and was considered by all, a hero. Senator Davis' first wife had died of malarial fever only three months after they married, then he married Varina, who was much closer to my mother's age than to her husband's. That's one reason they became such good friends, I suspect. The Davises hadn't been married long, so Varina was very interested in Mother's problems about her engagement. The Senator was still on crutches from the wounds he had received in the battle of Buena Vista, but he had a spirit about him that was infectious. His eyes looked at her so intensely that Mother knew he was paying attention when she spoke to him. She could certainly see why Varina had fallen in love with him.

Parties at the Cobb residence were a frequent event and Mother was the official hostess. She soon realized that as much political work got done at those get-togethers as took place in the official meetings of Congress. She longed to be a part of the discussion, but women were supposed to be demure and proper. That wasn't always the case, and on one occasion, there was real trouble in the Davis household over just that. Varina had been away, but Senator Davis had attended several parties in her absence. There was nothing unusual about that. He was a charming and handsome man, whose company was greatly sought after. When Varina returned home, she received an anonymous letter stating that, "Senator Davis had behaved in an unseemly and outrageously flirtatious manner with Mrs. Penelope St. John," a very attractive and seductive widow. Varina recounted the conversation she had with Senator Davis to my mother:

"Varina, I have told you there is not a word of truth in it," he tried to reassure her. "What more can I do? Whom will you believe?"

"Mary Willis Cobb is the *only* human I would believe," Varina told him.

"Very well," said the Senator, "I'll go and bring her this very minute."

"No, sir!" she exclaimed. "You will not leave this room! Have one of the servants go fetch her."

When the servant told Mother Senator and Mrs. Davis wanted to see her "right away, Missy," she had no idea what was going on, but when she walked into salon, she could tell there was trouble. "Read this, Mary Willis," sobbed Varina, handing my Mother the letter, "then tell me the truth!"

My mother had been at the party, and *had* seen what happened. She read the letter and immediately recognized it for what it was: a woman scorned. She put the letter on the sideboard, picked up Varina's fan and flounced over to Senator Davis. In her best imitation of the grieving Mrs. St. John, she batted her eyes over her fan, and said to the Senator, "Why, Senator Davis! Ah'm so glayud you were able to cum tonite. I know your lil' ol' leg must hurt you *terribly* and yet you're such a gentleman you just *had* to stand up when I walked up to you!" Then she snuggled up against him and said, "Why don't we go out on the verandah. Ah'll bring you a lil' glass of whiskey and you can prop yo' poor leg up on my lap." Then she changed roles to the Senator and dismissed the widow St. John's presence with the explanation, "Actually, madam, I stood to excuse myself and return home for the evening. My lovely wife, Varina, is visiting family in Natchez and I want to write a note to her before retiring." Then, with a sweeping bow, Mother closed with, "A good evening to you, Mrs. St. John." She snapped the fan shut and handed it to Varina. "And *that's* the truth!" she said, firmly.

Varina's tears turned into laughter and she walked to the sideboard, picked up the letter and tore it into tiny pieces. She came over to Mother, still laughing, and threw her arms around her. "Mary Willis Cobb, I've always loved you, but now I *adore* you!" They had been friends from the moment they met, but now they truly were sisters. Varina's maiden name was Howell. Mother once told her that maybe there was a family connection and that explained her brother's name.

That first year in Washington was filled with many wonders. President Polk, an austere man whom my Mother met on many occasions, valued Uncle Howell's judgment so they frequently were in conversation. The question of the Texas territory had led to the war with Mexico in 1846, although now a member of the Union, still had issues to be resolved. There were trade disputes with England. The settling of the northwest border of the Oregon

Territory continued to be a problem. It turned out *not* to be "Fifty-Four Forty or Fight," as President Polk's campaign slogan had promised, but rather the forty-ninth parallel. When Mother first met President Polk and his wife, she learned two things: The Presidency will kill anyone. Although he was a skilled politician, he looked defeated and worn down by despair. Having chosen not to run for re-election, he was saddened by his party's defeat, she felt sure. Looking at President Polk after General Taylor had defeated General Cass for the Presidency made her hope Howell was never in that position. The second thing she learned was never to underestimate the value of a good hostess. Mrs. Polk, Sara Childress from Nashville, was the best hostess Washington had ever seen. Mother, a marvelous hostess even at her young age, learned a lot from watching Mrs. Polk, and she was especially helpful since she was now in the position as hostess for the speaker as Sara Polk had been before her husband's election.

The final party of President Polk's administration was held in late February, 1849. It was to be a special occasion, even beyond the ending of the democratic administration. Zachary Taylor, a Whig and the hero of the Mexican war, was the incoming President. General Taylor, a great enemy of President Polk, had been the commander in the battle of Buena Vista where Senator Davis distinguished himself so brilliantly, saving General Taylor from defeat—almost at the cost of his own life. As far as Mother was concerned, the really exciting news of the evening was that Dolley Madison was going to attend the levee. Dolley was a great favorite of the Washingtonians and a living legend because of her heroism in the War of 1812. Mother had even a more personal reason for looking forward to meeting her: Dolley Madison had actually introduced my grandparents, Colonel John Addison Cobb and Sarah Robinson Rootes during one of my grandmother's visit to the White House during the Madison administration.

My mother had had great success with her duties as Uncle Howell's hostess. She tried to avoid thinking how much better than Mayon she had performed, although many of her friends told her just that. She did well in her job because she enjoyed it, but more than that, Varina Howell Davis and Sara Childress Polk guided her with firm hands.

When the final levee of the season was planned, Varina was quite busy making sure that Mother presented herself in the best possible light. It would be important for Howell's future, she told her, but she kept wondering if that were true; she was Howell Cobb's sister, not his wife! During all this time, she was trying to keep Mayon in mind and avoid having her upstaged by all she was doing. It came to a head the evening of President Polk's levee. Varina had selected the gown Mother was to wear. All the accessories, all the jewelry and the hat to set off the dress were the source of long conversations. When it was all done, she felt like a doll carefully dressed by a loving child. The gown was an emerald green silk and the hoops so large, she wondered if she could get through the carriage door. Varina's jewelry was magnificent: a beautiful necklace and bracelet, set with diamonds and emeralds that matched the gown perfectly. The final touch was long white kid gloves, soft as anything she ever felt. Before the carriage was to call for Howell and Mother, she was presented to Mayon for her approval. Mayon was *not* pleased!

"Mary Willis, take off Mrs. Davis' jewels! Your simple ones are in far better taste," she announced from her perch on the fainting couch. Of course, Varina was standing right beside Mother, prepared to accept Mayon's thanks for all her help she had given.

"You'll do no such thing, Mary Willis. You shall wear my jewels," Varina said. It was a command, not a suggestion. Her eyes were flaming. Uncle Howell was caught in the middle. He seemed to be in that habit when it came to Mayon and my mother. He simply smiled, took Varina on one arm, his sister on the other, and out they walked to meet the carriage. Poor Mayon, Mother thought. Stuck on that couch and her sister-in-law off to see the President . . . and the famous Dolley Madison.

When they reached The White House, the footman took the carriage. After she gathered up all her hoops and skirts, my mother, the nineteen-year-old belle from Athens, Georgia, walked in arm-in-arm with the Speaker of the house of representatives and General

Lewis Cass, the defeated democratic candidate for the Presidency. They walked slowly to the East Room. In the receiving line, immediately after President and Mrs. Polk, stood Dolley Madison. Although the President looked terribly tired, none could have guessed that after returning to Nashville, he would be dead in three months. Nor could they have known this would be Dolley Madison's last public appearance. She was a vivacious and lovely matron, even at her age. Her eyes sparkled with a sense of youth far below her years. Everyone had said, if you want to see real beauty look in the eyes of Dolley Madison. That was true. Mother still says she has never seen anyone with eyes like hers. When she was introduced to Dolley Madison, she immediately knew who mother was.

"Oh, my dear," she sighed, with a smile, "You must be the daughter of Sarah Rootes from Federal Hill down in Fredericksburg! Child, it was in this very room I introduced Sarah to John Addison Cobb. I knew they were made for each other, and now I can see I was right." Mrs. Madison leaned forward to kiss her, taking a number of sprays from her bouquet. "Give these to your mother, Sarah, for me," handing them to my mother before she could say a word. Such a gracious and charming woman! There have been few like her.

As she moved down the receiving line, meeting members of the outgoing cabinet, she thought to herself, "If John Lamar could see me now, he wouldn't believe it!" Athens and her plans for marriage seemed a distant, but pleasant, dream. General Cass was her official escort of the evening and they moved about the room meeting men whose names were legend. She had become accustomed to being in the presence of public figures, but a concentration of this magnitude was something special. General Cass and she approached Senator Foote, her neighbor. After a few pleasantries, the General excused himself and Senator Foote took Mother under his wing. They were well acquainted and she felt more comfortable with him than General Cass, whom she knew only by reputation.

"Mary Willis, there's a young gentleman I would like you to meet," the Senator said, guiding her down the hall leading from the East Room. Her engagement to John Lamar was well known; consequently, she had not been introduced to eligible bachelors. She was surprised that Senator Foote was taking it upon himself to look after her social needs, but she could think of no graceful way to decline. When they walked into one of the drawing salons off the corridor from The East Room, she was confronted with a man whose visage was, to say the least, arresting. He looked like a painting of Lord Byron. Tall and aristocratic, he had an aquiline nose that accented his high cheekbones and strong chin with just the right . . . what is the word? . . . she couldn't think of anything other than "magic."

"Mr. Lyons!" intoned Senator Foote, "May I have the pleasure of introducing one of Washington's newest and brightest young stars? Miss Mary Willis Cobb, sister and hostess of our esteemed colleague, Congressman Howell Cobb of Georgia, Speaker of the House." Then turning to her, as he offered her hand, he said, "Miss Cobb, may I present Mr. Leonardo Lyons of Lyonsdale?"

Mr. Lyons clicked his heels together ever so precisely, bowed slightly but gracefully as he took her hand, his eyes never leaving hers. After the kiss, he did not release her hand, but said, "Indeed, this shall be a moment to remember." She would have to admit that John Lamar, for all his charm and wit, was no match for Mr. Lyons of Lyonsdale. Senator Foote, apparently thinking his duty was done, left her in the care of her new escort.

It was immediately apparent to my mother that Mr. Lyons was immensely popular and sought after by young and old alike. Whenever his attention was required elsewhere, his eyes seldom strayed from hers. It was, as he had suggested, an evening to remember. She was overwhelmed by the attention she was receiving, not only from Mr. Lyons, but from many other men, most of whom she had never met and who knew nothing of her engagement. The preparation by Varina must have added to whatever natural allure she possessed. Across the room, she saw Varina. She waved and smiled. Mother could tell she was pleased with their success. When General Cass and Uncle Howell came to fetch her for their departure, the belle from Athens had garnered quite a retinue of young men who followed them into the porte-cochere. There was much scurrying about to assist her as she prepared to step into the carriage, trying to manage those large hoops.

After being helped to her seat by several of her new-found admirers, they all stepped back in deference to Mr. Lyons. He strode slowly through them, his cane tapping the cobblestone lightly, his head cocked thoughtfully under his silk top hat.

"Miss Cobb, my brow shall not rest upon my pillow until I have addressed a poem to 'The Maid of Modern Athens,'" he announced for one and all to hear. The Lord Byron image came to mind again. It was a heady moment. My mother didn't know who he was, but he certainly cut a figure and was obviously greatly respected by all. John Lamar was far from her mind that night!

When she awoke the next morning, the sun was already up and playing across her bed. She felt rested but still exhilarated from the night's success. She was luxuriating in the memory of it all when Aggie knocked on her door with more urgency than her usual faint tap.

She ran into the room, obviously alarmed. "Oh, Honey! Wake up, Missy! Whadda we gon' do? You done lost one of de settin's outta Miz Davis' bracelet." She held up the bracelet and to Mother's horror, she was right. One of the emeralds *was* missing. It had been nestled between two diamonds and now the bracelet looked like a snaggle-toothed child. She was so stunned, she didn't know what to say.

"Git up outta dat bedstead," Aggie shrilled. "We gotta find that hunk o' glass 'fore somebody else does."

Mother couldn't imagine where they would even begin to look, but she didn't have a better idea, so she got up and hurriedly dressed. She remembered that Senator Foote, as well as Varina and her husband, were coming for breakfast. There would be all sorts of people in the house. How in the world would she ever tell Varina, after she had been so kind to let her wear her jewelry? And Mayon! She would fall out in a swoon that would last all day, especially after she had told her not to wear Varina's jewelry! As soon as she could make herself look more-or-less presentable, Aggie and she started down the steps. Where to begin? Where could she have lost it? She knew the stone had been in place when they came downstairs last evening. Mayon had looked at the bracelet before demanding Mother remove it. At the bottom of the stairs stood Mrs. Tucker. She was a guest of the family's and had come down from Baltimore for the levee. There aren't too many people to whom my mother took an immediate dislike, but Mrs. Tucker apparently was an exception. Early in her visit, all had found what a gossip she was. The last person in the house Mother wanted to know she had lost a precious gem was Mrs. Tucker of Baltimore.

Mrs. Tucker had a smug look on her face. "Congratulations," she said.

Mother and Aggie tried to walk by with a hasty, "Good morning," but Mrs. Tucker wasn't to be denied.

"I said, 'Congratulations!'" she emphasized. "I didn't expect to see the acknowledged belle of Washington out so early after your brilliant conquest."

"Oh, yes indeed. I like to get out for an early morning stroll," she answered in a quavery voice.

"Ah, indeed!" Mrs. Tucker smiled, gloatingly. "And I had thought you might be out in search of THIS!" She held out her hand and snapped it open, the missing jewel sitting in her palm. "I found it in the foyer when I came down for breakfast. I knew, of course, that it came from the bracelet you borrowed from Mrs. Davis."

Mother was so relieved she even gave Mrs. Tucker a little hug, then she fled back up the stairs to replace the stone. She prayed that Mrs. Tucker would not tell Mayon, but it wasn't likely such a secret would be kept. The story of her losing such a valuable thing would be just the kind of news the chatty Mrs. Tucker would spread all over town. But at least Aggie and she were able safely to replace it.

"Lawd have murcy on me," Aggie sighed as they finished. "I 'spect dat green rock probably worth five whole dollers. Good thing ol' Miz Tucker don' know how vallable it is. She'd'a put it in her pocket and skidaddled right back out de Baltimo' pike." I don't think Mother thought that would have happened, but she was so relieved to find it that whatever Mrs. Tucker did seemed unimportant now.

After all of that, Mother was late getting to breakfast. Senator Foote was already seated and Senator Davis was just handing his crutches to the servant and seating himself. As he sat down, Varina helping him ease into his seat, he looked over at Mary Willis. "And whom did you captivate last evening, my little pet?" he asked, a twinkle in his eye.

"Yes, tell us everything," Varina added as she adjusted her skirt and seated herself.

As she was getting ready to answer, Mother noticed there was a letter on her plate. The parchment was heavy and ornately embossed. She turned it over and the sealing wax bore the imprint of a lion's head. Everyone was curious about the letter so she opened it. "Why, it's from Mr. Lyons of Lyonsdale. He's written a poem for me, "The Maid of Modern Athens." She started to read it:

> "Oh Maid of Athens, Modern Maid,
> I kneel in hope, a fear . . ."

That was as far as she got.

"Who dared introduce that man to you?" interrupted Senator Davis, angrily.

"Why, your colleague, Senator Foote," Mother said, waving her hand across the table toward him. "I found Mr. Lyons perfectly fascinating. Listen to the poem."

Before she could start, Senator Davis struggled to his feet, discarding his napkin with a flourish. His eyes shot fire and his tone was low, but frighteningly intense as he turned to Senator Foote. "Senator Foote! Mary Willis Cobb is a gentlewoman of the highest order and a warm friend of our family. She is betrothed to a fine Southern gentleman. To have you, my trusted colleague, expose her to such riff-raff as Mr. Lyons of Lyonsdale, I take as a personal affront, an insult of the highest order. You will answer to me for this!"

Senator Foote, who did not look the least intimidated, replied mildly, "Name your time, sir!"

What had started off less than two minutes ago as an intriguing letter now had turned deadly. The tension was enveloping the entire room. Mrs. Tucker, seated at the end of the table, had stopped eating, her fork poised in mid-air. She looked as though she had turned into a statue. Uncle Howell rose from the head of the table and led the way into the parlor, Senator Foote walking behind and Senator Davis gathering up his crutches to follow. As they reached the parlor door, Senator Davis raised his crutch and in a smooth motion caught the wig of Senator Foote, tossing it across the room. The challenge had been passed, like a flash. Howell made a fruitless effort to calm them both. Senator Foote was livid. He retrieved his wig and stormed out of the house. Mrs. Tucker's hand was still frozen in mid-motion toward her mouth, which, for once, was shut.

"What in the world is all of this about?" Uncle Howell demanded of Senator Davis. He motioned to a chair in which the Senator heavily seated himself, then he explained his colleague.

"Mr. Lyons of Lyonsdale is not what he appears. He is, in fact, a defrocked Catholic priest. Some years ago he, after hearing the confession of a nun, and it must have been of a most lurid and provocative nature, took the nun from the confessional and ran away with her to a secluded village in the mountains of Maryland. There, without benefit of clergy and with total disregard for his priestly vows, he fathered two children by her. They lived there in seclusion for several years until recently when he finally married the poor girl. Last year, Mr. Lyons established the small village of Lyonsdale down the Richmond road. He has gained himself a little coterie of influential friends, all of whom seem unaware of the existence of the woman, now his wife back in Maryland, who is the mother of his children before the marriage."

After Senator Davis had recounted the sorry tale of the fallen priest, Mother was aghast that she had been so charmed and taken in by him. She was horrified that harm might come to either Senator on her behalf. Surely, Senator Foote was unaware of Mr. Lyons' reputation. Shortly, Howell set out across the street to meet with Senator Foote.

"Spare me any message from Davis," was the greeting her brother received when he was shown into the Senator's study. Senator Foote was inspecting his dueling pistols by the window. "He will be hearing from my seconds in due time."

Howell told my Mother later he had forced Senator Foote to seat himself and listen to the facts of which, as she had been certain, he was totally ignorant. He was humiliated by what had happened and the delicate position in which he placed my mother. Finally both the Senators met with Howell and tried to find a way to punish Mr. Lyons, but they could think of nothing that would not place Mother in a compromising position. Finally, Howell came up with an agreeable alternative.

"Gentlemen," Howell said, "The only one who can settle this affair effectively and without adverse publicity, is Mary Willis herself. Her diplomacy is second to none. Leave it to her for the present, and let's see."

The potential combatants were still angry, but they agreed to wait and see what she could do. The need for the duel was abated since Senator Davis had come to believe that Senator Foote had acted in good, although ill-informed, faith.

The following day, the perfect opportunity arose. Mrs. Davis and my mother were out calling and had arranged an afternoon gathering at the Mayflower for a number of their friends. As they walked in, who should be standing by the entrance but Mr. Lyons, himself. Somehow, he didn't look nearly so charming as Mother had remembered him. Without speaking, Varina and she both walked by, as if they had not seen him. Shortly, as the tea was being served, Mr. Lyons presented himself to their group. Mother introduced him without identifying him further than his name.

"Miss Cobb, may I speak to you for a moment?" he inquired, the picture of dignity and solicitude.

She didn't know what would happen, but she knew an opportunity to embarrass him fatally was at hand. While the assembled ladies watched, recognizing that Mother was about to receive an extraordinary gift, Mr. Lyons said, "Lend me this for a moment," taking from her hand the fan she was nervously holding. He reached into his vest pocket and withdrew, with a flourish, an exquisite miniature of himself that was truly beautiful and surrounded by seed pearls. He held it out for all to admire, then he said, "Of course, Miss Cobb, you know for whom this is intended." A little smile of satisfaction crept around the corners of his mouth.

"Certainly, I do! It is a present for your wife or perhaps, one of your daughters." Then she turned to Varina and said, "Mrs. Davis, will you be so kind as to show the gentleman to the door?"

While she was escorting him, none of the ladies asked a single question, although Mrs. Scott did say, "Deftly done, my dear." That was the last anyone ever heard of Mr. Lyons of Lyonsdale. Fortunately, no blood had been shed.

The rest of that session of Congress dragged by slowly. Mother had received a surreptitious letter from a cousin in Athens telling her that John Lamar was pleading with her parents to allow their marriage to take place, regardless of Mayon's feelings. As usual, Aggie had an opinion. "You can't git married, Missy. You ain't got no trousseau!" She told Aggie she didn't care a straw about that. She just wanted to be with John.

"Well, if you gits married, I bet Miz Sarah got ever' pair of hands in Athens, white and colored, sewing up a storm to get ready for yo' weddin'," Aggie chuckled. Mother wasn't sure what John's intentions were, but she knew she needed to speak to Mayon personally. She was tired of walking on eggshells as far as her sister-in-law was concerned.

Mayon was reclining on her fainting couch when she consented to see Mother. Over the last few months she had gained back some strength and Uncle Howell had told his sister he thought his wife might actually give her blessing to the marriage.

"You're looking fine this morning, Sister Mayon," Mother said, kissing her on the cheek.

"I hope so," she sighed, without much conviction, her wrist held to her forehead. She was turning a letter over and over in her hands. "John wishes for your wedding to take place soon after our return," she continued. "I am trying to adjust myself to the idea. You have been very noble about all this." She stopped speaking and looked out the window for a long time . . . it seemed like hours. Finally, she added, "I am doing my best."

"I understand, Sister," Mother said, stroking Mayon's hand. The skin was thin and dry as any parchment; the veins looked like blue worms crawling over frail reeds. The interview was over. As she slowly left the room, she had the thought Mayon used her illness like a hammer on my mother's anvil to beat out her own will.

When they started southward, Mayon seemed serene and everyone thought all might be well, but when they reached Athens, Mayon had another collapse. Apparently the realization that Little Howell had never seen Athens and was lost forever was more than she could bear.

Word of the impending marriage had spread rapidly and all the family, far and near, were delighted. But the news of Mayon and her increased weakness wasn't far behind. Again the doctors said that John's marriage would be the death of her, but this time John refused to listen. They told him that he would bear the responsibility for whatever happened. The family was full of suggestions, ranging all the way from her marrying one of her former suitors to marrying John Lamar and letting Mayon take the hindmost.

Nothing happened. The longer they waited the deeper the divisions became until I think Mother realized the situation was worse now than before she had moved to Washington. Mayon's control over her life seemed complete. Looking back, my mother still doesn't understand why she felt so powerless in the face of this fragile woman who cloaked herself in the misery of her unhappiness and then demanded that all share the garment. Finally, after months of wavering, Mother capitulated.

Maybe it wasn't necessary to marry at all. Most of her friends had married and already she had seen unhappiness replace what had promised to be a blissful union. She had always assumed that she would become a wife and a mother. It seemed the natural thing to do. Women who didn't marry were roundly regarded as

"old maids," and in truth, most of them were never asked to marry.
My mother did not feel herself a part of the group, but she also
didn't want to be the cause of so much family strife.

"I will marry no one!" she announced. By that time, any
announcement, regardless of the direction, was welcome. Everyone
was worn out with the whole thing. The family and friends, ever
wanting to help, stepped into the breach. General Henry Jackson,
a cousin and confidante of the family, dispatched a messenger to
Colonel Frank Erwin, a pleasant gentleman whom she had seen on
several occasions before John and my mother made their plans.
The message to Colonel Erwin was right to the point: "If you ever
hope to win the hand of Mary Willis Cobb, now is your time.
Fly!"

It may sound as if this were a totally capricious act on the part
of General Jackson, but his motives were pure. The political
situation in the country was becoming increasingly polarized. Many
in the South, in fact most, were talking of radical action, possibly
even secession, over the issue of state sovereignty. The most
prominent part of that argument was slavery, of course, but
certainly not the only issue. The rule of the people—did it come
from Washington, or did it come from the individual states? That
was everyone's main concern and it involved much more than slavery.
Uncle Howell was in one of the most powerful positions in
Congress. His views were moderate and he was working very hard
to find a solution acceptable to all sides. General Jackson thought
that Howell Cobb, as Speaker of the house, could do it, as few
others had the respect and the power he did. If his life was seriously
disturbed by the death of his wife, there might truly be national
consequences. It was difficult for Mother to believe the fate of the
nation hung on her decision to marry John Lamar, but some well-
informed people convinced themselves that was true. If she were
married to someone else, the problem would be solved. Hence,
General Jackson's letter to Colonel Erwin.

In this state of confusion—it was bordering on panic—Mother
fled into the garden trying to find some peace with what was
happening to her. One of the servants, she suspected it was Aggie,

sent John out to where she was sitting. They stood there among the flowers, a gentle rain beginning to fall. John pleaded with her to run away with him. He had responsibilities. He was a planter with large holdings as well as a banker, but he said he would give them all up and they could go to the Northwest Territory. She couldn't do it. In what turned out to be a pivotal point in her life—and ultimately mine—she simply turned to him and said, "No, John. I can't do it. I'm so afraid. Please leave me." Then she ran helplessly into the house. Some of Aunt Mayon's fear must have rubbed off on her.

The next morning Colonel Erwin arrived. He was shown into the double parlor. My grandmother and General Jackson were in the adjacent room, talking quietly but earnestly. Mother couldn't hear what they were saying, but she didn't need to. She knew. As soon as she went into the parlor to receive Colonel Erwin, she heard John's voice in the hall. She thought he would come into the parlor, but something prevented him. She never knew if it were something my grandmother and General Jackson had said to him, or something in John himself. In any case, he did not come in to the double parlor where she and the Colonel were awkwardly seated.

She realized Colonel Erwin had been talking to her and she had not heard a word he had said. Finally, she recognized what he was saying. "I am only asking for the privilege of devoting my life to your happiness. I know that your love . . . ."

Suddenly, the earnest and eloquent words of this good man were in sharp contrast to the frantic pleadings of John, standing in the rain, the night before. She was powerfully struck by the extreme difference between the two. The voices of her mother and the General were more insistent. They had moved to the veranda where she heard the word, "Sacrifice." The General was saying, "Sacrifice . . . that's what is required here. A girlish romance must not be allowed to stand in the way of the resolution of a national crisis. The South needs every man, every vote, to stem the tide of the Abolitionists. Their strength is growing every day and it must be checked at all costs. In Heaven's name, don't allow this child to weaken Howell's position of leadership now."

The General was silent. Grandmother replied, but Mother couldn't hear what she said. She sat there a while. Colonel Erwin, resplendent in his dress uniform and sword, stood at attention at the bay window, looking out across the fields of Athens. She did not feel like a Modern Maid, but she turned to the Colonel and said, "Sir, if you are willing," she paused, then continued, "Colonel, if you are willing to marry a woman who admires you but does not love you, then I will be honored to become your wife."

In 1851, only three weeks later, Mary Willis Cobb and Colonel Frank Erwin were married in her home. The ceremony was performed, not with the usual festival of a Southern wedding, but a dignified gathering of close relatives. They assembled in the large drawing room, lined with the portraits of their forebears whose faces seemed to look down with approval and understanding. The guests listened to the stately words of the union. It was an alliance, not a marriage born out of love, but it met the highest standards of honor and loyalty. We put great faith in those virtues.

# CHAPTER II

I remember the rain that afternoon. I must have been about twelve at the time; at least I was old enough to wonder about all that had gone on in Atlanta. Mother and I were sitting in the front drawing room, looking at the river of muddy water flowing down the street toward Peachtree Creek. Things were being rebuilt, but the destruction from the burning was still on every side. Our house had been spared. I don't know whether that's because my father was a doctor and looked after wounded Union soldiers as well as our own or whether they were just lucky. Mother didn't seem to know either, but most of the other homes on our street had been burned to the ground. Some of my first memories are of playing in the cellars that had once been basements of beautiful homes. All that was left were the brick foundations and occasionally a charred column or two from a veranda. When I was a child, I didn't think much about the misfortune we had lived through; I guess that's true for most children: You take life as it comes and don't worry too much about it. When you get older and eyes are opened, then you have a sense of wonder about it all. That's what was beginning to happen to me. I had been off to Athens to visit some of my other relatives, the Rutherford family. Nothing there was in the shape it was in Atlanta. Up until then, I had thought the whole world looked like where I was living. In Athens, you couldn't tell there had been a war. The mansions were all stately and grand. The giant oak trees still had all their branches. The ones down on Peachtree Street were nothing but skeletons, half their limbs blown off by cannon fire. In Athens, the people didn't have any more food than we did, but it looked like they were getting along a lot better than we were. It made me curious about the war.

"Why don't we move back to Athens, Mother?" I asked as we sat there watching the rain. "It's a lot nicer than living here," I pointed at the flood in our yard. Mother had a sad look on her face.

"Too many memories, Sally. Too many memories." When she said that, I decided it was time to learn a little about what had gone on before I arrived on the scene. She had told me the stories about her growing up in Athens, about living in Washington and being such a good friend of Varina Davis, of knowing the President and his wife. I had heard all about John Lamar and how much she loved him, but ended up marrying the old Colonel instead, just to please her parents. I didn't tell her, but I *knew* I would never do anything like that . . . not to please my parents. Of course, Daddy would never make me do something I didn't want to. I could get him to agree to anything, just by cuddling up to him and batting my eyes at him. That's one of the nice things about your mother marrying an older man . . . they treat their own children like they're grandchildren. Mother seemed to like older men. After she didn't marry John Lamar, I guess she decided that romance wasn't everything.

"Tell me about your first husband," I said. She looked out the window. The rain was running down the panes like tears on a shiny cheek. I thought she wasn't going to say anything, but then she stood, walked over to the settee and patted the seat for me to join her.

"Frank Erwin was a good man. I was a child, only 19, but I knew that I was going to have to marry him just to make sure the family held together, especially Howell. If he hadn't been so famous, then none of that would have happened. I would have married John Lamar and been a war widow like everyone else I know. As it turned out, I was a widow even before the war. Frank had three plantations: one in Clark county, and two down near Macon. He had worked hard and his family was quite well off. There were more than three hundred slaves working those plantations. When we were married, it never occurred to me that I would end up running all three of the holdings. Since Frank was so much older, I suppose if I had thought about it I would have known that he might die and I would be left with all the work, but he was sick and couldn't get around too well, so right from the start I had to learn how to manage the affairs of plantation life and the slaves.

"Back then, there was a lot of agitation about slavery. The Abolitionists were getting harder to deal with all the time. Your Uncle Howell was trying to keep people from taking extreme positions, and he seemed to think that the Union could stay together. He worked really hard trying to get everyone to compromise, but he couldn't do it. I had understood a lot of what was going on when I was living in Washington and helping with Mayon, but after I married I didn't understand nearly as much as I should have. Howell made a lot of enemies who thought he wasn't being loyal to Georgia with his Unionist views. In 1851, I think it was, a man named McDonald was nominated for governor by the Southern Rights party. Howell couldn't stand him, so he resigned his seat in Congress and ran for governor supporting the Clay amendment—that was supposed to keep the Union together— and he won."

"Were you excited when he was elected?" I asked.

"I really hadn't thought about it. I was so busy looking after the plantations and the slaves, I didn't have much time for anything else. You can't imagine what a change that was for me. I had been the belle of the ball in Washington and I guess I thought it would always be like that, but when I had to take over managing the plantations, I had to grow up in a hurry. I had been raised by colored people who were our slaves, but I was brought up always to respect them and treat them kindly. When I became responsible for their lives, well that was something else! Almost everyone I knew treated slaves well, but after the war, we were hearing all sorts of things about how we beat the slaves and how mean we were to them. None of that was true, certainly not on our plantations. That's why so many of them are still with us today by choice. Everybody who works in the house was one of our slaves before the war and they chose to stay with us even when they were free to leave. That made me feel good about how we had looked after them. They were and are part of our family."

"Were you able to do anything to help them . . . back when they were slaves, I mean?"

Mother laughed and patted me on the knee. I remember that like it was yesterday. "There was one time I *know* I helped. We had just come back to Clark County from several months in the lower plantations. The slaves always had what they called "jollification" for us when we got home. They were all singing and laughing—all except Emma Lou. She was one of my favorites. I guess she was about twenty at the time; Frank and I hadn't been married long. She was sitting alone over to the side and looking ever so sad. 'What's the matter, Emma Lou?' I asked later that night. She told me that Josh was going to marry Hannah that night, and I could tell she was broken-hearted about it. Josh was the Romeo of the whole plantation. I thought about it and said, 'Emma Lou, how would you like to move to the Macon plantation? There are lots of handsome young men down there and they would love to see a pretty young thing like you.' The rest of the night she tried to join in the celebration, but I knew just how she was feeling. The man she loved was going to marry someone else and she wondered if she could stand it. Well, she did. She moved to Macon and, in time, married one of the men there; he was a lot better catch than Josh. But the day I decided to marry Frank Erwin, I had felt the same way Emma Lou was feeling."

Long after my mother was dead, I wondered if she understood the power they had over those people, their slaves. She certainly treated them well, the servants all loved her because she was genuinely kind to them, but it's hard to believe that times like that existed right up to my birth.

When Mother was just settling in as mistress of all those plantations, Howell was getting more and more involved in national affairs. Although he was powerful and had strong allies in the Unionist movement, bit by bit the problems of secession loomed larger. When he ran for governor, he thought he had a better chance of keeping Georgia in the Union than if he stayed in Washington. I can remember Mother telling me that as Governor one of the things he worried about the most was calling out troops to fight against the secessionists, should it ever come to that. The capitol was in Milledgeville in those days, and although Mother had her hands full with the plantations and three children of her own, she continued to help her brother with his entertaining. My Aunt Mayon never recovered from her depression, so Mother added being the governor's hostess to her list of responsibilities. She was still in her twenties then. I marvel at all she was able to do.

She told me the story of the first reception he had as governor. She was anxious for everything to be just perfect for him, and I'm sure it was, but there were a lot of things she couldn't count on. First of all, there had been invitations issued through the newspapers. That was a mistake. Milledgeville was a little country town surrounded by farmers and a lot of poor people. The party wasn't to start until late afternoon, but by mid-day the streets were lined up with mule wagons piled high with dirty children, dogs, and even a few goats. They surrounded the governors mansion like it was an invasion, Mother told me. The refreshments were being placed out on long tables on the capitol lawn and the country women with all their children and their tobacco-chewing husbands were leaning over the fence to see what they were going to have for their supper. The word "afternoon tea" probably was not in their vocabulary.

When the gates were opened and Governor Cobb stood at the head of the receiving line, the country ladies made a bee-line for the food like they hadn't eaten for a week. Mother excused herself from the line and tried wandering among the "guests" to restrain them from eating all the food. "Would you like to see the flower garden?" she suggested to a group who were filling their skirts with fried chicken and ham.

"I ain't too perticular about seeing no flowers. The woods is full of 'em," answered one.

"But these are cultivated flowers, grown specially. Some are very rare. If you like I'll give you some roots and you can plant them in your yard," Mother suggested, seeing the situation getting out of hand.

The lady laid her food-laden apron on the table and fixed mother with a stare. "Now, looky here! I didn' come all this way to see no flowers. We was asked here to eat and, by gawd, I don't keer to see nothin' till I've had my fill of these curious vittles." She scurried away to another table, loading her pockets with pickles, cakes, beaten biscuits, and everything else she could get her hands on. The *coup de grace* came when she shoved two huge dollops of ice cream into her side pockets. As she was leaving, she stopped dead in her tracks, an odd look on her face. "Lawd A'mighty!" she screamed. "Dis here food's alive! Hit's a'runnin' down my legs like a wet snake."

Compared to the dignity and majesty of President's Polk's levee, the contrast was beyond description. I don't think I ever heard Mother tell that story without tears of laughter running down her cheek. Some things just don't bend to dignity, and the country women of Georgia were certainly in that class.

One of the advantages of living through and far beyond a period of history is the possibility of retrospection. Looking back, some things seem very clear that, at the time, were terribly confusing. My family, having been in government both nationally and in the state, has left me a legacy of which I have become increasingly aware as I have grown older. That my mother, Mary Willis, lived through such a critical time and told me so much about it, has left me with a sense of gratitude for all they went through and a need to carry on the belief in public service that they held so closely.

In 1856, the country was becoming even further divided over the states rights issue, and Howell was feeling on the outside as governor of a state that was leaning more toward secession. James Buchanan, an old friend, was running for President, and Howell campaigned for him vigorously in the north. Although there had been support for Howell when he ran on the Unionist party line for governor, that was eroding, and he made many enemies in Georgia and the South because of his support for Buchanan and a compromise solution to the issues. When Buchanan was elected, he named Howell Cobb as Secretary of the Treasury. Poor James Buchanan. By then, the die was cast and no one could have averted the dissolution of the Union. Probably no one *should* have averted it, although it's terrible to think there could be no solution other than war. Every debate on the floor of the House and Senate devolved into the slavery and states' rights issue. Friends parted, right and left, over it. I have a letter that Mother gave me that shows the depth of the division. It was written to Chancellor Andrew A. Lipscomb of the University of Georgia and it reads:

August 15, 1858

My Dear Friend:

We leave tomorrow for Nahant where I shall be happy to have you, and where we shall talk about everything but slavery, and even that, if I thought we should get in sight of each other, which at the present, I fear we should not. For you look upon it rather as a blessing than otherwise. In my opinion it is the meanest sort of tyranny. What use can it be to discuss it? I can never make it rhyme with "do unto others as you would have them do unto you." Nor do I think you can meet it face to face. One thing we do agree about is your estimate of the newspapers as a power in this country. Of this we will talk, and all other things pertaining to literature.

With greatest regards *quand meme* we disagree,

Yours faithfully,

Henry W. Longfellow

Little did she know how radically things would change for her, not only because of the war but because of personal life. When Lincoln was elected President, the secession movement began in earnest. Howell resigned his Cabinet position and returned to Georgia, still hoping to keep the state in the union, but he had lost much support because of his political views. When the seceding states met in Montgomery in 1861 to form the Confederate Government, Howell was the chairman of the convention and considered for the Presidency, but his stand for preservation of the Union and his lack of military experience kept him from the post which went to his good friend and colleague, Jefferson Davis.

In trying to understand all that took place during those years, I asked my mother, about her early years if marriage. As the country was coming apart, so was her life. Her husband, Col. Erwin, died in 1859, leaving her with three plantations to run and three small children to raise.

"How in the world did you survive?" I asked her one day when she was well into her later years.

"I knew that war was coming and I stayed at the plantations in Macon until it actually started. Then I moved to Atlanta with three children and no husband. I thought we would be safer there than out in the country, but I had no way of knowing what would happen in 1864. When you're in the midst of a crisis, you really don't think about it in those terms. You see what needs to be done and you do it," she answered, as if that explained everything.

"I understand that, but still, there must have been terrible things to overcome."

"Well, there were . . . no doubt about that, but when you don't have any access to the fine clothes from Paris we were accustomed to, when there is no money, when you have to think about the simple feeding of the children, that occupies most of your energy. We were making coffee out of sweet potatoes, we used molasses instead of sugar. As the war progressed the shortages got even worse. I was working in the hospitals then, mainly because I could get extra food for the children. After the war, then most of the land, except for the bit around Athens, had been destroyed. When Sherman started for Savannah, he didn't leave much intact. There were no plantations to oversee, no slaves to be concerned about . . . all of that was gone. I remember once going back up to Athens to attend to something or other, and saw a sight I will never forget. It was in the spring of 1863. Things weren't going well with the war and every man, every young boy available was off fighting. As I was walking by the university grounds, I saw some really old men, lined up and trying to drill. Most of them should have been on a porch in a rocking chair, but there they were, rifles in one hand, walking stick in the other, trying to march. There was an old crippled-up French officer trying to lead them. They were all lined up in their Prince Albert coats and alpaca suits, following his commands with surprising enthusiasm. I stopped to watch. When the old soldier told them to "break ranks and fall to the ground, roll over and fire," things began to break down. At first they refused. One fine looking man said he would not permit himself to engage in such indignity, but the officer convinced them that it wasn't a matter of dignity, but a matter of survival. They talked among themselves for a minute, then painfully began to fold their rheumatic legs beneath them and began to fire wildly in all directions. It was pretty frightening. When they had finished, their servants helped them to their feet and with one accord turned to their commander and gave him to understand they would dispense with his absurd rules and regulations, as they intended to stand up and fight like men. I guess I knew then the war was lost, although it wasn't for lack of courage."

All of that was made worse by the news that John Lamar, now a Colonel, had been killed in the battle of Crampton's Gap, Maryland. I tried a number of times to get Mother to talk about how she felt about having given up her love for family reasons, and how she felt when she heard John was dead. Did she regret the decision she had made? Mother wasn't one to re-plow a furrowed field.

"If I had married John Lamar, then, of course, my life would have been different. My children with Frank would never have been born. I can't imagine how my life would have been without them. Frank Erwin was a good man. He loved me totally and I respected him completely. That bond made up for a lot of things. You can't always have everything the way you want it, Sally," she told me for the hundredth time.

Of course I thought a lot about my mother's life. Had she married John Lamar, I would never have been born. If Colonel Erwin had lived, there would have been no Sarah Johnson and I wouldn't be finishing up a life that has been, for the most part, glorious. In 1863, about the time she heard of John's death, she began working in the hospitals in Atlanta. The warehouses around town had been turned into receiving stations for wounded from the battles in Tennessee. As the war came to Atlanta, every available space, including private homes, was filled with wounded. Mother was good with her hands, good in the midst of chaos, so she helped with the surgery. It was there that she met Dr. John M. Johnson, post surgeon for the district. He was a widower and nearly twenty years older than Mother who was about 33 or 34 at the time. She was his assistant at surgery and became quite skillful, my father would tell everyone. His daughters by his first wife were grown and gone but his family became very important in my life as a young woman, and I have kept up with them. He was from Kentucky, which as a border state, had more difficulty within families during the war than those of us in the deep south. My father's younger brother, Richard, was a graduate of West Point and had remained in the Union Army, while my father chose to join the southern forces, as did the remainder of the Johnson family. Maybe all those years Uncle Dick had spent fighting Indians and Mexicans in the West had broadened his views.

Just after the first Battle of Bull Run, Uncle Dick was asked by Congressman Jackson of Kentucky to become a Lt. Colonel in the Kentucky Volunteer Cavalry. Dick went to Washington to ask General Thomas for permission to accept, but was emphatically refused. When Congressman Jackson got the news he said, "Well, we won't give up yet. We'll go see President Lincoln." And they did . . . the very next morning. President Lincoln suggested that they all go to see General Thomas. When they arrived at the White House, President Lincoln greeted uncle Dick with, "Good morning, my confederate friend." Confused by the greeting, the President clarified himself. "We're both from Kentucky. Doesn't that make us confederate friends?"

When they arrived by carriage at General Thomas' headquarters, they were received politely, if coolly. When President Lincoln suggested to General Thomas that he wished Captain

Johnson released to command a unit in Kentucky, the General simply stated, "It cannot be done."

The President stood up and appeared about ten feet tall. Looking down at the General, he said, "I didn't come to discuss if it *could* be done. I came to tell you it *will* be done!"

The General looked up at President Lincoln, and said, "Ah! Well, I see. It will be done." And so it was that my uncle was assigned to a Union force in Kentucky and the breach between him and my father-to-be became wider.

I still have some of the letters they wrote back and forth before the war, each trying to convert the other. They respected each other's views, but neither was willing to give an inch on what they believed.

February 26, 1859

Dear Dick:

Don't be eternally bristling for a fight just because you're a West Pointer. Please, Brother, vote for Bell or Breckinridge as against Lincoln. Bell stands for the Union, the Constitution, and the enforcement of law.

Affectionately,

John

Years later, Rachel, Uncle Dick's wife, recounted the conversation they had when the letter arrived in Kentucky.

"Bristling for a fight, Rachel?" he handed the letter to her. "Brother John is standing by the Union until it touches states' rights, then watch out! He'll be the first man in the field."

"But how can a man of his intelligence even *consider* secession?" she asked.

"You can't understand because you're from Minnesota. But watch what I say. The West Pointers from the South who married Southern women will join the Southern army and those who married in the North will stand by the North. See if they don't!"

Shortly after Lincoln's election, Uncle Dick sent my father this letter.

March 14, 1860

Dear Brother John,

 I am writing to tell you that I am standing on the platform you stood on in your letter: the Union, the Constitution, the enforcement of law. Surely, you are not the Johnson who is urging a vote in the Kentucky Senate for secession. Scramble back to your old platform.

              Dick

Even though their views were totally different, Uncle Dick managed to get parcels of food and clothing from the North sent to his brother all during the war.

For whatever reasons, and they were ones he held dearly, if Dr. Johnson had not stayed with the Confederacy he would never have been in Atlanta and fallen in love with Mary Willis Erwin, and I would not have arrived on the scene in 1865. The story of their marriage reflects how spontaneously things can happen during war. In the spring of 1864 President Davis asked Dr. Johnson to go to France as an envoy to seek their aid. Mother told me of the day that letter came.

She was working in the area where men were waiting for their surgery when Dr. Johnson came to her. In his hand he held out a letter. "Please read this, Mary Willis."

She thought about the implications of Jefferson Davis' request. Varina and Jefferson Davis had been great friends during her Washington years. That seemed like a century ago. She thought of the grandeur of those days as she looked around at the dead and dying, the tattered dress she wore, the gnawing hunger she felt. Could there ever have been a time when things were as simple and wonderful as they seemed back in 1848? Of course, there were all sorts of difficulties then, but compared with this . . . her eyes swept around the huge warehouse. There was nothing but misery as far as she could see. And now the President was asking John to leave all this and go to France.

"Will you go?" she asked, fearing what the answer might be.

"That all depends on you, Mary Willis."

"On me? How?"

"If you refuse to marry me, then I will go."

"And you mean . . . ?"

"That I will decline if you agree to marry me at once."

With the Union army growing closer by the day, who knew what would happen when they reached Atlanta. They might all be killed if they stayed there, but stay there they would. The idea of John's going to France filled her with a sense of loneliness. She thought back to another time she had turned her back on a man named John, a man she had loved, one who now lay in some nameless grave in Maryland. She thought for a while, then said, "Give me time to inform the family."

They lived in my father's house after they were married. He had been living there for months, but now it became her home as well. I can imagine falling into each others arms after another day at the hospital in the midst of carnage, of rotting flesh, of the moans of the dying, the screams of those having a leg removed. What a peaceful interlude that must have been, what a tiny harbor of safety from reality.

The letters that went back and forth between John and Dick detail the progress of the war. My father had been the post surgeon for the Atlanta district, while Dick, soon a general, was advancing through Tennessee toward the pivotal Battle of Atlanta.

I was always curious about the past, and none more so than the terrible year before I was born. It is difficult for anyone to imagine what my mother's life must have been like as the Union forces drew closer to Atlanta. The number of wounded increased and the ability to care for them diminished. I remember her telling me of operating with her husband for thirty-six hours at a stretch; then, after only a little food and a few hours' sleep, they were back at it again. The news came to them from the front through what the wounded soldiers told them. It was obvious the Union forces were going to take Atlanta. The soldiers gave accounts of the bravery of the Confederate forces at the Battle of Lookout Mountain, and the intervening battles coming down from southeastern Tennessee toward Atlanta, but the underlying message was always the same: The day of the Battle of Atlanta was soon to be at hand.

One night, in the summer of 1864, mother was helping the wounded get ready for their surgery. She told me the story of a young soldier with a mini ball through his thigh. As she was cleaning the dirt and mud from the wounds, she always talked to them, trying to take their minds off what lay ahead when their turn would come.

"Where's your home, son?" she asked.

"Down near Smyrna Church, but I don't 'spect to ever see it again," he said looking at the shattered bones sticking through his trousers. Most of the soldiers didn't want to talk about what happened to them, but this one was different. "I was up on the other side of Kennesaw Mountain. I'd gotten separated from my company and the next thing I knew, I was right in the middle of the headquarters of the Kentucky Volunteer Cavalry." He paused. "Do you think I could have a little snort? This leg's hurtin' somethin' fierce."

Mother gave him a bottle of whiskey she kept handy. He took two big swallows and wiped his mouth with the back of his hand.

"Right there in front of me was the Union General, big as life. His horse was wheeling around and the General was shoutin' orders this way and that, directing his troops best he could. I don' know how anybody could understand anything; you never heard such a mess of noise. The General, he didn't see me comin' and I was sure I was going to be killed any second but, by God, I was goin' to take that Yankee General with me, even if it was the last thing I did on this earth. I bayoneted a couple of soldiers while he was spinning around on his horse. He didn't even know I was there. When he turned back to me, I stuck his horse right under his neck and he reared up, kicking at me. The General fell off and landed on his back. He was stunned, but I was on him before he could move. He had his pistol out and took a shot at me, but I got him with my bayonet right in the liverlights. He grabbed at my rifle with one hand and shot me in the leg all at the same time. I stuck him three more times before I fell. My rifle hadn't been loaded for an hour; the fightin' had been so thick I couldn't take the time. I'd'a blowed his head off for good measure, if I could've. When I rolled over, the General was lying right next to me.

"'Reb,' he sez to me, 'I'm goin' to die. Get me to my brother. I want him to close my eyes for the last time.'

"Well, I didn't have any idea what he was talkin' about. Why'd he think I would be takin' him anywhere, since I'd just killed him? He lay back and was bleeding all over the place. I figured I was dead too, but I took his pistol. I planned to kill me a few more Yanks before I died. That's the last thing I remember, Ma'am. I don't know how I got here. I guess the Yanks thought I was dead and when they pulled back, the Rebs found me. I still got that General's pistol." He held it out to my mother. She stared at it in disbelief. It was a standard issue Colt, but engraved just below the cylinder was a name. Richard Johnson, Kentucky Volunteer Cavalry, General, USA.

"Are you sure he was dead?" Mother asked, her blood running cold.

"Oh, yes, ma'am. I stuck him real good. Wiggled that bayonet all the way to the good Georgia clay. Pinned him like a bug to the ground. He's dead, all right."

Mother said she finished getting his wound cleaned and his leg ready for amputation. She wondered if she should tell John. Though it seemed unlikely, maybe the soldier was wrong. When she told her husband what she had heard and showed him the pistol, for a time he was totally silent, then he said, "It won't be long before we're right behind him."

"Maybe it's a mistake," mother told him. But it wasn't. Word came the next day that the Yankee, General Richard Johnson, had been killed. Mother said her husband sat down on a feed sack and put his head in his hands, then he looked up. "Dick was doing what he had to do. and so are we. Let's get that Reb in here and, at least, try to save his life." So even with the terrible news they continued to operate through the night, the artillery to the north becoming louder by the hour.

Everyone had been hearing about General Sherman, a fierce

man who was in command of the Army of the Cumberland and
the Army of Tennessee. He was a ruthless soldier, or that's what all
the wounded soldiers were saying. He had more than 110,000
men, and General Hood, the Confederate general on whom everyone
was depending had only 70,000. My father had a lot of respect for
General Hood; he was a brave man, but stubborn. His men called
him, "Old Woodenhead." In the middle of July he took command
of the defense of Atlanta, but right in the middle of the siege,
President Davis replaced him with General Joseph E. Johnston.

By that time, there was such a state of confusion that no one
really cared who was in command. It was a foregone conclusion
that Atlanta was doomed and there was a terrible rush to escape to
the south. Thousands had, although there were many more left
behind, my parents among them. Since they were desperately
needed in the hospital they felt they had to stay. "Why didn't you
leave and go down to the plantations in the south, near Macon?" I
asked Mother.

She gave me a long look, then said, "You don't know what
you're asking. First of all the Macon plantation, like all the others,
was deserted by now. The slaves had all left, so there were no crops,
no one to help look after the place. And even if there had been, I
was Mrs. Johnson now, not the widow of Frank Erwin. We could
have run somewhere, but your father would never have left his
post. I wouldn't have left without him. In fact, I probably would
have stayed even if it hadn't been for him. I kept thinking about
John Lamar and Crampton's Gap. Who had looked after him when
he was hurt? Maybe he wasn't killed outright, but just mortally
wounded. If that had happened, I hoped that somebody, Yankee
or Reb—it didn't matter—was there to help him. In a sense I was
paying back a debt that I hoped was owed."

"What was it like when the Yankees finally got there?"

"Well, it all happened by stages. The fires up north of the city
were burning brighter every night. We were out of food, almost
out of water, and it was hot as could be. When the first Yankees
started running through the streets, everyone thought they might
start shooting and killing anybody in sight, but they didn't. They

ransacked all the stores, although there was nothing left for them to take. They broke out all the windows, then set fire to the buildings. Townspeople were told that our 'property would be respected,' but that turned out to be a lie. The soldiers took everything they could. One of the main things they did was destroy all the railroads. By the middle of July only one line was running, the Macon & Western, and by the end of the month, that had been shut down, too. When the city fell in early September, they totally destroyed the terminus and all the train yards even though there were no tracks that led anywhere. The mills for weaving, the rolling mills where weapons were being made, everything that could used for anything was set afire.

"And here we were with thousands of wounded boys. We packed them up as best we could and took them out of the city by the wagon load. If I live to be a hundred, I'll never forget that. Those children . . . and that's what they seemed like to me . . . half blown apart and banging down the roads with thirty or more of them on board. Some were too close to death to even know what was going on. They were the lucky ones. Many is the time I heard boys screaming to be taken off the wagon and left by the roadside to die. That was better than being tossed about on a hip half shot away."

"How in the world could you have lived through that?" I asked.

"Didn't really think about it. By that time I was so numb with all that I had seen, all that happened to me, I just put one foot in front of the other. After the city burned, we moved from the hospital where we had been staying back to the house which, somehow, had been spared. We settled in and looked after ourselves as best we could. Your father was always busy because he was willing to help whoever needed him. There was no money, but people brought us what little they had to share and we managed to get by. To compare that with life on the Athens plantation just ten years before was too painful to bear. By that time I was expecting you. I thought long and hard about what it was to bring a child into the world we had found, but somehow I thought there might be a special hope in new babies born after the war was over. That gave me a sense of courage about you, Sallie."

Mother never said much more about the war, although I asked her a lot, even when she was old and dying herself. I wanted to learn as much as I could about it. I do recall one story that stuck out in my mind. After General Sherman had started toward Savannah, the Yankees were burning everything in sight. At New Hope Church they were preparing to burn a mansion they had surrounded. Just as the torches were being lit, an old Negro woman came around the corner and sat in the middle of the road. She hid her face in her hands and cried over and over, "Lawd have murcy! What gonna happen to Miss Cecelia now?"

General Sherman rode over to her and said, "What's the full name of your mistress?"

The old mammy got enough control of herself to tell him. "Miss Cecelia Stovall Shellum."

General Sherman looked stunned. "Cecelia Stovall!" he exclaimed and took a page from his notebook on which he wrote the following note:

> My Dear Madam:
>     You once told me you pitied the man who would ever become my foe. My answer was to you, Cecelia, that I would ever protect and shield you. That, I am now doing. Forgive all else, as I am but a soldier.
>                                       Gen. W.T. Sherman

A guard was posted to save the house from destruction. All those years after as a West Point cadet when the lovely Cecelia had been his love, General Sherman had a chance to make good on his promise. I always liked that story. Things that showed any humanity were hard to come by and, when found, seemed a special treasure.

Through the rest of the war my parents carried the burden of the deaths of so many of their friends, made all the worse by members of their own families who had died, none more precious than my father's brother. Early in the summer of 1865, the war just barely concluded, my father was sitting in his office, tending Union soldiers who were stationed in Atlanta. His nurse came in and said there was an officer who insisted that he see Dr. Johnson immediately, that he would not wait his turn. Impatiently, my father told the nurse to have him take a seat and he would be with him shortly. After she delivered the message, the officer burst through the door, standing in front of my father's desk, unable to speak. He was using a cane and thin as a worn rail, but he was— unmistakably—General Richard Johnson. Neither of them spoke, but fell into an embrace. I don't suppose there has ever been a happier reunion, although any family who ever had a son erroneously reported as killed in action can understand the depth of that feeling. I was only four months old then, but I have heard that story so many times I feel as though I was there. Uncle Dick and his family became such an important part of my life that I can feel the blessing of that moment as if it had happened to me.

Stories of horror were at every hand. In listening to them years later, I wondered if they were exaggerated, but I have come to believe they were not. Although great efforts had been made to evacuate the city before it fell, thousands were left behind. Many of them were too ill to move, many too defeated in spirit even to try. Although the wounded were a major problem, there were just as many who were ill from disease. Typhoid, dysentery, lockjaw, low camp fever—those problems disabled and killed as many as the bullets and cannon. Those who died had to be buried. My mother, organized anyone who could wield a shovel to put them in shallow graves, frequently in groups. It wasn't uncommon in the least when we would be digging in the back lot of a house to come upon a skeleton. The idea now seems horrifying, but we just went and told our mothers who would come cover him up again.

The first time I realized what lay in those fields down toward the creek, I was picking blackberries and saw a funny looking rock sticking up in the middle of a little bush. Mammy Sophy was with me. I went over to the rock and tried to pull it up. It was a shoe! Worse than that, there was a foot inside. "Oh, Mammy! There's a dead person here," I yelled. She came waddling over, took a look and said, "Sho' nuff. I thought we'd got all 'em outta here, but guess we done missed a few."

"You mean there were more than him," I said, pointing at the shoe and backing away.

"Lawd, yes, chile. Dis heah field right down to da crick was fulla dead boys. I remember yo' mama and her friends got up a load of lumber from out at Stone Mountain and had Jim and all the mens makin' coffins and diggin' up what they could find and den buryin' 'em. I said to Jim after dey got started, 'Lawd, Jim, you say dem dead soljers arms 'n legs is scattered off from der bodies?'"

'Dey sho' is. I nuv'r seen as many jints layin' off to derself in m'life.'

"'What does you do wid'em?'" I asked.

'Do wid'em?' Jim sez, 'We picks'em up an' give ever' soljer two arms and two legs. Dat's what we does wid'em.'

"I won't satisfied wid dat answer," Mammy Sophy told me. "I sez to Jim, 'But 'spose you gives de wrong jints to der wrong soljer? Dey'll hant you sure as da day you wuz born.'" Mammy was always suspicious about ghosts.

'Dat's whut I says, too, when we first started gittin' dirt off'em, but atter me and Josiah talk it ober, we decided dose soljers wouldn' need no feets until Jedgment day an' . . . '

"I stopped Jim from talkin' foolishness right dere. 'How dey gonna rise on der wrong feets on Jedgment Day? Dat's what I wanna know.'"

'Dat's whut I'm tryin' to tell you, Mammy.'

"'Well, tell it, man!'"

'As I wuz sayin', dey gwinna lie still 'til Gabrel blow his trumpet' and by dat time, Miss Mary Willis'll be up in heb'n an' she'll git der right feets fo' all'em.'

Mammy laughed and slapped her ample thighs. "Jim sho' nuff right 'bout dat, Miss Sally. Dere ain' nuthin' yo mama can't do!"

Mammy wasn't through with her story, though. "I recollects after Miss Mary Willis heared 'bout da feets and da jints, she hadda dream dat somebody wus gwinna steal dat lumber she done found down at Stone Mountain. Da next mawnin' she make Dr. Johnson hitch up da buggy and drive her all da way down dere to make sure nobody wuz gitten her coffin wood. And don' you know, chile, da carpetbaggers had two loads of dat wood and wuz high tailin' outta dere when she got dere. Dr. Johnson, he tuck care of dem, right now, das a fact. Dey brought da wood home and ol' Jim and Josiah made coffins till dey 'bout needed one demselves."

By that time, the blackberry picking was done, but Mammy Sophy wanted to talk some more about Mother. "Miss Mary Willis, right afta da war, tol' allus to stay on da plantation till she could figger out whut to do wid us. We didn' wanna do dat. Some of da field hans', dey stayed, but da house servants, we all come up heah to Atlanta to be wid yo' folks. Yo' papa, he find places for mos' of us to stay, but only three-four of us could stay right here. Da rest of'em wuz off wherever Dr. Johnson could find a place for'em. But dey wuz neber happy. Dey all wanna be right here wid yo' folks.

"I remember old Malviny and her three chillun showin' up one afternoon, all crying and bawling. 'What's wrong?' Miss Mary Willis say. 'Is der chillun hurt? Is you sick?'

"When Malviny stop cryin' she finally say, 'Lawd, Miss Ma'y Willis, dey ain' no use tryin' to live wid no po' white trash.'

"Yo' mama say, 'Whatchu talkin' 'bout, Malviny? Dose folks is rich and we don' have enuff to feed ourselves. You gotta have a place to stay."

'I can' hep dat,' Malviny whined, 'We jes' come to you an' we'll starve together. It don' make no diffrence how much money he got, dey's still nuthin' but po'white trash. Dat man hit me. He whupp'd my chilluns, an' I sez to him, "Mister, you rich, but you gimme da first lick I ev'uh had from white folks. I wuz born a slave, but my white folks neber laid a blessed han' on me. I'se goin' back to *my* white folks," and heah I is.'

"Yo' mama, Miss Sally, she come ober to us an' asked Phyllis, Kitty, Miranda and me to double up so's Malviny an' her chilluns would have a place ta live. We did it. Wuz like a jar of pickled beets in dat cabin, but we got by."

It was comments like that which let me know my parents had been good to the slaves and the servants who stayed with them. I get impatient with people, particularly from the North, telling tales they don't know anything about. Some terrible things did happen. Slavery was terrible, the war was terrible, the way the Negroes were treated by some after the war was terrible, but not everybody was the same. Those servants loved my parents and they loved me right up till the time they died. That's because they knew we loved them.

After the war, all sorts of new problems arose. The difficulties of Reconstruction were beyond imagination, but during those terrible times, I was a little girl. A more immediate problem was who would be my playmates. There were many people from the North brought into Atlanta to administer the occupation. It was not unusual for an Atlanta family to find northerners living next door. In many cases the children were forbidden to play with them. I suppose that was a natural way for our parents to feel about the conquerors, but it certainly made no sense to me. A child is a child and they are to be played with. That's what I thought from the very beginning. It was through the playmates that the adults began to speak to one another. When sickness came to a playmate, mothers would begin to compare notes, to make suggestions or to help with the care of the other children while the mother attended the sick one. Out of such encounters began to grow the first tentative healings of hatred that ran too deep for words. Looking back on that and remembering it was my playmates and I who began to make things better, I realize that was an important lesson for me, too; one that I have carried into my old age. Sometimes it was more serious than children's games. Young southern women were falling in love with handsome Yankee officers. I remember when my cousin, Elizabeth Overby, announced that she was going to marry Yankee Lt. Williams. The family was appalled. I remember her family saying, "It cannot be!" It was an ultimatum.

"Why, Lizzie," said her mother, "We gave our all, our wealth for the cause of the Confederacy. Your dear father fell on the field of battle! And now you're going to marry . . . a Yankee?" She could hardly get the words beyond her teeth.

Lizzie threw herself in the arms of her uncle, General John B. Gordon, weeping inconsolably. "I know! I know, Uncle John, but I love Lieutenant Williams so. I love him with all my heart!"

The General raised his hand and looked into her face, said, "Then you shall marry him, Elizabeth."

Healing was taking place, although slowly, on many levels. I was too young to remember all of that, but I heard the story many times over when, as a young woman, I visited them in their home at West Point, New York. Happiness and love filled that house and did till the end of their days. I often think about their happy marriage and how it grew out of a conflict that shattered countless others, my own mother's the closest to my heart

The horrors of Reconstruction lived on until I was in my early teen years. The tragedy and turmoil of the time, the brutality and corruption were on every hand. The carpetbaggers and the scalawags made life miserable for everyone. My family was very lucky. Compared to many, we lived exceptionally well. Not until I was grown and had seen some of the world did I realize how terrible life in the Atlanta of the 1860s and 1870s had been for most. We still had a house and clothes to wear. We did have food, but never much of it. Most of Daddy's patients paid their bills with vegetables, fruits, eggs and chickens. There was little or no money and even today, even after a wonderful meal served in the most elegant homes in Washington, New York, Vienna or wherever, I still remember how hungry we sometimes were. As a child I was grateful to get any food, never thinking that other children had given up that meal for me. I was often hungry, but I learned not to talk about it.

I remember one night after playing in the hot sun all afternoon I came in to dinner. I must have been about seven or eight. The meal that night was cornbread and molasses. That had been the meal for the past week. I took one look at it, and when Daddy took our hands to ask the blessing, I said, "I don't think God expects us to be thankful for this." I felt his hand tighten on mine but he went ahead and blessed it anyway. As he took his napkin, shook it out and placed it in his lap, he looked at Mother. She looked at me. Then, Daddy said, "Sallie, there are children not five hundred feet from your chair who have never seen a meal like this. Tonight, they will have clay for their supper. It won't help them, but it will swell up in their stomachs and they will feel full. You think about that, and then you can say your own blessing that you don't *really* know what it is to be hungry." Then he took up his fork and said to mother, "Mary Willis, sitting opposite you makes any meal a feast."

Even then, I knew I was the favorite of my father. He'd been through the loss of his wife, of some of his children; for a time he had thought his brother was dead. My father was old enough to be my grandfather, and he treated me that way much of the time, but I loved him so much that when he spoke to me as earnestly as he did that night, I paid attention. It didn't take away the hunger. It did lead me to sample some clay that I knew some of my friends ate regularly. To this day, I can remember the feel, the taste of dirt. Those were hard years, but they were a time when I learned a lot about living. It certainly gave me an appreciation for all the things that would come my way in later years. Had we not known the deprivation of the Reconstruction years, I don't think the good things of my later life would have been weighed on an accurate scale. The loving nature of my parents made up for much of what we lacked, and that was a blessing beyond measure.

# CHAPTER III

War makes treasures of common things. When all the grandeur that once was as enfolding as a warm comforter is stripped away, then what really matters stands out in bold relief. I've never had to live through any hardship that remotely approached what my parents went through during the war. The wars and those lost in them that I have experienced have been, while close to my heart, thousands of miles removed from my home.

Dr. Johnson's home on Pryor street was on the front line. Down the street from our house was The Terraces, one of the most magnificent homes in Atlanta. It took up an entire city block and had belonged to Rawson and Elizabeth Clarke before the war. They were in the hardware business and owned Rawson, Gilbert & Burr. Like so many wonderful homes during the occupation, it was taken over by the federal government and used to house important families or as a headquarters. The Terraces was occupied by Brigadier General John W. Geary. The Rawson's had four daughters, all nearly grown when I was born, but Mr. Rawson kept an accurate record of the Battle of Atlanta and the subsequent evacuation. Reading those documents helped me as a young woman to appreciate what actually had happened.

In the summer of 1864, Mother and her husband were working in The Calico House, near the center of town. It served not only as a hospital, but as a supply depot for clothing, ammunition, food and medical supplies. It is a beautiful place, two stories, flanked by wings and a veranda overhung with a balcony supported by

four scrolled columns. Somehow, the gingerbread around the eaves
even managed to escape the destruction. A cupola sits atop a four-
pitched roof and was used for a lookout as General Sherman's troops
approached the city. As the shelling became more intense, Mother
and Dr. Johnson moved from The Calico House or whatever hospital
they were working in, to his house. During the rare times they
were not operating, getting away from the carnage became necessary
for sanity. The lot and the yard behind the house took up nearly
two city blocks. Just beyond the blackberry fields were the cabins
where Mammy Sophy and all the servants lived. Many of the homes
on Pryor Street, The Terraces probably included, had built shelters
in the back yard to protect the family, as well as the servants, from
the increasing shelling. They were simply called, "The Pits." The
one at our house was converted into a storage room after the war.
Mammy Sophy would never let me play in there. "Dere's snakes
down dere bigger'n yo' leg, Miss Sallie. One of'em grab you and
drag you off fo' supper. Yo' mama have a fit if'n she find out I lets
you in dere."

But I was curious and would, full of fear and excitement, sneak
in when she wasn't looking. It was entirely below ground, and not
more than six feet tall, as I recall, and probably ten or twelve feet
square. At the time it seemed large, but I can hardly imagine adults
and children staying in there when I think about it today. The
roof was made of large timber and the walls re-enforced with logs.
There was no ventilation and, even below ground, it must have
been stifling in the summer. Most of the wood was later taken
down and used for fuel after the war was over. I went back into The
Pit as a young woman. I thought about my parents, my mother
thirty-eight when I was born, and my father in his late fifties.
Looking back as an adult, I can understand how precious a new
baby would be, given all that they had lost.

My father, with grown children of his own, my mother with
children by her Col. Erwin had come together and fallen in love in
the worst of circumstances. It seems natural to think a child born
out of all that hardship would occupy a special place in the hearts
of the parents. As a little girl, I certainly didn't know that, but

when I think back to my earlier years, particularly how my father adored me, then it becomes a little more understandable that I felt favored as a child. It would have been entirely possible to have grown up completely spoiled and self-centered in such a setting, but the overall hardship of our lives probably saved me from being totally self-absorbed. Then of course, there was Mother and Mammy Sophy.

If my father was going to spoil me, then Mother and Mammy were going to make sure that didn't happen. While the idea of slavery is totally abhorrent, the servants who stayed with families became a part of those families. The blessings of my parents were great, but hardly more than those of Mammy Sophy and Mammy Phyllis, who was with Mother from her days in Washington until her death.

My Uncle Howell, I scarcely remember. The stories of him are legend.,and it is through those often-repeated family tales that I recall him. In reading over his life, I wonder what might have become of him had he lived. Although he left national politics and wore the uniform of the CSA, his belief in the importance of fighting the Reconstruction policies of Congress was unshakable. After the war he opened a law practice with his cousin, Henry Jackson, the son of General Jackson, who arranged the marriage of my mother to Colonel Erwin. Uncle Howell's wife, Mayon, continued in poor health. He spared no effort to find help for her. In the fall of 1868 when I was just three years old, he took her to Saratoga Springs, New York, for the baths. The idea of healing baths was still widely enjoyed. On October 9, returning to Georgia, he died suddenly in New York City.

Although he was fifteen years older than my mother, they shared an unusual bond, especially strong because of her help to him during his years in Washington and as governor. Her grieving, as well as her age and general fatigue, may have made her less patient with the antics of a three year old, but her sternness coupled with the firm loving of Mammy Sophy was more than tempered by my gentle, old father. All things considered, every child should be so lucky!

There's no question about it: I did get by with a lot because of
my father. One morning as we were finishing breakfast, I recall an
especially blatant example. As a rare treat, Mammy had served
scrambled eggs, fried ham, grits and biscuits with red-eye gravy. It
was shortly after Uncle Howell died and I suspect she was trying
to cheer up everyone. Mammy didn't like gloomy faces around her
table. We certainly didn't eat that well very often . . . that's one
reason I remember it so vividly. When I had finished the meal,
there was still a little red-eye gravy mixed in with the grits, so I
just picked up my plate and licked it clean. Mother was horrified.

"Sallie! Put that plate down this instant. You're not one of the
yard dogs. Where are your manners? Mammy!" she called, "Come
get this child and take her to her room."

"Oh, please. I won't do it again," I wailed, but my father came
to my rescue.

"It's all right, Mammy, I'll take care of this," and placing his
hand on the back of the high chair, and turning to Mother, said,
"She shall not be sent from the table. If little Sallie licks her plate,
I'm going to lick mine, too. Whatever Sallie does is right."

Mother threw up her hands with a groan of despair.

"You just watch me, my dear," he spoke seriously, as picked
up his plate, licked it clean, then headed for the porch and the
morning paper.

I was out of my chair and right after him I went, Tabby Cat in my
arms. I certainly didn't want to be left alone with Mother and Mammy.
I sat down on the top step and watched him shake open his paper. He
was sitting in his rocking chair reading intently when our next-door
neighbor, Colonel Scruggs, walked by. He was editor of *The Atlanta
Sun* and a great friend of the family. Even as a little girl I knew he was
a man to respect. "Good morning, Dr. Johnson," he called out. He
waved his gold-headed cane in the direction of the porch.

"Ah, good morning to you, Colonel. Good morning, indeed."
He laid his paper aside and said, "Oh, by the way Colonel, I have
a new thought for you today."

"Really? Let's hear it." He paused, resting his cane on his foot
just on the other side of the picket fence.

Father glanced at me. "Little Sallie has just introduced us to an important idea. We're all going to lick our plates when we finish eating."

Colonel Scruggs looked puzzled, not having any idea what the point was. "Yes," Father continued, "This morning Sallie licked her plate clean after breakfast. Her mother was upset, but of course, you and I know that Sallie never does anything wrong, so I think we should all follow her example. Think of all the water we will save by not having to wash dishes! Isn't that a fine idea? Tell Mrs. Scruggs You might even want to write an editorial about it."

Father smiled at me, but there was something in his face that made me think I was missing the point. Colonel Scruggs had a peculiar look on his face, one that let me know without his saying it, that I had done a bad thing. I drooped my head into Tabby Cat's furry back. As soon as the Colonel had left, I jumped into Father's lap and said, "Oh, please don't lick your plate! It's bad manners. I won't ever do it again!"

"Well, well! You see how we must be careful about what we do and say. Since you are a perfect little girl, you have to set a good example." He squeezed me tightly in his arms and said, "Your mother and I will follow your example in everything."

I remember that lesson well and far better, I suspect, than if I had been sent to my room as Mother had demanded. But that wasn't the only example. From relatives, I heard comments about the way he treated me. My Aunt Mildred was visiting one day and I overheard her in the drawing room.

"Mary Willis! I just don't understand it. Dr. Johnson is a beloved physician. He's the friend and confidante of powerful statesmen and scholars, respected by everyone, but when it comes to the raising of Sallie, he trails off into a line of apparent insanity! Why, just the other night he interrupted a conversation with General Toombs and Senator Stephens just so Sallie could say 'Good night.'"

Mother could see both sides. She smiled at Aunt Mildred. "Yes, he did. And it was the cutest thing you ever saw. Everyone just went wild over her."

"My heavens, Mary Willis! You're as bad as Dr. Johnson!"

"No, no, Millie. I gave her three switchings yesterday. I know when to punish, but she's such a good little thing she never tells her Father that she's had a whipping."

"But why do you allow her at your dinner parties?" Aunt Mildred demanded.

"Oh, that's an exaggeration. She just sits beside her Papa for a few minutes, then Mammy comes and puts her to bed."

"But why don't you put her to bed before the guests arrive? No one likes to have children underfoot at a seated dinner."

Mother laughed. "I did that once and the first thing the guests did was ask, 'Where is little Sallie? We must hear one of her little songs or speeches before dinner.' So I had to go get her dressed and bring her into the parlor."

Aunt Mildred was not convinced. "Well, all I can say is only the Grace of God will save that child!"

As the only child of these unusual parents there's no doubt I was treated differently. The three children of Dr. Johnson by his first wife were all grown and gone. The two surviving children of my mother's marriage to Col. Erwin were years older than I was, so I was really treated as though I were the only child. Lucy Erwin, my half-sister, was away in school most of the time, so I didn't have much contact with her until my teen years. I suspect, had she been younger and living in the house, things would have been different.

Mother had a way of getting her point across by having me teach myself the lesson she wanted me to learn and making a game out of it at the same time. The game was called "Playing Lady." I would get dressed up in whatever grown-up clothes I could find, and would appear at the front door for an afternoon visit.

"Come in," Mother would chime from the front parlor, and in I would sashay. "I don't believe I caught your name, madam," Mother would comment. That was always part of the game—a stranger at the door.

"Mrs. Evergreen is my name," I would answer, with a toss of my head, "and I have heard that you have a very bad little girl, Sallie Johnson."

"I certainly have. Do sit down, Mrs. Evergreen, and tell me what I'm to do with her."

"Well," Mrs. Evergreen laughed. "You've heard about *my* terrible little girl, Sallie Cobb, I'm sure. She's the worst child in all of Atlanta."

"Isn't that strange! We both have such naughty girls and they're both named Sallie. What makes your Sallie so bad, Mrs. Evergreen?"

"Oh, it's her father," she said with a deep sigh. "He spoils her so and I have to whip her every day to make up for it."

"I switch my Sallie, too," Mother said, "but it does *no* good!"

That was the way the conversation usually went. Mrs. Evergreen was forever trying to make my mother feel that little Sallie Johnson couldn't possibly be as bad as little Sallie Cobb and that Mother should be grateful for what she had. Of course, it never influenced the way Mother disciplined me . . . or the way I behaved, for that matter, but it was great fun.

I saved my Mrs. Evergreen performances just for Mother. Mammy, who spent a lot of her time chasing after me, was much easier to handle. While she was full of blusterings and bluffs, I knew that I could have my way with her. Many was the time I would run out to play in the mud, no respect for my good clothes and after Mother's stern admonition to Mammy, "Now, don't you let Sallie out of this house with all that mud around. You know exactly what she'll do." And she was right. Mammy would drag me back in, change my clothes and we'd go through the same thing again.

"Miss Sallie, I gwinna tell yo' ma sure as' da day I wuz born. I gwinna have her wear you out," she would say, washing me off yet another time.

"You wouldn't tell on me, Mammy, would you?" I would throw my arms around her and kiss her cheek, her skin soft and smooth as any brown velvet. "Would you tell? Would you?"

"You knows I ain't gwinna tell . . . but I oughta!"

But even with all the collusion, Mother was hard to fool. "Why are you changing Sallie's clothes, Mammy? She was perfectly clean when I left and now she's a mess," she said, picking up the muddy clothes Mammy was trying to hide from her. "Well, I see. I think I'll just follow Mrs. Evergreen's advice and give Miss Sallie Johnson a good switching. Mammy, go out there and pick me a nice long forsythia switch."

"Oh, Mama, please let Mrs. Evergreen visit one more time. I'm sure she has a better idea." She looked at me, trying to suppress a smile. "Well, all right. I'll listen to what she has to say."

Into my costume I hurried and knocked on the door.

"Come in," Mother answered, sternly. "How do you do, Mrs. Evergreen?"

"Don't call me Mrs. Evergreen," I answered, frothing with indignation. "My name is Mrs. Tom Thumb. I wouldn't be like that mean Mrs. Evergreen. Everybody hates her. She's the meanest woman in town, even her own little Sallie Cobb hates her." With a change of voice, I said, "Now, Mrs. Johnson, I have a little Sallie, too, and she's the best little girl you ever saw!"

"How in the world did you make her so good, Mrs. Tom Thumb?" Mother was trying hard not to laugh.

"Why, I just stopped switching her. No, Ma'am. I never switch my little Sallie. Whenever she's bad, I just talk sweetly to her, let her have tea with Mammy, and she's the best thing you ever saw." I jumped up in her lap and said, "Now, Mama, what are you going to do? What Mrs. Evergreen said, or what Mrs. Tom Thumb said?"

Mother laughed. "Today, I'm not going to do either, but in the future, I think I will follow Mrs. Evergreen's advice."

By the time I was nine it had been ten years since the Battle of Atlanta. There had been only about six thousand people living there before the war, but it grew quickly after the occupation began. Bit by bit, the rubble was cleared away and new buildings began to appear. It reminded me of a spring garden: One day, there's nothing but bare earth, and then the ground is all but obscured with new growth. The old buildings that had been left standing were filled with the occupation forces, but by the mid 1870s the number was dwindling. Peachtree Street, Whitehall, and Pryor were filling the vacant lots with new buildings. The railroads, which had been the reason Atlanta was founded in the first place, were being rebuilt. The rails the Union soldiers had heated over the bonfires they made with the cross ties, then twisted like pretzels, were all cleaned up, re-smelted and new rails fashioned. I was particularly interested in the railroads. There was something special about those ribbons, glinting in the afternoon sun and disappearing around the curve or into the distance. I would lie in my bed at night and I could hear the trains, shifting and blowing their whistles as they started out of town. That sound gave me a sense of adventure. Mother had told me of her train trips before the war, the long rides with John Lamar to Washington, the special times they had together. That planted in my head a romantic notion that adventure lay just up the road on those trains.

Travel by other means was tedious and uncertain. The country roads were deeply rutted, bumpy beyond belief in dry weather and a river of mud, red as liquid brick, in the rain. Even with good horses and fair weather, a trip of 20 miles was a good day's journey, while the trains would sometimes cover that much in an hour. The trip to Athens where the family lived was almost a hundred miles, so it was a long journey for anyone, particularly a child. Speed is something you become accustomed to. I never thought carriages were particularly slow until I rode on a train, then trips that had seemed manageable by horse and buggy began to seem interminable. I was delighted when I was old enough to ride the train by myself.

In 1874, I began to spend each summer with my cousins, the Rutherford girls, in Athens. That was the beginning of lifelong friendships with those girls, particularly Lamar. In the summer of that year, my first trip, Mother and Father loaded me into the buggy with Jim and Mammy to take me to the train station. In later years, it seemed odd that they didn't take me themselves, but sending me off with Mammy and Jim was virtually the same as if my parents had gone along; that's how much trust they had in them. We hadn't gone a half mile before Jim and Mammy had a chance to prove that. All up and down Peachtree were dozens of saloons, houses where women seemed to be standing around with nothing to do, and a lot of people just milling in the street. We were trotting along when a pair of drunks stepped out of a saloon and saw me, all gussied up in fancy clothes—Mammy dressed me like I was going to church whenever I rode the train. "You're Miss Sallie Johnson! You gon' look like you's a real lady 'fore I lets you outta my sight." Then she would add, "An' you better act like one, too!"

The two men started toward the buggy. "Looky there, Billy." Them darkies got themselves a little white doll. Don't they look like they think there're somethin' special, sittin' up there all high and mighty?" He skipped up to the horse and grabbed the bridle. The other one started toward me, but Jim was out of the carriage before he got half way across the street. Mammy said to me, and in a voice that I knew she meant it, "Sit right where you is, chile. Don' you move a inch," then she hopped out of the buggy with amazing grace for such a heavy woman. She walked up to the man holding the bridle, pushing up her sleeves as she went. He was a runty-looking little man, Mammy made about three of him. The man walking toward me stopped, and so did a lot of people on the street. Mammy put her face about an inch from the little fellow and said, "You don' wanna see me get mad, does you? Oh, I don' think so, 'cause when I gets mad, strange things happ'n. I don' know what I'se likely to do." His eyes were getting big, but he still held the bridle.

"Dat's sho' nuff de truth," Jim volunteered to his partner. "Why, jes' las' week she got so mad I seen her bite de head off a live rooster. An' you see dis piece of missing ear I got?" Mammy pulled her lips back and showed her teeth, made funny noise in her throat, and said, "Lissen to what he say, po' white trash. You let go dis here hoss, or I'se gonna have both yo' ears." She looked at him without blinking. He dropped the bridle and stepped back unsteadily. His friend, happy not to be the center of attention, tried to melt back into the crowd, all of whom had enjoyed the scene.

"Good thing 'tweren't you out there," one of them said to him. "Big as your nose is, it would have been a nice mouthful for her." Everybody laughed as Jim and Mammy jumped back in the buggy and off we went toward the station.

"Mammy, would you have really bitten off both his ears? I asked.

"Oh, yes, Miss Sallie. She'd'a don' it and spit'em on his boots."

"You jes' shet yo' mouth, James. Miss Sallie don' need to hear nuthin like dat."

I wasn't satisfied. "Would you have done that?"

Mammy shook her head and said, "If'n anybody tried ta lay a hand on you, sweet chile, den dey'll cuss de day dey drew dere first breath. Dat's all I got to say."

We rode along in silence for a while, then Mammy said, "Miss Sallie, you knows I don' tell yo' mama everything you gets into. 'Bout goin' down into da Pit, playin' in da mud, an' sech. Now I wants you to do der same thing fo'me. Don' you go tell yo mama how mean ol' Mammy Sophy can be."

I nestled up close to her. "You're not mean, Mammy, but I won't tell." And I didn't, but I didn't forget that day. After that, I never doubted Mammy would have died in that street—or any other—before she would let harm come to me. She was that way as long as she lived.

When we got to the station, the train was sitting there. It was hot, so of course all the windows were open. I would be covered with soot by the time I got to Athens four hours later. Mammy carried my bags and Jim had my trunk on his back. When we found the conductor, Mammy gave him money for the ticket and said, "Dis here is Miss Sallie Johnson. She de little girl of Dr. John Johnson. I 'spect you knows him. He a famous man. Her mama, she knows de prezident of dis here railroad, so I knows you gwinna take good care of her and see dat she get to Dr. Rutherford in Athens without no harm comin' to her."

The conductor smiled at her, bent down and said, "Well, I've got a little girl just about your age, Miss Sallie, and I'm going to take care of you just like you were her." Mammy seemed satisfied, reached down and gave me a hug, then said, "Come on, James, let's git on back up der street."

The conductor carried my trunk up to the baggage car, then helped me on the train. The seats were dark red velvet . . . at least that's what they had been once. Now they showed the dirty imprints of thousands of bottoms and the nap of the velvet was a crushed and sooty-looking maroon. I wondered if Mammy had ever ridden on a train. I knew she would never let me sit on a chair that dirty in a store. The conductor put my bag up over my head, pulled up the window next to my seat and said he would be back and check on me soon as the train started. There wasn't a breath of air stirring in the train shed. Flies were everywhere, and when I ran my finger along the window sill, it came back as black as if I had cleaned the ashes out of my bedroom fireplace. I was so excited about the trip, I didn't really pay any attention to the heat and the dirt. I was just settling back in my seat, my legs barely touching floor when I saw Mammy waddling down the platform. I stuck my head out the window and called to her.

"Dere you is, Miss Sallie," she panted. "I jes' wanna tell you, don' you go talkin' to no strangers! I knows whadda friendly little lady you is, but don' you say nary a word to no menfolks."

That seemed to be a dumb bit of advice. There wasn't anyone on the train that I would know. And most of them were men. Did she expect me to sit quietly by myself all day? I'd never done anything like that in my life.

"You heah what I say, chile?" she demanded.

"Yes, I do, Mammy. I will be a good little lady." She seemed satisfied, not realizing that I hadn't promised to do anything she said.

"Good. I'se gwinna miss you so, Miss Sallie." She reached her hand up and took mine. She gave it a squeeze, then I heard Jim calling her to hurry up.

"I got work to do, Mammy. Cain't be standin' 'round here all day watching you blubber. Miss Sallie, she be fine. Don' you worry none."

After Mammy left, I began to feel sad. I would miss Mother and Father, but all my aunts and uncles and their children would keep me company while I was in Athens. But there wasn't going to be anybody to take Mammy Sophy's place.

Soon, I heard the conductor shout, and the engine, just ahead of my car blew its whistle and with an awful belch of smoke and steam, the train began to move. Through the streets of downtown Atlanta, heading north, we went. I could see the back of Pryor Street and The Terraces. I could even see Mammy Sophy's cabin and the blackberry brambles where we still were finding pieces of soldiers and broken weapons. The houses began to thin out, then we were in pine thickets, interrupted by the fields. I'd seen cotton growing before, but there were all sorts of other plants, people bending over, picking and weeding. It made our little garden at home where we got most of our vegetables look tiny. As the train went, by the people, working in the fields would straighten up, their black skin shiny as wet licorice. I would wave to them. Sometimes, they wiped their brows and just stared back, but every now and then, they would wave. The children in the fields would stop their work and run along beside the train, but soon they were left behind, panting in the hot sun. I wondered what it would be like to work like they did. Some of the children were much younger than I. Did they look at me, laughing and waving, wishing they could change places with me? I remember that thought because of all the thousands and thousands of miles I would ride on trains in my life, I frequently thought of those children out near Stone Mountain on that first train ride. I wondered how their lives had turned out. Of course, I never knew the true answer, but as I grew older, it wasn't hard to imagine that most of them died in or near those fields where their first memories took form. Traveling, even as a child, began to give me a sense of how different life is for some.

Although Mammy had given me a good breakfast, I was soon hungry and opened the picnic hamper she had fixed for me. It was enough food for several days. I looked around the coach. No one else seemed to have any food. Across the aisle sat a man about my mother's age. He was looking straight ahead, never looking out the window or at anyone else. I slid over to the aisle and asked him if he would like some fried chicken. At first, I thought he hadn't heard me, but then he turned to me and said, "Didn't you hear your Mammy tell you not to talk to any strangers?" He was smiling when he said it.

"Well, if we talk and you take some of my chicken, then we won't be strangers, will we?"

The other men in the coach were looking at him and I wondered if I had made a mistake. I didn't have enough to feed the whole car.

"That would be nice," he said, and slipped over to the aisle seat. I handed him a drumstick. "My name is Mr. Yarborough and I'm going to Athens, too. I'll make sure you get there safe and sound. I certainly wouldn't want to make your Mammy mad."

"That's a good idea. She bites the ears off men she doesn't like." Everyone within ear shot, turned and looked at me again. "Well, it's the truth," I said to the assembly.

Mr. Yarborough was a nice man. He had a picture of his little boy who looked just like him. We talked and ate the fried chicken, the stuffed eggs, and the shortbread cookies. "Your Mammy is a good cook," he said and he ate enough to appreciate it. It turned out he knew my Aunt Laura Rutherford and he worked at the University in the office of Chancellor Mell. The trip was long and hot. Just as it seemed the train was going really fast, it would stop, sometimes at a station, other times in the middle of a field of cotton. We would sit there waiting for another train to go by, and when we finally started up again, sweat was running down my face like I'd been in the creek. My frilly dress, my shoes, everything about me was a mess. I had been so proud of the way I looked when I left home, but by the time we got to Athens, I looked like I had never had a bath, that the clothes had been worn for a month. Everyone else looked the same way, so I supposed that was the normal appearance for travelers. I was glad that I wouldn't be seeing Mammy or Mother when I got off. They would have a fit.

In late afternoon, Mr. Yarborough said we were almost there. He helped me with my bags and somehow produced a clean washcloth for my hands and face. I did the best I could with it, but asked him to see if I had left any smudges. He laughed and said I looked like a raccoon around the eyes. I handed him the cloth and he finished the job for me. That was the first time anyone except Mammy or mother had washed my face. I would never have asked a stranger to do it, but there's nothing like a five-hour ride in an open day coach in the middle of a Georgia summer to make friends out of strangers.

My Aunt Laura and her four children were waiting at the station when I arrived. Mr. Yarborough handed my bag to Mister Robert, the old gentleman who had been in the Rutherford family since he arrived from Africa. He was stooped with a fringe of grayish cotton around his head, all that was left of what must have been thick hair when he first saw the harbor of Charleston. His eyes were rheumy and the color of old acorns. I can't imagine all they had seen in his life. Despite his age, he hoisted my trunk to the back of the wagon like it was no more than a sack of feathers. Lamar took a look at my luggage and said, "Goodness, Sallie, you brought enough clothes to last a lifetime. Are you moving in?" We both laughed and hugged each other.

Lamar, the oldest of these four girl cousins, was just my age. We enjoyed swapping clothes back and forth. She knew she would be wearing most of what Mammy had packed and I would be enjoying her new outfits. I had begged Mother for a sister, but she let me understand there would be no more children. Lamar was and remained through all our lives as close as a sister would ever have been. Moving to Athens to be with her was much more appealing than the gracious life they seemed to lead. The absence of the destruction of war was wonderful, but the friendships were even more valuable. As Mister Robert hopped up to the driver's sit and clucked to the horses, we settled in the back of the carriage for the ride to their home.

The streets were lined with live oak trees, draping down into a green tunnel. Compared to Peachtree, this looked like the gateway to heaven. The hooves of Daisy thudding long in the dust like a muffled drum cadence, Mister Robert humming to himself and talking to her as if she were human, the chatter of all of us, and the sense of summer excitement made my life in Atlanta seem more distant than the long train trip. We went through the university grounds. This wasn't my first trip here, but somehow, it seemed different now. I was far enough along in school to know that education was going to be a big part of my life. Reading had begun to be something I enjoyed. Lamar and I shared our love for books. Mother had told me, many times, as long as I had a book I would never be lonely. It's odd how little, off-hand comments like that turn out to be so important. In the sadness that would come to my life, in the joys that were so common, the ability to write about that, to read my own words in books and articles was a source of comfort. In that summer with Lamar and her sisters, those foundations were laid even deeper. What a blessing books were to become to me. When we passed the University Library, I asked Aunt Laura if we could go there and look at the books. Look at them, we could, but she said there wouldn't be any we would be interested in reading. That's the first time I realized the wealth of information in libraries was beyond anything I could hope to master. That would always be true, but in my life, I made a little progress in learning and books were the foundation.

The Rutherford home was a beautiful mansion. It sat back from the road almost a hundred yards and the drive up to the columned veranda was flanked by crepe myrtle, the bushes looking like clumped columns of purple fire. Mister Robert pulled Daisy under the porte-cochere and we all hopped down. Mammy June, Mister Robert's wife helped us out of the carriage and led us into the foyer. The ceilings were fourteen feet high or more, with the front parlor off to the left, and from the right, the broad staircase leading up to the first of two landings. In the center of the foyer ceiling hung a wonderful crystal chandelier. The afternoon sun was streaming through the parlor side windows across the foyer and casting hundreds of tiny rainbows on the stairs. It looked like walking into a fairly land. Lamar saw me looking at them. She picked up a feather duster on a long pole and stuck it in the middle of the chandelier. The rainbows danced as if possessed.

"Pick out a rainbow and make a wish," Lamar whispered. "If it's the last one to stop moving, your wish will come true."

"Really?" I knew it wasn't true, but it was so beautiful, I hoped that it was. I put my finger on one. "I choose that one."

"Too bad. That one's going to stop real soon." And she was right. The ones on the edges of the chandelier—they were the lucky ones. I soon learned to choose more wisely and I always made the same wish: that Lamar and I would love each other forever. So who's to say that chandelier *wasn't* magic? I picked the right crystal more than once and the wish certainly did come true.

Things weren't always entirely smooth between my cousins and me. My Father never let a day pass without telling me I was the prettiest girl God ever made. If he said it, it was bound to be true. I knew that for a fact. One day Bessie, Lamar's sister just a year younger than she, sidled up to me and, out of the blue, announced that Lamar was prettier than I. I was stunned at first, then recognized that Bessie, only a child, had made a natural mistake.

"No, she isn't. She's pretty, but I'm prettier." That should settle it, I thought.

"What makes you think so?" Lamar asked, walking up to us. I wondered if Lamar had put Bessie up to her comment.

"My father says I'm the prettiest girl in the world. He's famous and he always tells the truth." What more need be said?

"Well, my father is more famous than your father. He thinks I'm the prettiest. Besides, Chancellor Mell, who's the most famous man in the world, they *both* say I'm the prettiest thing they ever saw."

It was clear this matter would have to be settled. It wasn't possible that both of us were the superlative in appearance. Lamar felt the same way.

"Come in here and let's look in the mirror. I'll show you exactly why I'm right and you're wrong." It was a daunting challenge. Lamar seemed to have thought this out carefully. She led the way into her mother's room. Her sisters, along with Lizzie and William, Mammy June's grandchildren who were always with us, traipsed along behind.

We had to stand on chairs to get our faces close to the mirror and I soon knew this was a contest I shouldn't have entered.

"Look at your nose, Sallie. Now look at mine. Can't you see you don't have a cute little turn-up nose like mine."

"But I don't want a turn-up nose! Papa says my nose . . ."

"Well, Uncle John may like your nose the best, but everyone else likes mine." She turned to her allies and they universally nodded their heads. "Now look at your mouth. Don't you see how beautiful mine is?"

"No, I don't see any difference."

"And my eyes—see how big they are?"

She was right about that. They were so large and deep you could see forever looking into them. "Mine are just as big," I suggested.

"Are not." Her audience concurred. "You've got little pig eyes."

I was getting mad. "They are not! Papa says . . ."

"Well, make them big like mine," she demanded.

No matter how much I stretched my brow and bugged them out, I could never come close to matching the beautiful brown eyes of Lamar. I was crestfallen. The disappointment Papa would feel when he learned I had "little pig eyes!"

Lamar hopped down, satisfied that her point had been made. Everyone was scampering out of the room, headed down toward Mammy's cabin for hoecake she'd promised to make. Lizzie stayed behind. She took my hand and said, "Don' you pay no mind to Miss Lamar. She be pretty, das a fact, but you is jes' as pretty as you needs to be. So dere!" Learn to be happy with what you are. Another little lesson . . . and this one from a servant's child. Lamar would laugh about that morning for years. "Don't forget those little pig eyes," she would tease. By then, I could laugh, too.

The Rutherford home was a magical place, and it extended beyond the chandelier and its rainbows. The back lot, probably three or four acres, included the smokehouse, the spring house, the servants' cabin and the cook house. I looked around for The Pit and then realized that artillery shells had never fallen on this quiet place. We spent as much time in Mammy's cabin and following her around as we did anywhere else. Just behind the cabin was a cane field. By mid-afternoon, we would be hungry. We would get a stalk of cane and have Mammy or Mister Robert peel it for us. Under the shade of the two-hundred-year-old oaks we would listen to the July flies, the breeze soughing through the leaves, and suck the cane until all the sugar was out of it, the juice dripping down our chins like a sticky river. Mammy would be sitting under the tree, patching and darning the clothes of her children. She acted as high tribunal for all disputes, and when real disagreements occurred she would set her needle and thread aside, then she would pass judgment and that was the end of the matter. More often than not she would tell us a story of some tragic end that had befallen an unruly child who had failed to heed her advice. Whether or not the stories were true, I never knew, but she had an endless supply that were cautionary tales for anyone so foolish as to ignore her advice

But it wasn't always laughter and playing. Frequently guests would arrive and we would be herded into the house for a quick clean-up and presentation. Chancellor Mell lived next door and there was a constant parade of buggies coming and going. We would sit on the veranda or out under the trees and watch them arrive, then tell each other stories about the grand men and the lovely women who accompanied them. We had everyone from Napoleon to George Washington's sister visiting. Never mind they had all been dead for a century. We didn't care. That's who they looked like to us. One particular afternoon, Lamar and I had been in the fig tree, eating more than was wise. We could see across into Chancellor Mell's garden. There was an unusual amount of activity, so we decided we should see who was visiting. Could have been Jefferson Davis, or Julius Caesar—someone important, that much was clear. Seated in shade of the trees was a group of adults, all paying attention to a little man who sat at the head of the circle. He was quite old, we guessed about a hundred and fifty, and there wasn't much left to him. He wasn't any taller than we were, very thin, and his skin had a dry, papery look to it, like he was getting ready to shed it like a snake but just hadn't gotten around to it. We crawled through the bushes between the houses and heard someone mention his name: Alexander Stephens. I didn't know who he was, but I had heard my father talk about "the great Alexander Stephens," so I knew he was somebody important. Whatever they were talking about didn't interest us, so we headed back to the see-saw. After a few minutes, Lamar hopped off while her end was on the ground and sent me crashing to the ground rattling my teeth right down to the roots while she laughed as if it were the funniest thing she had ever seen. I was trying not to cry when I saw Mammy rushing over toward me.

"Laud, chil. Jes' look at you," she said, brushing the dust away from my face and trying to straighten my skirt. "Come on heah, Miss Sallie. Miz Laura wants you to get cleaned up and come out to da front. Mr. Stephens, he fixin'to leave and he say he wants to see you."

"My head hurts and I'm all dirty. I don't want to go see anybody."

"Don' make no neber mind whut you wants. Miz Laura sent me back heah to fetch you and dat's what you gwinna do." She took me in the house, got me cleaned up and dressed in a hurry, and down to the front gate of Chancellor Mell's house she took me. "Now, let Mammy see you smile," she demanded. I made a weak attempt as she handed me over to Aunt Laura.

"Mr. Stephens, this is Sallie Cobb Johnson," Aunt Laura solemnly introduced me.

The little old man stepped up to me and took my hand. He was very old; maybe he *was* a hundred and fifty, but he had very kind eyes. I could feel the bones in his hands as he held mine, the veins showing through the skin like purple worms.

"I know your father, of course, Dr. Johnson, but it's through your mother and her family that I heard about you. I was visiting your parents several days ago and they told me you were here staying with the Rutherfords. Mammy Sophy said I should check and make sure you're behaving. What shall I tell her?"

"Oh, yes sir! I'm being very good." I hoped he hadn't heard anything to the contrary.

"Of course, your Uncle Howell and I were great friends. He was a wonderful man. In some ways, I can see the Cobb resemblance.

You have such a cute little nose! Mary Willis Cobb was one of the prettiest women Washington ever saw and she gave you her beauty."

I looked around to see if Lamar heard this endorsement of my nose from one of the most famous statesmen of the day. She was standing with her mother and I smiled knowingly at her. See, I told you so! was the message I intended.

"Very well," said Mr. Stephens. "I shall give a good report of you. And when I next see President and Mrs. Davis, I will tell them I have at last met the daughter of their wonderful friend, Mary Willis. It makes me feel confident of the future." He patted me on the shoulder, and Chancellor Mell helped him into his waiting carriage.

I wasn't sure why I had been singled out for his special greeting, but later I learned Mr. Stephens had been Vice President of the Confederacy. Then it all made sense. My Uncle Howell and Aunt Mayon, my mother and Jefferson Davis, along with his wife, had been key figures in a part of history that altered the course of the nation. I was the child of that time, and Mr. Stephens had known that. I had thought it was idle curiosity, but I came to believe that these men who had sacrificed so much for a cause in which they believed, rightly or wrongly, had a more-than-passing interest in the children of the leaders of that movement. It was a legacy that I was happy to claim in my later years when veterans of the war were falling on hard times of their own. I remember the dignity and bearing of that old gentleman on a hot summer afternoon in 1874. He knew of a time when dreams had died a hard and bloody death, when justice took a turn different from what he might have imagined or hoped. My family had been part of that. My summer in Athens opened my eyes to that message. It made me think that I should pay attention not only to history—things that had happened in the past—but what my future might hold.

My cousins from other parts of the state often came to Atlanta to visit our family. Although mother had in-laws from two husbands, she did not lose sight of the importance of keeping all the cousins in touch with one another. The sense of family, a belief that had marked her early life so indelibly, continued with her.

That worked well for me. I always enjoyed having cousins visit, and although Atlanta seemed far less exciting to me than Athens and the wonderful homes there, my cousins seemed thoroughly enchanted with the city life in which we found ourselves in the middle. Railroads, carriages, houses of trade, the markets for selling of cotton and indigo, all of that was as different to them as the live oaks and mansions of Athens were to me. We made up our own entertainment, and when we ran out of games to play around the house, I had the whole of downtown Atlanta as my stage.

Several blocks down Pryor Street the homes of the neighborhood gave way to houses of commerce. I always enjoyed going in the dry goods stores and looking at the dresses, the fabrics, the fashions that were being sold. This was a major adventure for visiting cousins who had never seen such stores. I was well known to the owners who allowed me to wander through. I would hold up grown-up dresses in front of the mirror and then pick out a broad-brimmed hat that I thought would look stylish. When they weren't busy, the clerks would often let me play dress up and listen to the stories I made up about parties that I planned to attend. When my cousins would visit, I would take them on a tour of the downtown stores. I was allowed to come and go without Mammy Sophy by the time I was ten or so. It was quite liberating. She would never have allowed me the freedom that I was coming to enjoy, and as I found out on several occasions, the consequences of my forays went beyond what I had imagined.

I particularly remember my cousin Blanche Lipscomb's visits. Blanche was four years younger than I, but always ready for any entertainment I might devise. In addition to the adventuresome spirit we shared, Blanche envisioned herself quite an actress. She was very quick to memorize a poem I might teach her or to rise to the part I might cast her in for a backyard production we would stage for the always-willing audience of Mammy and her grandchildren. There was one poem that was my favorite: "The Maniac." I have long since forgotten the poet, but it was a wonderful piece of work, complete with ravings and screams. Blanche was a natural for the part. I quickly taught it to her, and after several successful performances around the house we were ready to take her act on the road. We were out for an afternoon walk, all turned out in white dresses, frills and bows in abundance. Father had taken me to a stage show several weeks before, and I had been highly impressed with the glamour of the performing arts. Before Blanche knew what was happening, I had her in Harper's Dry Goods and up on the front counter.

"And now, ladies and gentleman," I announced, "Harper's is pleased to present for your entertainment and amusement Miss Blanche Lipscomb and her rendering of "The Maniac."

Whatever else might be said of Blanche, she was *never* one who did not know an audience when she saw one. Without further prompting, Blanche launched off into a premier performance. Amidst the screams and rants of the performance, the front of the store was soon packed. Everyone already shopping had come to the front and all passersby had stepped in to see what was happening. The more people gathered, the more energized became Blanche, all of six years old. When she finished, there was noisy applause, and if Mr. Harper had initially been displeased, he got over it in a hurry since many of the people off the street stayed to congratulate him on "the entertainment," then stayed to shop. Emboldened by our success, and the money that had been thrown on the counter, we proceeded down Peachtree, giving several renditions, each better than the last, before arriving at The Big Bonanza. I didn't notice that most of our following, trailing along behind us, dropped away when we went in.

I had never been in The Big Bonanza, but as a budding producer of theatrical acts, I could tell this was the place for a wonderful performance. The ceilings were high, there were numerous round tables, all filled with nicely dressed gentlemen. Some were playing cards, some just seemed to be visiting and behind nearly every chair stood a woman dressed in a lovely gown. In the back of the room was a perfect stage: A narrow platform covered with green marble, and on each end was a dark wood column that rose all the way to the ceiling. There were stools with rungs that allowed Blanche to climb onto the stage, with the help of a friendly patron, and while she was awaiting my introduction which, by this time, had gotten considerably more grand, the room had grown strangely quiet. As soon as Blanche was getting warmed up with her ravings, there was a major commotion in the back of the room. Through the crowd broke Jim Jason Love, Mammy Sophy's husband. With one monstrous arm, he swept Blanche from the stage, and grabbed me with the other. He had murder in his eyes.

"Come outta heah dis minute. I gwinna make yo' ma whup you 'till you can't stand up."

"I haven't done anything, Uncle Jason," I wailed.

"You ain' done nuthin'? You been in dis heah bar room an' hoe house!"

I was confused. I looked around and didn't see an garden tools, let alone any hoes. "What's a bar room?" I asked, truly innocent.

"Yo' ma'll tell you 'bout dat," he growled.

He fussed under his breath continuously until we got home where he faithfully preferred charges in the sitting room before the entire family and guests, ending up with, "An' when I found Miss Sallie, she was makin' little Blanche stand up on de bar, 'mongst de julep glasses and likker bottles, telling a story to all dem likker men folks and dere wimmens."

Still tingling with the glow of our triumph and having no idea what we had been into, in enthusiastic ecstasy, I pictured our successes, one after the other, ending up with, "And, oh! It was better than the circus that we saw."

I could tell the family took a different view from Uncle Jason who was truly outraged. Mother and Father, as well as the guests, were having a hard time controlling their smiles, much to the bewilderment of Uncle Jason and Mammy

"Sallie," Father said, "We will see one more performance of 'The Maniac,' then you must promise never to do anything like that again."

As Blanche was getting ready to perform, I head Mammy Sophy say to her husband, "Dat Miss Sallie! She gonna be de deff of me sure as da sun do rise!"

She probably thought that was true, but neither one of us

could have gotten along without the other. Most of my education, at least in the early years, was done at home. Mother taught me to read and write, the beginning of arithmetic, spelling, and all the things my children learned in a regular school. When Reconstruction ended, the school system was very shaky, at least for the beginning grades. The university systems had remained intact and I knew that I would someday be going to one of those. Mother had a little classroom set up in the house where she taught me and some of Mammy's grandchildren, too. Without making them feel badly about their families, all of whom were illiterate, she told them that learning to read books and to write letters would make things much better for them when they grew up. As it turned out, it really didn't improve their lot noticeably, but at least they had the rudiments of learning. It was certainly more fun for me to have classmates rather than having to be by myself for the better part of each morning. I enjoyed being a teacher myself and set about to educate Mammy. That didn't work out too well.

"I don' need no book larnin.'" she told me when I was trying to get her interested in reading. "I knows how to git along in der world, an' dere ain' no book what's gwinna teach you dat. You better not get so big for yo' britches wid dat schoolin' dat you don' know nothin' 'bout cookin' vittles. Ain' got no vittles for der table, ain' no book gwinna fill yo' belly." She laughed and shook herself at me. "But you pay 'ttention to what Miss Mary Willis tells you. I knows dat's important stuff for you. You gon' grow up to be somebody and den ol' Mammy gwinna be so proud she'll strut her stuff when you gets to be famous like eberbody in yo' fambly."

Mammy was a great teacher. She taught me how to cook, how to sew, how to pick out a sweet, ripe cantaloup from a tasteless one, how to keep house and make up a bed so you could bounce a marble off the covers. She told me that I might not always have somebody to do all those things for me, and if I wanted to be a good woman, then I would need to be able to look after myself. The lessons that Mother taught me were vital, but the kind, gentle things that I learned from Mammy have stood by me in a way that keeps her in my mind every day.

The time came when my parents decided that I needed to go away to school if I were to be well educated. I wasn't excited about the idea. Atlanta suited me fine, but I knew they were right. If I was going to learn the things that would be important to me, I would need to leave home. The children of our neighbors were all being sent off to boarding school. Reconstruction was officially to end in 1878 and no one knew how the local schools would be operated. I knew that I was lucky to have this chance. In our neighborhood, which was well-to-do by comparison with most of the city, there were some families who couldn't afford to educate their children in the way they would have liked. I suppose I did my share of complaining about school work, but seeing some of my friends having start looking for work when I was off to school in Washington was another reminder that I had a lot about which others could only dream.

On a fall morning 1879, when I was fourteen, my cousin Lamar Rutherford and I set off by train for Washington and Waverly Seminary. As the train went north, I thought of the same ride my mother had described in 1848 going to live with her brother, leaving behind John Lamar and the dreams of a life with him. I wondered if my life would be as altered by this trip as hers had been. Having Lamar along soon took my mind from any serious thought. Of all my cousins and relatives, none could match Lamar in her willingness to venture into the unknown. She was a beauty (as she frequently told me) but she loved me as if we had been sisters. The idea of going off from home without her seems unthinkable now, just as it did then.

Waverly Seminary was a girls' school long noted for its prestige. They prided themselves, probably more than deserved, in taking children and turning them into young women. To this end, there was endless instruction in the niceties of gracious living, all of which we had seen in our own homes, probably far exceeding anything our teachers had ever experienced. The emphasis on education in the classics was strong, and with the combination of these two disciplines, many of the students came to "think more highly of themselves than they ought," as I once heard Mother tell

Lamar's Mother. The two of us certainly did our part to uphold that bit of negative philosophy. We were a handsome pair, we had come from families that had survived the war and continued to prosper, we had credentials that included powerful people and, sad to say, we weren't above playing those cards when it suited our purpose. I suppose we were no more snooty than some of our classmates, but I'm sure our parents and families must have found us insufferable.

One of our more ridiculous affectations was that of Shakespearean scholars. We took to learning long discourses of Ophelia and her general craziness, Lady McBeth, and whoever else struck our fancy. When dinner conversation lagged, we would be off and running with a soliloquy which seemed to amuse all. It wasn't until I was grown that I understood the amusement had more to do with our opinion of ourselves as scholars than at what we were actually doing.

More often than not, Lamar and I found ourselves in the office of the Headmistress. We were generally involved in some adolescent prank, which seemed uproariously amusing to all of us, but usually was greeted with an equal amount of official displeasure. The Headmistress, a lady with the warmth of gray iron, would have us stand at attention in front of her massive desk. Eventually, she would creak around to where we were standing, making an attempt at looking chastened. Her hair was twisted into a bun, so tightly it made her eyes bug. The glasses she carried on the end of a little stick were used more as an implement of gesture than for actually seeing. She would pace back and forth in front of the two of us, the glasses nodding forward with each tentative step. Finally, she would position herself in front of one of us—I always hoped it would be Lamar who could control her giggles better than I. She would bend at the waist, the glasses now held in front on her rheumy eyes, and would always say the same thing: "Well, young lady. What do you have to say for yourself?" If her glasses helped her vision, I cannot say, but they magnified her eyes to the point that they truly appeared ready to pop right into your face. If Lamar could contain herself, she usually wouldn't answer anything, to which the Headmistress would solemnly intone, "We are not amused . . ." then would follow with a condemnation of whatever the most recent infraction had been . . . a frog in the flower arrangement at the faculty table in the dining room, a cowbell on the Headmistress's bedsprings . . . it didn't matter. The session always ended in threats of letters to parents, no more trips to the park, or whatever punishment seemed Draconian to her. Nothing ever really happened. In talking with my friends who had attended boys' schools, we were very lucky. There were no whippings, nothing that really was difficult for us to bear. I think the Headmistress really enjoyed our little get-togethers. We were never rude or impolite. I suspect that sometime before the War of 1812, she might have been not so different from Lamar and me. I hope that's true.

I didn't realize that all our high-flown manners, particularly in the letters we wrote home, were making us the family laughingstock. It came to a head the summer I was sixteen. Mother had decided it was time to "present me to Atlanta society." My sister, Lucy, by now Mrs. Wellborn Hill, was put in charge of the arrangements. She had visions of me wafting across the ballroom, dressed in a medieval costume and playing Ophelia to my escort's Hamlet.

When I arrived home for the summer, there was a family conference about the upcoming festivities. We gathered in the parlor after dinner to discuss it. Lucy was in a high state of agitation, probably not made any better by the tales I had recounted at the dinner table.

She was very direct in her approach. "Sallie, this is an important matter. It will determine who you marry and what kind of life you will lead. You have the family reputation to think of, even if you usually don't think beyond amusing yourself. If you don't behave like the lady we want you to be, I'll *die* of embarrassment. If I don't kill you first," Lucy said, fanning herself nervously. "Everyone will think we've turned loose the village idiot at a debutante ball. I can just see you now, sweeping into the hall, wrist to your forehead and quoting some mad verse from a play no one ever saw!"

My father was amused and that didn't help matters any. Lucy was the most handsome of all of us. She had a beauty that could not be emulated and she had the carriage to match. When she entered a room, without saying a word, everyone knew a belle had arrived. Lucy apparently thought I should follow in those dainty footsteps, but that never was my style. Action and fun—those were the things that appealed to me more than acting the coquette with all the intelligence of a morning glory. Lucy wept when I told her I was much more interested in being accepted in the literary set than the Society of Southern Belles, a name I made up and infuriated her even further. Woodrow Wilson and Mr. Gross— those were the literary figures that I wanted to impress. In exasperation, Lucy shouted, "If Mr. Gross, whom I know, or Mr. Wilson ever hear you read Shakespeare, then maybe you will understand what I'm trying to tell you!" And she stormed out of the room.

It wasn't long after that when Lucy and I were waiting for the Athens train when a wonderful thing happened: Into the waiting room walked my idol, Mr. Gross! He saw Lucy and—joy of joys— walked over to us. Lucy had no choice but to introduce me. He was as courtly and grand as I had imagined. Dressed in a morning coat, with an ebony cane in one hand, a top hat in the other, he bowed as if I were someone special which, of course, I was *sure* I was.

"Miss Johnson. Such a pleasure to meet you, a young person about whom I have heard so much. I wonder if you would do me the honor of allowing me to call this evening?"

The look on Lucy's face was a sight to remember. I was nearly speechless, but managed a curtsy and said, "We will expect you with pleasure after dinner." Lucy rolled her eyes and shook her head in disbelief.

I thought the evening would never come, but finally, Mr. Gross pulled up in his carriage. I had envisioned meeting in the large salon, but Mother seated him on the porch in a large rocking chair. I sat opposite him, a feeling of being in over my head growing stronger by the moment. Lucy looked remarkably at peace with the whole affair. I was determined that my family would hear of my brilliant interpretation of Hamlet, to be confirmed by Mr. Gross, and put to an end all the ridicule I had been receiving from them. As I launched off into my dissertation, Mr. Gross sat very quietly, rocking slowing, stroking his magnificent beard thoughtfully. He listened attentively until I was finished, then he commented.

"Oh, Miss Johnson! If only you could take the platform and teach the world Shakespeare."

I took what he said as absolute truth, failing to notice the smile he was trying to hide. I was seriously considering this wonderful approval when a burst of laughter came through the sitting room window just behind us. It was Wellborn, Lucy's husband. He was beside himself and rushed out on the porch.

"How soon can you start, Sal? None of us want to miss that circus."

Everyone on the porch was laughing, including Mr. Gross. I was furious. I never did know if this was something Lucy had set up to convince me that if I were going to amount to anything, I should give up my theatrics and concentrate on batting my eyes. I was sorry that Lamar wasn't there. At least *she* knew what a talent I was. If Lucy's purpose had been to have me focus on the upcoming social season, she succeeded. Mr. Gross, a kind gentleman, had better things to do than deal with a stage-struck young woman; but I didn't see it that way at the time.

The entire idea of "of being presented to society" seemed artificial and out of place. I knew that I was leading a life of privilege. It wasn't something that I had earned, that any of us had earned. Our families had been lucky during and after the war. Not a half mile from Pryor Street were families living in the worst imaginable conditions. Their houses were thrown together with whatever they had been able to find. The sides of a burned boxcar for a wall, railroad ties for steps, hand-hewn shingles for a roof . . . and these were families who, according to Mother, had been just as well off as ours (or even more so) but now were reduced to living on the ragged edge. The daughters of those homes were not going to

Waverly Academy, they weren't prancing around in hoopskirts fussing about what to wear. They were on their hands and knees working in the garden, trying to get enough to grow to keep body and soul together. In most of those cases, there were only women in the household. Brothers and sons, husbands and fathers were all dead and gone, more often than not in unknown battlefields. And those families weren't thinking "of being presented to society." I spoke to Mother about it.

"I don't feel right about all these parties and things. So many people don't have enough to eat, let alone do the things we do. Maybe I should just skip all this."

"I can understand how you feel, Sallie. It doesn't seem right in some ways. We're no better than anyone else, but we have had a lot more luck than most. Your Father realizes that particularly. That's one reason he works as hard as he does. He feels like he owes a lot because of all he has received. More than half of his patients are never charged. He knows they don't have the money, but he'll go to the worst house on Whitehall just as quickly as he goes to The Terraces if someone needs him. And I try to do my part, too, although it seems precious little."

"Then why don't we do something different with our money, rather than have big parties?"

"There's more to it than just big parties, as you put it. The war changed everything, there's no denying that, but we have to work to preserve what we can. There were terrible things wrong in the South before the war, but there was a lot of good, too. There were good manners and courtliness, there was a gentility that had to be set aside during the war, a special quiet beauty in our way of living that was shot to pieces, literally, then burned to the ground. Those traditions still live on, though, and we need to make sure that heritage is passed on to our children as you must pass on the good things about our living to your children and your grandchildren. I have no patience with those from the North, the carpetbaggers and scalawags that were such a problem during Reconstruction. They were always trying to make sure that no memory of the South survived. Well, they were wrong. There are a lot of things about the South that shouldn't survive, and they won't, but that doesn't mean that we're going to become a bunch of barbarians living under the heel of people who have no idea what we were *really* like or what we *really* stood for. That's why these parties are important. It's not because we're living in the past, but that we're determined, all of us, to bring into the future—your future, Sallie—the graciousness of our heritage."

I thought about how ridiculously anxious Lucy was over the whole thing. I thought about how I had made so light of all the pretentiousness of it. After Mother explained that to me, I understood a little better.

"Just remember," she concluded, "We're not doing this because we're special, because we think we're better than anyone else. We're doing it because we owe it to all those who died alone in some honeysuckle patch in Virginia or had their legs blown off at Gettysburg. You're a Southern lady, Sallie, and no one is ever going to take that away from you—not unless you let them."

The "being presented to society" sounded positively patriotic when I listened to Mother talk about it. I wondered if Lucy knew what a *cause celebre* she was fostering. Dinners, with a carefully selected guest list, were the usual format. Occasionally, there would be a major ball with a cotillion type setting, but more often than not, the gatherings were held in private homes. The belles would be much on display in such company with no more than two or three being the honored guests. That had the disadvantage of each of us being highly visible. It was not possible to hide one's ignorance. And as I learned so painfully in my performance for Mr. Gross it was dangerous to pretend to be something you were not. Even though everyone was extremely cordial and gracious, I felt—and rightfully so—that I was a show dog being trotted in front of a group of canine fanciers. It may well have had all the altruistic overtones mother had listed, but still it felt artificial.

There was nothing artificial about what would happen if a debutante turned out to be a dud or committed a major *gaffe*. The invitations to the receptions came one at a time, and if one did poorly, then there would be no more knocks at the front door with a handsome servant dressed in morning coat holding out the silver tray with the invitation carefully placed in the center.

Lucy, still beside herself over the thought that I might show up with a purse full of lizards (which, I thought, would be just the thing to see who really had a sense of humor), enlisted the aid of Emma Mims and Mary Couper to get me ready for the first evening. I had to admit Emma and Mary had learned their lessons well. They were several years older than my 16 and had been down this path four years earlier. Emma, a beautiful woman, had left a mark to which we were all supposed to aspire. Mary wasn't far behind. They had stepped through the process as delicately as a cat stalking in chrysanthemums and emerged on the far side of the garden with the enviable title of "belles of Atlanta." I was far from convinced that I needed to follow in their train, but they were both so charming and lovely, I couldn't help but want to be like them. Their arrival on the scene must have seemed to Lucy like the appearance of the cavalry when the line is about to fall.

"All will be well, Sallie, now that Emma and Mary are going to help." I wasn't sure whether that was a promise or a threat, but it certainly had power of some sort backing it. The assembly of the dress and all the accouterments took Mammy Sophy to the limits of her skill, but she settled into the task with the same sense of resolution I had seen in her whenever she set her mind to anything.

"You gwinna be der belle of dis heah ball, I'se seein' to dat. Don' you go cuttin' no shine when you gits in front of all dose impo'tent folks. You heah me, Miss Sallie?"

I laughed. I admit I was enjoying keeping everyone a bit on edge about what I would do. Although I was determined to do my best, I wasn't going to give them the satisfaction of knowing that.

The first formal dinner was to be held at the home of Major and Mrs. Livingston Mims. What an elegant sounding name, I thought the first time I heard it. As Mammy was laying out the dress, Lucy, Emma and Mary were bustling about the room getting things together. The dress had so many hoops and skirts, it looked like a peony blossom turned upside down. I wondered if I could even get near the dinner table with it, but my tutors gave me careful instructions about all maneuvers I might be called upon to make. The whole thing took on the atmosphere of a theatrical production. I whirled around in front of the mirror and let off a fine line from Ophelia, dancing on the margins of madness. Lucy was on me in an instant, but with a new tack.

"Oh, Sallie," Lucy cooed. "You look just marvelous." She handed me my overnight bag. "I want you to remember Daisy Breau will be at the dinner this evening. She's the true belle of New Orleans and is visiting the Mims. This is her first trip to Atlanta, and we're anxious to show her we're not a bunch of crackers." She looked up quickly at Emma and Mary for support, then went back to her instructions. "Please don't let her think you're crazy. Please darling, *do* be charming. We understand how you are, Sallie, but strangers might not. They might think you are . . . , you are . . ."

"Crazy," Emma added

"Mad as a March hare," suggested Mary.

I smoothed out my voluminous skirt, hiked it up a bit, stuck out my ankle with its little bracelet and said, "Don't worry, ladies. I won't disgrace you." Then, as I walked toward the stairs, I patted my purse and called over my shoulder, "I'll keep most of the lizards in here."

The entourage of my helpers followed me into the front parlor where Mother and Daddy were waiting to review me. Lucy, less than reassured, immediately began to catalogue her concerns.

"And remember, darling, you must eat something of every course, even though it may be something you dislike."

That was enough. "Look here, Lucy Hill! Do you think I know nothing of proper form at a dinner? This may be my first debutante dinner, but it's not the first time I ever sat down to a plate of food," I shot back.

"Oh, I didn't mean that." She kissed me on the cheek. "I was just thinking. For example, about the raw oyster course. You know how you detest them, but you must eat . . . ."

"For heaven's sake, will you *please* hush? Papa, tell Lucy to leave me alone!"

He laughed. He could always put a tense situation at ease. "Well, well, dear little Lucy is anxious for others to appreciate you as we do." He hesitated, then went on. "But there is one thing I would like to add to your sister's advice, although I know it's unnecessary, but that is to abstain from wine."

"Why, Papa! You know I've never had anything to drink except for the sugar left in your early morning julep glass."

"I know that, sweet Sallie, but you are a young lady now and I always want it said that your *bon mots* are not the product of stimulants, but of your quick mind."

"What he's saying," Lucy added, "is that your spirit is so free, some might think you're drunk, the way you say ridiculous things."

She had a point there. I threw my arms around Daddy's neck and ran my fingers through his soft gray hair. "Don't worry, Daddy, I'll not eat with my fingers or lick my plate!" The carriage was waiting. Mammy Sophy made her final adjustments of the sash, patted the crinolines into place and gave me a long look—no advice, but a look that told me how much she loved me, too. I hugged her, then kissed her cheek, smooth as a polished buckeye, and was down the steps and on my way to a new world.

# CHAPTER IV

The carriage ride to the Mims took about a half hour. I had plenty of time to think about where I was going. Lucy's husband, Wellborn, was my escort, but he sat there like a stone stature. I suppose he knew I was lost in my own thoughts. No longer could I banter and parry with Lucy and all her nervousness. Now, I was nervous enough for the two of us. I would know only a few people and certainly couldn't spend the evening with them. I was expected to mingle, to be charming and gay, to laugh at the proper times, to be suitably coy if the occasion called for it. It was a daunting prospect. If I made a huge *faux pas,* if the evening ended up in shambles, then what would I do? My life up to that point had seemed to be a game, one played on ground that had been difficult for those who went before me, but one in which I had always felt in control. No longer. I was on unfamiliar terrain and it seemed terribly important, despite all my previous comments. Looking back, I can't say that it really was an epiphany. I could never have been invited to another party and my life might have turned out the same. But who's to say that it wasn't the beginning of a life that opened to me so many opportunities?

When we walked up to the stately mansion, Old Ben, the dignified butler, bowed as if I were the Queen of England. He took my bag; Wellborn held the door for me. I picked up my skirts—all ten of them—and stepped into the foyer. It was filled with elegantly dressed women, men in dazzling attire, and servants walking among them. I was a little girl in the midst of the mighty. That was the feeling that overwhelmed me. No wonder Lucy had been upset. *I* would be upset to turn someone like me loose in a place like the Mims' mansion. I was shown up the circular stairs to my room which was Emma's double room, to be shared. Ye gods! Daisy Breau, the Belle of New Orleans! She was my room mate. I looked around the room. A pair of tester beds, overhung with Belgian lace, stood in the center against the far wall. Matching chifforobes of mahogany inlaid with ash and ebony stood in front of each bed, and these were flanked by dressing tables. The room was softly lit by a large chandelier with a dozen or more whale-oil canisters. On side tables by the beds were silver bowls of magnolias and gardenias, their perfume cloaking around me like a satin shawl. It was a magical scene. All I wished for was a high-arch connecting door, behind which I could conceal my incompetence from Daisy, the Queen of Debutantes.

The magic was shortly dispelled. Emma arrived with the vaunted Daisy in tow. They took a look at me and exclaimed together, as if by practice, "Ah, there stands the debutante!"

"My, but you look lovely," Emma said, coming over to admire my dress. Then she added, "Remember, now—no Shakespearian foolishness."

"Oh, stop it, Emma! I'm sick of hearing about that."

"You listen to Emma," Daisy advised, seating herself on the swooning couch near the door. "Men just hate intellectual women."

"That's absurd," I said sternly. "A man who thinks wants a woman who can match his wit."

Emma and Daisy both shrieked with laughter. "Sweet innocence," Daisy sighed, arching her impressive eyebrows.

I took a good look at this woman, "The Belle of New Orleans." She was something to see. Probably two or three years older than I, she had a grace that set her aside as something special, a fact that had not escaped her notice. I knew immediately that she would brook no competition, not that I had any to offer. Nellie, Emma's maid, was adjusting the hooks on Emma's dress and had been taking in the whole scene. She looked up from her work and said, "Miss Sallie, dese ladies is right. Don' you know a man hates a woman who knows mo', or thinks she knows mo' than he do? You wants to git 'long wid da mens, you got to fool'em into thinkin' dey got mo' sense than a hog got slop."

"Fool them?" I gasped, not believing what I was hearing. My mother would never try to fool Daddy. Not in a thousand years. She was every bit as smart as he was and he knew it. He liked it. He was always asking her opinion when they were talking serious business with the governor or a senator.

"Dat's right! You bes' fool'em," Nellie repeated, as if I hadn't spoken.

Emma stepped in. "She's right, you know. A woman's role is that of clinging vine. You know how the wisteria runs up a trellis and it gets so thick and strong the trellis can fall down and you'd never know it. That's the way to get a man to do anything you want. Make him think he's the ruler of all creation and seek his wisdom in everything. Soon, he'll begin to think you're absolutely dependent on his brilliance, that you don't have a brain in your pretty head, then he's putty in your hands."

"That's ridiculous. Stop teasing me. I'm looking for real advice and you're telling me all this rot."

"Oh, no, you crazy girl," Daisy joined in. "It's the absolute gospel. The most successful men in the world are ruled by women. The men don't know it; they think they're the most powerful things God ever made. And you do everything you can to make sure they keep on believing that. Do you think all the coy, eyes-behind-the-fan are because we don't know what we're doing? It's to hide your mouth. You can't lie with your lips and eyes at the same time . . . one or the other, but never let them see both at the same time when you're pruning the vine to wrap around your trellis. And unlike what Emma said about the wisteria, men need your trellis more than they need feet to stand on."

None of this fit with any of the men that I had seen, or the way they were treated by their women. Mother and Daddy were, of course, the best examples, but the Rutherfords in Athens, to say nothing of Chancellor Mell and his wife. Those were powerful people and they seemed like they treated each other with mutual respect. I sat down on the bed and wondered how in the world I could pull off such a charade when I thought it patently stupid. I did have to wonder if the girls I had seen as debutantes before me were as vapid as they sometimes seemed. That fit in with what I was being told. Before I could puzzle it out, Mrs. Mims came into the dressing room. She looked as elegant in a midnight blue satin gown as a swan on a moonlit lake.

"Sallie," she said, walking toward me, "I'm changing somewhat the arrangement of my guests this evening. One of the ladies is ill, so I'm putting Captain Harper and Mr. Patrick Calhoun on either side of you." She said "eye-ther" side. Miss Standridge at Waverly was always trying to get the girls from the South to use that affectation. Here it was right in the mouth of Mrs. Mims. "I will expect you to fascinate them both."

Things were going from bad to worse. Now I had a specific assignment of whom to fascinate and no idea how to go about it. I knew I would appear a fool if I followed the advice of Emma and Daisy. That seemed to be the purpose of such behavior, so I decided I would rely on my instincts. My mother was no fool, I was sure of that. Captain Harper and Patrick Calhoun! They were both reputedly brilliant; I had been endorsed by my own family as crazy and by my friends as a foolish child. I surely felt like the both as I thought over the prospect of the evening. Captain Harper was deaf as a post and whoever sat with him had to lean into his ear trumpet and relay the table conversation by shouting. I couldn't think of a worse situation. To ignore him would have been unspeakably rude, and I had heard that he would tap his seat mate—none—too—gently—on her wrist with his ear horn if he wasn't getting the attention he wanted. There was nothing to do but make the best of it.

As I walked very carefully down the spiral staircase, a dozen or so gentlemen were standing in the foyer, watching my progress. I tried to read the eyes of the one closest to me. Was he looking expectant, hopeful, bored, hungry? I couldn't tell. A more impassive bunch I never saw. How charming would I need to be? I had the feeling I would be addressing an assembly of corn shocks. Mr. Calhoun stepped to the front, and with a courtly bow extended his right arm. With surprising grace, he spun me in front of the onlookers who smiled broadly, then clapped with approval. Maybe this wasn't going to be as bad as I had thought. Mr. Calhoun led me to the dining room. As we passed under the arch, the table appeared to extend halfway to Macon.

I was to be seated in the middle facing the large sideboard which was already loaded with food. To my horror, right in front on my seat was a silver tureen packed with ice on which sat the largest collection of Lynhaven oysters I have ever seen—before or since. I had thought that I could manage a tiny oyster. All one had to do was close one's eyes as the repulsive thing passed between the lips, then tilt the head slightly back as if studying the ceiling candles, and down it went, like a greased bullet. But these were monsters! They would have to be chewed or risk choking to death. The thought of sinking my teeth into that gray, slimy, boggy thing took my breath away.

After everyone was seated, I was served three largish ones and waited until the last possible moment to start eating. Everyone else was slurping them down like they hadn't eaten in a week. Captain Harper finished his before I had gotten the first one speared. He turned to me, a little gray trail trickling down his chin.

"Aren't these grand?" he shouted. Everyone was waiting for my reply, so I got the thing half way to my mouth when Mr. Calhoun said something that everyone found uproariously funny. I was too nervous to pay much attention, but Captain Harper, right on cue, tapped me with his horn and shouted, "What did Calhoun say?" Each time I would try to eat one, the same thing happened. Eating the oysters was bad enough alone, but having to deal with Captain Harper and his horn was making it impossible to get it done. When everyone had finished and the plates were being collected, Mrs. Mims saw the problem.

"Sallie, you poor dear! You've been so busy helping the Captain you haven't had time to eat a single oyster. Dolly, wait just a moment before clearing the table while Miss Johnson has time to finish." Well, there was no escape now. I would probably be doomed to

life as a charwoman and certainly Lucy Hill would never speak to
me again. Into the mouth it went and began sliding from side to
side across my tongue as if looking for the exit. I demurely picked
up my glass of sherry, never giving a thought to Papa's advice about
wine, and washed it down with an amazing gulp. From that
moment on, the oysters, the sherry bottle and I became the best of
friends. It was a rite of passage in more than one sense.

I think everyone knew what a problem I was having with that
oyster. I even wondered if it were a little test. In any case, the
evening improved considerably after that. Captain Harper learned
he had a woman at his other elbow and seemed delighted for me
to share him with her. Patrick Calhoun turned out to be as brilliant
as his reputation . . . and a lot more fun than I would have
imagined. When I had something to say, I spoke and, to my
amazement, people listened, not as though I were a child or a
brainless belle, but with real interest. The conversation flowed in a
manner quite different from anything I had experienced earlier. I
felt that they were interested in what I had to say, and I certainly
learned things from them. After the oyster found a new home and
I was convinced that it would stay there, I enjoyed myself
thoroughly. The time went quickly. As we were standing in the
foyer and the guests were leaving, the parting comments were light
but sincere. I knew that I had passed the test, at least the first one.
I felt a sense of relief that all my anxieties had been for nought.
There would be times in the future when I faced a situation with
trepidation and after it was over found that my fears had been
groundless. Not to say there haven't been many times when I failed,
but by then I had enough confidence to accept failure as a lesson
for growth. That first night at the Livingston Mims' home, failure
would have carried a different message. Many is the time I faced a
challenge that I would think back to that night, remembered how
unprepared I had been, yet how well it had gone, and gained
confidence for the task at hand. The frivolity of debutante parties
needs to be measured against the important learnings that can
happen when a child is thrust into an adult world. It is a real
opportunity for growth, but only if the young lady involved

recognizes it. I realized that night as the last guest left why my family had been, and justifiably, so concerned.

I took a deep breath and let it out slowly with an audible sigh as Uncle Ben stepped up on his stool and began snuffing out the chandelier candles. "You sho'nuff turned into a lady tonight, Miss Sallie," he said, smiling down at me.

"You don't know the half of it, Uncle Ben," Emma laughed. "Come on, girls, let's go to bed," taking Daisy and me by the hand.

The servants had laid out our night clothes and lit a fire in Emma's fireplace. We took off our gowns and sat down on the big fur rug in our wrappers. Our shadows danced on the far walls behind us like phantoms. Emma poked me in the ribs, then said to Daisy, mimicking my voice in an irritatingly accurate way, "Why, Papa! You *know* I've never had anything to drink except for the sugar left in your early morning julep glass."

Daisy laughed. "You saw the way she gulped that sherry on top of that oyster. I thought she'd be dancing on the table before the evening was over!"

"Tell me I didn't act like I was drunk!" The thought had never occurred to me that the sherry had headed north while the oyster headed south.

"Of course not, but you're not supposed to *swallow* them," Emma explained. "You just put it in you mouth, let it run around for a while, then deftly put it in your napkin then toss it under the table. Only men actually *eat* the things! They think it makes them more . . . manly. Can you imagine such stupidity?"

"That's probably why the men thought you were so wondrous. They'd never seen a woman swallow a whole one!" Daisy laughed, and added, "I may try that when I get home. How much sherry did you take with it?"

"The whole glass, I think it was," and I realized that Emma and Daisy, despite all their big talk, weren't much more experienced than I was when it came to some things.

The rest of the season sped by and although I assume Lucy received good reports, she was unrelenting in her advice and concern about my "appearing normal."

"What do you mean," I finally demanded, *'appearing* normal?' I *am* normal."

"Oh, Sallie, dear, you poor child. You must dance the cotillions instead of seating yourself and gathering a gallery of gentlemen about you. I've seen what you do: You refuse to dance with them, then they all sit with you and, before you know it, you look like the Queen of England holding court. The beaux want to dance."

"They don't seem to mind sitting and talking. That's so much more entertaining than twirling around in the arms of a dancing bear, which is about how most of them manage the music."

I don't know how long her ceaseless cajoling would have gone on, but a totally unexpected event changed the course of the season . . . and much more.

Uncle Dick had "risen from the dead" at war's end. The story of his sudden reappearance had been told to me, but there was still great enmity between my father and his brother, Dick. The initial euphoria of their reunion had quickly paled, according to my mother, when they realized the differences they held still lived, although the war was supposed to have settled those issues. His portrait, in his army dress uniform had been taken to the attic and turned to the wall when the war began and there it remained. Uncle Dick went back to Minnesota, and through the years there was little contact between them. Why that should have been so was hard for me to understand, but it all began in an era about which I had only heard.

In the summer of 1881, Uncle Dick had written my father, pleading with him to put aside their differences and have a reconciliation before it was too late. This story was played out in thousands of families, I'm sure, particularly in the border states. Sadly, I did know of families where brothers remained bitter enemies 'til the day one died, and even then the hatred lingered on, a fire with no new fuel, but banked against extinguishing.

"I reach out, not as Union general, not as the victor," Uncle Dick wrote, "but as an old man, as your brother reaching out for a touch of those vanished days."

So it was that he came back from the North, not with a sword, but with a cane. When he arrived at the station, we all went down to meet the train. From Chattanooga the train had come right down the rail lines that seventeen years earlier had been the site of so much carnage. Just north of Atlanta, Uncle Dick had passed within a few hundred yards of where the Reb had pinned him, writhing, to the "good Georgia clay," where he watched his life blending in with the red dirt. Now he was here to heal the deepest wound of all.

The train hissed and creaked to a stop. Of course, I had never seen Uncle Dick and there were no pictures of him that Papa allowed to be in the house, but I knew him the minute he stepped to the door of the coach. He was tall and angular. He had the strong chin of my father, his height, and the same sense of bearing that must have come from their parents. We wondered what Papa's reaction would be. The two old men stood and looked at one another, several feet separating them. Then they folded into each other's arms—a pair of grey-haired patriots—their bodies shaking with silent sobs.

Papa looked up, held his brother at arm's length, then said, "Peace. Peace at last!"

We were all ecstatic over the reunion. It marked a special time in the life of the whole family. After almost twenty years of separation, each thinking the other was dead for part of that time, now they were reunited. The emotions about the officers of Sherman's army still ran deep. Too many deaths, too much destruction, too many horrors to be forgotten by some. Within the family those things could be overcome. But what about others who did not have the tie of family blood to strengthen them? What about our friends and neighbors where the only memory was one of shed blood? What would their reaction be to General Richard Johnson? He was my uncle whom I came to love instantly, but he might well be viewed by others with at least suspicion if not outright hostility. The parties of the season provided a forum where all those questions were answered.

My father, so widely loved and respected, brought an acceptance for Uncle Dick that otherwise might well have been impossible. He was widely entertained, but there was a coolness, a certain distance that clearly marked him as a different man. Southern hospitality had a character of its own: You knew it when you saw it—like an old friend met on the street after an absence. But for one who had never been exposed to it, the coolness that met Uncle Dick might not have struck him as odd. He didn't mention it. He was cordial and gracious; we didn't speak of it, but all the family knew there was tension in the air at social gatherings that was different from the usual feeling of warmth and relaxation. Fate has a way of straightening things out. In a way that we never could have conceived or engineered, the ice was broken most remarkably.

Uncle Dick discovered General Aldophus King, a retired Union officer, was wintering in Atlanta. Officers from the North frequently came South in the winter but they lived in their world; we lived in ours. Social exchange between the two was rare. Lucy and her husband, Wellborn, had invited guests to the Hill home for dinner and Uncle Dick asked Lucy if General King might be included. Wellborn had no desire to have yet another Union General in his home—one was one too many except that he *was* a family member, but as a cordiality to the family, the invitation was extended.

The dinner was held on a Saturday evening, with about two dozen guests. General King and Uncle Dick were seated together— I suppose Wellborn thought he could keep an eye on both of them if they weren't separated. Across from them was seated Captain Evan P. Howell, editor of *The Atlanta Constitution*. He was a brilliant conversationalist and always enjoyed meeting people from a different background. Soon volleys of interesting matters were flying back and forth between General King and Captain Howell. In addition to his personal accomplishments with the newspaper, Evan Howell was known for his strong support for the Confederacy, his understanding of military tactics and his remarkable bravery in battle.

"Is this your first visit to Atlanta, General King?" he asked.

"No, indeed. I have wintered in Marietta for several years." He refrained from mentioning that had been after the battle of Atlanta and that he had been in command of the division in which Uncle Dick had been so terribly wounded.

Turning to Uncle Dick, "Well, I know it's your first visit, General Johnson."

"Indeed, it is not," laughed Uncle Dick. "You tried to kill me on my first visit and now you're trying to freeze me to death. I brought a winter fur coat to show the family what we wear in Minnesota, but I've hardly been able to take it off!"

General King, wondering where all this might lead, said, "This is unusual weather. It will warm up shortly. Wonderful climate."

Captain Howell dismissed the remark with a wave of the hand. "You fought in Georgia, General Johnson?" he persisted.

"I did, sir. I fought, bled, and nearly died just outside your city."

After a pause, the Captain said, "Will you give us your angle of the battle?"

Uncle Dick laughed and said, "My angle from the ground was very acute! I had my horse shot from under me at the beginning of the engagement on the second day. As I fell to the ground, a Reb, whom I sure was killed moments later, decided to take me with him."

"The beginning of the battle on the second day? That's when you were wounded?" Captain Howell had lain his napkin beside his plate and was leaning forward toward my uncle.

"I was."

"There was a fusillade into the middle of your ranks? And the first shots cut a man in two?"

Now it was my uncle's turn to lay his fork down. "Yes."

"And a second burst almost took the leg off a man standing next to your horse?"

"Right, again."

The entire table had fallen silent, wondering what was coming next.

Captain Howell continued, "And with the third, your horse was shot from under you and then a Reb jumped you with his bayonet? Didn't he?"

Uncle Dick was growing pale. "He did. And after he had done what he could, I asked him to take me to my brother, John here, to close my eyes for the last time."

There was silence for a moment, then Captain Howell rose from the table and walked around to uncle Dick grasping his hand when he reached him. "That third volley went awry. I was the one who shot your horse. That Austrian musket was meant for you! The Reb who tried to finish the killing was my first sergeant. Thank God we didn't kill the brother of our beloved Dr. Johnson!"

There was a stunned silence. Fate had brought these two men together twice. The first time with the mentality of killing or being killed; the second, at a gracious dinner party where sectionalism had been an unwelcome guest and was ushered out by the embrace of two men who, once sworn enemies, could now become friends. The story from that evening spread like wildfire. The attitude of everyone who heard it was changed. To be sure, it took years before bitterness became isolated to pockets of people who had not been able to reconcile their hatred with the need to get on with life. I remember that evening as the beginning of my understanding that the opportunity to bridge the gap between North and South might present itself in surprising events. I would keep my eyes open if it happened in such a way that I could speed the process.

I was surprised how soon such an opportunity would arise and, even more so, at the circumstance. During the time Uncle Dick spent with us that year, I learned to deeply love him. He had many of the same gentle characteristics that I so admired in my father. They were both men of great intellect, a keen sense of humor, and devotion to their beliefs. The latter had nearly killed them both, but that part of their lives was behind them. When we took Uncle Dick to the station to begin his long trip home, I wondered if I would ever see him again.

"You should move your family to Atlanta, Dick," my mother told him. "I've spent winters in the north and that's not something a normal person would do. Now that you've seen what a pleasant people we are, why don't you become one of us?"

He hugged her. "But I already *am* one of you. Kentucky isn't exactly the frozen tundra although I would have to say Minnesota can give a pretty good imitation of the North Pole. My sweet wife is the real reason, of course. Her roots are in those northern, green hills and around those lakes. To ask her to leave all that beauty . . ." He stopped himself before he said what was probably in his mind, ' . . . for this ugly red clay . . . ,' well, that would be asking too much. I have a better idea. Let Sallie come visit and she can bring back such a colorful report that maybe you all will move to St. Paul!"

"My joints would freeze solid before November," Papa laughed, "But Sally, she's young and lithe. She could stand the cold."

"I would love to come visit, Uncle Dick. Do you think the Yankees would treat me as well as the Rebs treated you?"

"No doubt about it, little lady. It would do them a world of good to see a Southern Belle whose charm is exceeded only by her quick wit. Most of my friends think all the women in South do is pick cotton and drink mint juleps."

So it was decided that I would go to St. Paul, but not until the spring thaw was over and the rivers were back in their banks. When my friends heard of my upcoming trip they were quick to have their say. Having a Union general visit in the south was one thing, but to have a young Southern lady venture into the north—well, that was quite unthinkable. Mrs. Marshall, from down the street, was the first to issue what would become a common refrain.

"Why, Mary Willis," she chirped, "I simply can't believe you're going to let that child go up there with those . . . . those . . . *people*! She'll get up there and charm the sideburns right off some Yankee fool and that's the last you'll ever see of her. You mark my words. You remember Lizzie Overby married that Yankee officer out at Ft. McPherson and the next thing you knew, she was living in a mud hut in the desert fighting Indians!"

It hadn't been quite that bad, although Lizzie was off somewhere in Texas with her husband. The last I had heard from her, she had two little children and seemed happy. She didn't mention anything about carrying a gun to protect her family from savages. I could hardly wait until springtime came. Mammy Sophy and I were preparing for the trip when I received a message from Mrs. Samuel Hall. Her husband was chief justice of the Georgia Supreme Court and she was a lady of great reputation for courage and initiative during Reconstruction. The furor about my plans had died down over the winter, so I wasn't prepared for her invitation to tea, nor what she would say.

After we had settled in her drawing room, the tea and biscuits had been served, she got up and closed the double doors leading into the hall. I knew then I was in for more than a social chat.

"Sallie," she began, laying her silver spoon on the china saucer, "Is it true that you're going to visit among the Yankees?" Her lips clamped into a tight little line. She made it sound as though I were about to step off the wharf into the Okefenokee Swamp.

"Why, yes. I'm going to see my dear uncle. He's invited me . . ."

She held up her spoon as if she were about to use it as a director's baton. "Wait one moment, child. I do not blame you for going. General Johnson is your father's brother and it would be hard for your father to do otherwise. In fact, I am glad that you're going, Sallie, for I have a little favor to ask of you." She paused a minute, set her spoon back in the saucer and looked out the window for what seemed an interminable time. When she turned back to me, there were tears in her eyes. "Promise me, Sallie. Promise me just this one thing."

I had no idea what she was about to ask, but I gladly agreed. "Of course, Mrs. Hall. I would do anything you ask." Then the truth began to surface.

"As you no doubt know, that demon Sherman is going to visit St. Paul while you're there. My duty as a Southern Christian woman prevents me from saying what I *really* think of him and you, as such a proper girl, have never heard such words, I'm sure. "Demon" will have to do for the moment. Since your uncle is a Union General, he is certain to be an acquaintance of Sherman; God forbid that they are friends! In parties that will be given in your honor, the Demon will be invited. I'm sure of it. When that happens, I want you to promise me that you will insult him in the most grievous manner. I don't care what you do. I don't care what you say. I just want you personally to demolish him in the presence of his friends."

I was horrified. It had never occurred to me she would ask such a thing. I didn't even know I might meet General Sherman, to say nothing of his being a friend of my uncle. The look on my face must have betrayed my astonishment. Mrs. Hall held up her spoon again. I knew that meant to listen.

"Wait, child, before you answer. You must hear the story." And the tears started again. She composed herself once more and started over. "When Sherman and his hoodlums swept through Atlanta, leaving nothing but fire and death on every hand, they came through this very house where my father was on his death bed. My sisters and I, along with some of the faithful servants, were in his bedroom, doing what little we could to comfort him. He knew what was happening all around him. His dying was going to be hard enough, but the carnage all around was more than any of us could bear. He was giving us last messages to my brothers, all of whom were in the battle, either in the streets of Atlanta or off somewhere else; we didn't even know where they were. Right in the middle of this, in burst eight or ten of Sherman's soldiers. They came through the doors, they knocked out all the windows and came in that way. They charged right into the bedroom, laughing and yelling like crazy men. I pled with them to leave us alone, to have some respect for the dying. One of them pushed me to the floor and the rest turned over every piece of furniture in the room, looking for money and jewelry. My father, in very near his last words, said, 'Give them the treasure chest.' He pointed under the bed. They jerked the bed away, dumping him on the floor, found the chest and set it on the table. One of them shot the lock off. The chest was filled with deeds to property and the like, all of my mother's jewels and all the pieces she had given to us. They scrambled into that chest like a pack of rabid dogs on a cornered fox. By the time they had filled their pockets, my father, still lying on the floor, was dead. One of them even had the temerity to tip his hat to me as they romped down the steps." She stopped and looked at me.

I was filled with righteous indignation. I could not imagine anyone behaving in that way. I promised her that I would speak personally to General Sherman if I ever met him and it would be an encounter he would not forget. I would verbally demolish him.

She smiled wanly. "That would be nice, Sallie. But not enough. Insult him! Scratch the Demon's eyes out."

I didn't know what I would do, but poor Mrs. Hall had put the spirit of the Crusader in me. I would invade the land of William Tecumseh Sherman. I would seek him out. I would right the terrible wrong done by his army. I would vindicate the desecration of the Hall family. I would be like their hideous battle song . . ."the terrible swift sword." In my wildest dreams, I could not have predicted how differently this would turn out.

The long train ride was exciting. The anticipation of travel to new places has always filled me with excitement. It still does. I did have some apprehension about how I would be treated. Suppose people ignored me or were rude? Shortly after arrival, my fears were laid to rest. Uncle Dick was one of the world's most charming men. Why did I think that he alone was not a savage. I don't think I ever encountered a more charming, more gracious group of people. I asked Uncle Dick if he had been surprised by the cordiality with which he was received in the South.

"Not in the least. Of course, I knew there would be some tense times, given my history, but I had spent much time in the South before the war. I knew them to be a kind and gentle people at heart."

I had only heard of the loud brashness, the boisterous bawdiness of Northerners. I had no way of knowing what they were really like. Uncle Dick's wife, Rachel, was somewhat of an exception. She, like me, had little knowledge of what lay beyond her home. The wit and charm of my uncle was balanced by the imperiousness of Aunt Rachel. I suspect she viewed me as a pampered and spoiled child, and there was some truth to that, although I was trying to overcome it. She took it upon herself, a sense of duty, I suppose, to train me properly. If that were her goal, she certainly succeeded. To this day, I still use some of her aloofness when the occasion calls for it.

Whenever guests were in the home, I was always called in for an introduction. Governor and Mrs. Ramsey, the Cornelius Livingstons and many others who seemed to me to be the luminaries of Minnesota, frequented the home of General and Mrs. Johnson. It never occurred to me that I was the object of their visit. Aunt Rachel brought it to my attention.

"Here in St. Paul,"she began, as if decorum had a different set of rules from the red clay hills of Georgia. "Here in St. Paul, it's necessary for a young lady to return the calls that have been paid to her. When the Governor takes time from his busy schedule to visit you, Sallie, you must extend to him the courtesy of a return visit." She wiggled her fan as if to make sure the words flowed over me.

Of course, I knew that! That anyone would have the slightest interest in visiting me was the furthest thing from my mind when the Governor or anyone else, for that matter, called at the Johnson home.

"I've made up a list of those whom you must visit in the next few weeks. I shall, of course, accompany you to make sure . . . ." Her voice trailed off. I wondered if she were going to say " . . . to make sure you wear shoes." In retrospect, I'm making more of this than it really was. Had I been in her position, I would have done exactly the same thing. Years later, when our children were to meet William Jennings Bryan, President Wilson, or someone of that stature, I was forever making sure everything was just so, even though they were nearly grown at the time. My own children were as patient with me as I was with Aunt Rachel, whom I realized was going to an extreme to see that I was well received.

Uncle Dick's youngest son, Harry, was my age, and as is often true of cousins, there can be differences of personality that are difficult to reconcile. Harry, a handsome man, carried the chilly elegance of his mother like a mantle. His interest seemed confined to the cotillions, the lawn parties, the regattas, and all the social occasions attendant to them. I was determined to see that he was educated in the ways of literature. My graduation from Waverly Seminary had not dulled my appetite for reading and sharing views of the classics. As far as Harry was concerned, Hamlet was the back leg of a small pig. I finally gave up and found a more relaxed atmosphere by spending my weekends at nearby Fort Snelling. Captain Alfred Johnson, the eldest son of Uncle Dick, was on the staff of General Terry, the commandant of what can only be described as "an adorable fort." It looked like a set of buildings designed for a child's playroom. It had none of the grim singleness of purpose of the forts I had seen in the South. Those looked little better than a prison. Fort Snelling looked like a comfortable rustic resort nestled in a grove of balsam. Alfred's wife, Kitty, was just a few years older than I and we became wonderful friends. Their baby, also named Kitty, added hours of enjoyment to my weekend visits. Additionally, there were numbers of young lieutenants about, all of whom struck me as quite handsome. I remembered the admonitions my mother had received about even allowing this trip. I could imagine the furor it would cause should I arrive in Atlanta on the arm of a Yankee officer.

Cousin Harry and I continued our standoff. He refused to be interested in literature and I refused to be interested in his silly social life. The problem came to a head one morning at breakfast.

Harry, shoveling his eggs in with his fork inverted (why didn't Aunt Rachel worry about *his* manners?) announced, "Sallie, a German is going to be given in your honor. You are to lead it with me." He stopped with his fork in mid-air, expecting me to whoop with delight.

"Oh, Harry," I said, daintily fluffing my napkin and doing my best imitation of Aunt Rachel, "I cannot descend to round dancing, not even with you."

His eyes bugged slightly. "What's the matter with you? Can't you dance?"

"Dance?" looking down my nose at him, "Of course I can dance. I've been taking dancing lessons since I was five years old."

"Well, what's wrong with you, then?" he demanded.

"Nothing is wrong with me. I simply think it is silly for a high-toned educated girl to be hopping around a ballroom with a man acting as though he knows what he's doing." Aunt Rachel's head was going back and forth like watching lawn tennis.

Harry stood up. "Well, listen, young lady and listen well. You'll dance this German with me or I'll see to it that you spend the time in your room. I'll have no wall flower on my hands." And he stomped out of the room.

I was furious. Who did he think he was . . . my father? Papa would never have spoken to me in such a tone. Treating me like a child. I was almost as old as he, and twice as smart, to say nothing of having better table manners. I went to my room to mull it over. I had backed myself into a corner. I suspected that Uncle Dick and Aunt Rachel were on Harry's side, although neither of them had spoken. I needed a conference with cousin Kitty. I was trying to figure a way to get down to the fort when, wonder of wonders, I heard her in the hallway.

"Kitty, I need your help," I called to her. It didn't take her long to see what I was about. I wanted to put my arrogant cousin Harry in his place once and for all, but I had probably gone about it in the wrong way.

"True," she said, after musing for a minute. "I thought the best way might be to get you down to the fort, but that won't accomplish your purpose. You certainly don't want to upset your uncle. He's so proud of you and wants everyone to meet you. This is a perfect chance for that. You simply need to rise to the occasion."

I didn't know what I was going to do, but decided the best approach was to "out—Harry—Harry." That evening after dinner, Harry came to the table, hat in hand. I knew my chance was approaching.

"Well," he demanded, twirling his hat by the brim like it was a child's hoop, "Are you going to the German with me or not?"

I gave a trilling little laugh. "Of course, I'm going. Men are such dumb creatures."

He stopped his twirling. "What do you mean—dumb?" He looked astonished. "You certainly blistered me with the most emphatic refusal I've ever received."

"Harry," I said, with infinite patience, "Don't you know that girls have to fool men, even those in the family, to make them take a real interest. If I had been all excited about going, then you would have taken me for granted. You must *never* let a girl think you take her for granted—even if you do." I smiled condescendingly.

"And you were fooling all along?" The hat was beginning tentatively to twirl again. "Well, I'll acknowledge I *am* dumb, if that's the truth. I'll say this for you: You should be on stage. That's the best act I ever saw." His eyes brightened. "You know, you almost ran me crazy with all that talk. I couldn't figure it out at all! And you were just playing with me," he shook his head ruefully.

"And you see how happy you are in consequence of it? You're much more pleased with me than if I had jumped at the chance." I moved over on the sofa to make room for him. He sailed his hat in the general direction of the hall tree and sat down beside me. He told me of all the activities of the upcoming German, which would last the better part of a week. It would culminate in my christening a new boat in their yachting club. Everything was falling into place. I was counting on one thing: that Harry's friends could read and write, a pair of skills I wasn't sure my cousin fully possessed.

The week progressed like a staged play. Not only could his friends read and write, most of them were excellent dancers and could do any step that I suggested, all of which flew by Harry as if he had only one leg. To make matters even better for me, Randall Jackson, a youngish looking Colonel was a Shakespearean scholar who appreciated all my interest in the theater. We spent hours discussing what Iago really had in mind, how mad was Ophelia, was there *ever* an instance that Polonius knew what he was talking about; it was delightful. The most delightful part of it was watching poor Harry treading water while the rest of us swam right by him. By the time we got to the boat christening, I knew I was in the final lap of my victory. I coyly asked Harry, "Now you must tell me exactly what to do. I've never seen so much water before. This doesn't look like the Chattahoochee."

By then he knew the jig was up. "Don't think you're fooling me for one minute, Sallie Johnson. I know precisely what you're up to. Before this is over, we'll probably find out that you christened the *Monitor*."

"Don't be silly. I've *never* christened a Yankee ship before today. And besides that was before we were born."

"Well, the *Merrimac,* then. It wouldn't surprise me if you had been here in another life. You've learned too much to be just nineteen years old."

That was enough. I knew I had vindicated myself and he would regard me as more than a brainless cousin from the God-forsaken State of Georgia. All this sounds frightfully petty to me now, but at the time I thoroughly enjoyed it.

The week of the German must have been satisfactory, for the following Monday I learned an elaborate reception in honor of General and Mrs. Johnson's niece was to be given.

During that week, Aunt Rachel and I had many calls to repay and I heard little of the news. We returned home for luncheon one day and Aunt Rachel instructed the coachman not to remove the harness as we would be leaving shortly after eating. We didn't even remove our hats as we sat down for chilled lake trout in a dill sauce. "Should anyone call, tell them we're not home," Aunt Rachel called out to Rose as she returned to the kitchen. Evidently Rose did not hear as she returned very shortly with a calling card on the silver tray.

"Oh, who is it?" aunt Rachel asked, impatiently. She held up the card, then fetched her glasses and read it again. "Oh, dear, Sallie. I'm afraid we will have to receive them," she said looking distressed.

"Who is it?" I idly inquired.

"General Sherman. It's General Sherman, Miss Rachel Sherman, and Master Tecumseh Sherman."

My heart nearly stopped. I could see Mrs. Hall standing in front of me. "Now's the time, dear Sallie. Do what you must do for the honor of us all. Slap his face, Sallie. Then, go after him with those beautiful fingernails of yours. How *lovely* this is going to be!" It was almost as if she *really* had said all those things. Aunt Rachel must have seen the look on my face.

"Now, Sallie, you remember . . ." she trailed off.

That was the whole problem. I *was* remembering. Ye Gods,

the Arch Fiend, the Demon was in this very house! My formidable aunt faded from my mind and the words of Mrs. Hall were ringing in my ears. I felt like Joan of Arc at Orleans.

The best way to handle this was to take charge of the situation, so I strode into the drawing room, not waiting for an introduction. What I was expecting, I have no idea. What I saw was a charming scene. General Sherman was standing by the window, his daughter and son on either side. He kneeled down between them and was showing them a bird's nest in the bushes just beneath. The baby birds could easily be seen and the mother was busily trying to feed them all at once. The general was talking quietly to his children who were leaning against him in that special way little children do with their father. I had come this far. There was no turning back and I wasn't going to be altered by this little display of fatherly gentleness.

"Are you General Sherman?" I demanded.

"Yes, and who are you?" he responding, rising.

"I am," I said, with a little more imperiousness than needed, "Miss Sarah Cobb Johnson."

"Well," said the General, "And what kin are you to Dick?" He had a quizzical look on his face.

"I am the niece of General Johnson." I was beginning to sound haughty.

"Well, well! Rachel. Come here and meet General Johnson's niece. Cumpie, you come, too."

The children scampered over to us. Rachel gave a little curtsy followed by a dignified bow from Cumpie. General Sherman had a hand on the shoulder of each and, even in all his finery, he looked like nothing more than a loving father. I had expected a giant, I suppose, someone with a gleaming glare and bad teeth but he was scarcely taller than I. His beard, said to be red from blood, was full and white. His eyes, those steel blue eyes, the ones said never to have blinked when killing children, were so deep, so clear, that it felt as though I were looking into kindness itself. I was losing my train of thought. The General was standing, expectantly.

In my mind Mrs. Hall sidled up behind me. "Sallie, dear.

Remember what I said . . . first, slap his face, then the fingernails."
This man was now the Commanding General of the entire United
States Army . . . I could handle that much. It was the children
standing there, holding his hands, the total look of gentility about
him—that was what froze in my mind as surely as a mid-winter
Minnesota lake. I shook my head to clear my thoughts.

As I recovered, I said, "I didn't come in here to converse, General
Sherman. I came to take the measure of the man who burned my
home. Will you please remain standing while I look you over?"

With surprising grace, he turned fully around, then smoothed
his uniform jacket slightly, looking very amused by the whole affair.
"And what home of yours did I burn?"

"Atlanta! Atlanta! And everything before you on the way to
Savannah."

"Why, child, didn't you know that I burned Atlanta to make
the home of Miss Sallie Johnson famous?"

I didn't know what he meant by that remark. Surely we all
could have done without that kind of fame. "I wasn't even born
then," was the only reply I could bring to mind.

"Of course you weren't. You're much too youthful and vivacious
to have lived in those terrible times." He laughed heartily just as
Aunt Rachel was coming into the drawing room, a look of lightning
about to strike on her face.

She started with chilling dignity to introduce me to the General
but he waved her off with a hand. "Don't bother with all of that,
Mrs. Johnson. Miss Sallie has introduced herself in a most original
and charming way. Now you sit over there and talk to Rachel and
Cumpie while I get to know Miss Sallie from Atlanta better." He
pulled a piano stool over to the settee where I was standing and he
sat down, his sword brushing my skirt as he did.

Aunt Rachel seemed at a loss for a response, so she took the
children across the room, leaving us to our own devices. Oh, how
I longed to launch my attack so I could bring back a glowing
report to Mrs. Hall! But he was so affable, so pleasant and charming.
He had been so tolerant of my impertinence that we both sat and
drifted into conversation.

"I'm really a Southerner at heart," he mentioned. He paused, waiting for a response and getting none, proceeded as if that had been his plan all along. "After I graduated from West Point, I was assigned to St. Augustine. It was there I first learned the charm of the Southern Belle and it heightens my sense of youth to see that same loveliness in you, Sallie Johnson."

He went on to talk about his four years in Charleston as some of the happiest of his life. He asked about my schooling and was very familiar with Waverly Seminary, and laughed with great appreciation at some of the stories I told of my years there.

"I can see they educated you well but did not break your spirit. What a beguiling combination: wit, charm, education and humility, all in one package." He had taught school in Louisiana before the secession, "The best job I ever had," as he described it.

By then I knew he had figured me out, but I didn't mind. We did talk of the war. Of his phrase, so often quoted, "War is hell," he denied authorship although he said he certainly believed it to be true.

"I have often told the children," he gestured toward them, where Aunt Rachel was trying to listen to our conversation and them at the same time, "that war is a demonstration that men are blind and crazy. I have done more than my part to prove that statement true. There were times during the war when it was publicly stated that I was insane. I may well have been. How could a sane person ever do the things for which we were called to execute?"

The visit passed most pleasantly. Mrs. Hall, ever in the back of my mind, would have behaved no differently, I felt sure. When the Sherman family rose to leave, we noticed there was a large crowd around the fence in the front yard. The General looked through the curtains. "It appears we have been discovered," he said to his children. As they parted and he began to wave to the cheering crowd, he turned to say good-bye.

"Don't forget! I'm from Georgia," I called out with a smile.

"I don't think I will forget that . . . or anything else about you, Sallie Johnson." He snapped his hat in place, gave me a salute then took the children by their hands and walked out to meet his public.

As it turned out, General Sherman had come from Washington for a special celebration, and on arrival at the station, had slipped out a side door, avoiding the welcoming crowd and the committee that had arranged his trip. They had been frantically scouring St. Paul to locate him when someone realized that he might have gone to General Johnson's home. He had missed seeing Uncle Dick, but there would be adequate time for that, he assured Aunt Rachel, who looked as though she need a dose of her salts by the time the crowd had cleared the yard.

That evening, we all went to the ball being held in honor of General Sherman. When we arrived the entertainment was in full swing. As we got to the receiving line, General Sherman, resplendent in his dress uniform, saw us some distance from the podium He winked in recognition and, although I couldn't believe I did it, I winked back. Without ever breaking his stride in shaking hands, he called out, "Hello, Dick. I met your niece."

"You did?" Uncle Dick called back.

"Yes. She's pretty, and she's damn pert, too."

Everyone turned and looked at me, laughter washing around us. Aunt Rachel rolled her eyes and looked for a place to hide. The evening was a complete success as far as I was concerned. To see the great affection in which General Sherman was held confirmed my earlier impression that the man, when seen in his full dimension, was something quite beyond the ordinary. In Georgia, we had seen only one side . . . and the worst side of any man, to be sure. Over my life I would meet many more generals; some of them famous, others hardly known beyond their jurisdiction. In none did I find a more encompassing personality than that of William Tecumseh Sherman.

During the rest of my visit I saw much of the Sherman family. Rachel and I were the joint honorees at numerous parties given in St. Paul as well as at Fort Snelling. My experience in army life before my trip to Minnesota was nonexistent. I didn't realize that the rules of military protocol were quite different from those in civilian life . . . "normal life," I used to tell the General. Rachel, although much younger, knew all the proper ways to do things at a formal military function. In Washington, she had done it all. I tried to follow her example, but made frequent mistakes, much to the merriment of the officers and their wives. General Sherman was ever patient with me, always gently protective. Although he would join in the laughter, he never made me feel ill-at-ease and would explain to his staff, "That's not the way they do it in 'normal' life." Rather than enjoying a joke at my expense, we all participated in my gaffes in a congenial way.

One afternoon Rachel and I had been invited to see Guard Mountain. We stood around on the parade grounds at Fort Snelling while several detachments of troops rode around in a curious pattern in front of the main building. It looked quite intricate, but I was anxious to get off to Guard Mountain. I hadn't seen anything that remotely looked like a mountain in all of Minnesota, so I was looking forward to a little lesson in geography. After a furious drum tattoo, the soldiers rode off in different directions and my party began to drift toward to officers' quarters.

"Wait," I called, "When are we going to Guard Mountain?"

The group stopped and as one, turned to look at me. Lieutenant Biddle, one of my favorites, said, "Guard Mountain? What in the world are you talking about?"

"Guard Mountain!" I repeated. "You said we were going to the mountain. I've brought a picnic."

I didn't understand the roars of laughter. General Sherman took me by the arm and said, "Quite a natural mistake, my dear. We have just seen Guard Mount-ing, not Guard Mount-ain. Lieutenant Biddle, perhaps you will be good enough to explain to Miss Johnson at tea what she has just seen." He said it kindly, but with the tone suggesting there would be no more laughing at the Southern lady.

"Yes, sir!" snapping his heels together and extending an arm to me, we walked off to the officers' mess (I won't mention what came to pass the first time I heard *that* term).

There were other times when I would have appeared to be

playing the stupid Belle for all it was worth. Emma Mims and Daisy Breau of New Orleans would have been proud of me. But I wasn't playing. There really *wasn't* a bull at whose eye they were shooting their rifles.

General Sherman's family ended their visit as I was preparing to return to Atlanta. They came to see me at Uncle Dick's the morning of my departure. What a contrast between my huffy entrance on his first visit and the genuine sadness that I would likely not see the Shermans again.

"Of course you shall, Sallie," the General said. "You must come to Washington and visit Rachel. She's grown so fond of you . . . as we all have."

Mrs. Hall, who had been relegated to the back corners of my mind, now reappeared. What in the world was I going to tell her? She obviously had been confident that I would actually meet him and deliver her "message." I remembered the tears on her face that afternoon. I recalled the horrible story of her father's death and the Yankee soldiers looting his death room. How could I ever tell her of the different man I had come to know?

"Will you come to Washington, Sallie?" he asked again.

"Oh, I couldn't do that, General. Don't you see, I can associate with you up here, but if I went to your home, they would find out in Atlanta. They would think I was a traitor."

General Sherman smiled kindly—very kindly—and said, "I don't see it that way at all, Sallie. You can build a bridge to help heal all these terrible wounds. You may choose to do it in another way than visiting the Shermans, but I believe you will find the way."

As their carriage pulled away, I was torn between the duty I felt I had owed Mrs. Hall and the admiration, the true affection, I had for this understanding friend. The arch fiend, the monster Sherman had faded—that image was as dead as the thousands of boys from both sides left in the swath of his terrible swift sword. For me, his memory will always be one of a loving and protecting friend.

# CHAPTER V

When I think back to the time in St. Paul, I realize one of the greatest lessons I learned there was that of self control. Had Mrs. Hall not spoken to me before my going, had I not been so filled with righteous indignation, my meeting with General Sherman would have been little more than a pleasant interlude. It could have degenerated into an ugly scene that would have marred me for years to come. For General Sherman, it would have been an embarrassment, but no more. A foolish girl from the South had attacked him, verbally and physically. Although I never heard of it happening, I would not be at all surprised to learn that it did. Thank goodness it wasn't I. The self-control to look a situation over rather than acting on impulse saved me that day. It was the beginning of a lesson that I have tried to enhance with each passing year.

My experience in St. Paul seemed at such variance with the vapid personality Lucy and others seemed to think was essential if a woman was to succeed in life. It led me to wonder what type of success they would find gratifying. Surely, there was more to being a woman than acting coy and seductive, beguiling men to do your bidding. The older women whom I most admired seemed to have avoided that path. My Aunt Laura Rutherford, my mother . . . especially my mother . . . they led lives of quiet dignity that seemed to bear none of the marks of the superficiality which seemed so common in my closest friends. Any talk with them about more serious matters was always dismissed with a wave of the hand. I certainly didn't think I was smarter than they, but I was beginning to notice that my interests were different. To spend the rest of my life "allowing" myself to be entertained by men seemed a colossal waste of time.

I was, however, enjoying the social whirl just for what it was . . . a diversion. In St. Paul, in the debutante parties of Atlanta, I found myself energized and full of excitement. How did that enjoyment match up with a life that was more directed? I wasn't sure. I did realize that if I didn't "fall in" with the society in which I was expected to be a part, I would most surely "fall out."

Then there was the matter of Lucy. I had thought once I completed the season she would get back to her own life; I was mistaken. Apparently, she had taken me on as a lifetime project. She missed no opportunity to tell me what I should be doing, whom I should be seeing, where I should be going—all of it directed toward a destination for which I had no aspiration: to become a Southern Belle.

Lucy presented me with The Five Commandments (I was grateful there weren't more!).

First: Never permit a man to take a liberty. Always keep
    them at arm's length.
      (That sounded exceedingly dull, I thought.)
Second: Never reject a man when he first proposes.
      (The inference was, I suppose, you can reject him later.)
Third: Keep all men dangling. Make each one think he has
    an equal chance.
      (Unfair. Some were such dolts I could scarcely
        keep from telling them.)
Fourth: Be lovely and charming to all but remember—no
    favors.
      (At least *one* commandment made a little sense.)
Fifth: Remember, the larger the following, the greater the
    Belle.
      (It sounded like the description of a good sheep dog.)

Thank goodness for Mammy Sophy. She overheard much of

the cajoling, the whining, the pleading, the advice of which Lucy seemed to have an inexhaustible supply. One afternoon, she was ironing in the kitchen and I was making a cobbler from the peaches behind her cabin.

Mammy was putting her iron on the stove-top to reheat, and I had stepped out to the back porch, thinking about all Lucy had been telling me

"Oh, well," I said to myself, "I guess I'll have to try this life for a while. I'll string along as many beaux as are crazy enough to be strung, and then I'll . . ."

"Who you talkin' to, chile," Mammy said, sticking her head out the kitchen door. "You ain' keepin' comp'ny wid no hants, is you?"

"I was just thinking out loud, Mammy."

"Well, you better take care or you'll git yo'self conjured."

Mammy was convinced that witches and hants were always looking for a way to "git a—holt of somebody," and talking to yourself was a perfect invitation for a hant to answer. She came out on the porch and pulled up a chair for herself. Then she reached up and pulled me into her lap. She put her arms around me, rocking and cuddling me as she had done when I was a little girl.

"I heer'd all dat foolishness Miss Lucy been puttin' in yo' head." Her hand went up and her eyes got big. "And I's gwinter give you some advice. Chile, you better look out 'cause menfolks is dangersome critters."

I stroked her cheek. It made me sad to see wrinkles beginning around her eyes, her skin not quite so firm as it had been. "I'm too heavy for you to hold, Mammy," I said, getting up. I stood beside her chair rocking it slowly. "But you're right about Lucy and all her foolishness. Still, I suppose I've got to try it for a while."

"How come you gotta try it? You ain't no dummy. You don' have to fool nobody. Any mens worth havin' oughta figure dat out."

"You don't understand, Mammy. It's too complicated to explain. Either I have to get in the boat or be left stranded on the shore by myself."

"Well, de Lawd knows I'd ruther set on da dry land than git in de water wid a bunch of crazy menfolks, 'specially wid all da stories

you fixin' to twist around'em." She got up from the chair and
went to the stove to get her iron. "I'se glad I gots work to do. I ain't
got time to be settin' 'round here and studyin' about Miss Lucy
and all her foolishness."

"I'm not telling any stories, Mammy. I'm simply going to say
I'm not in love with anybody. When I do fall in love, I'll tell the
truth."

"Well, all I got to say," Mammy laid the iron on a damp shirt
as the steam rose up from her hands and in front of her frowning
face, "I'se glad you projeckin' yo'self with white mens 'cause if dey
was colored mens da whole she-bang of em would be kilt off 'fore
da week was out!"

I knew that was true. The fights that took place over the
affections of one of the servant girls could be unexpected and vicious.
When Mother saw trouble like that coming, she was quick to step
in and move the men to different jobs, but that didn't always
work. I remembered the story about the servant girl on the upper
Erwin plantation and how upset she was when she lost her man to
another girl. No fights ever came out of how the women felt—just
the men. Women were supposed to stuff their feelings inside and
go on with their work.

It wasn't many months before I realized that Mammy Sophy
had been right. The servants may have had serious fights, but the
gentlemen with whom I was associating surely wouldn't act that
way. But they did. They would fight for what seemed to be no
rhyme or reason. Sometimes it was as simple as a comment about
a family's war record. A man might take exception to another
questioning the battle record of his family. Often, the remarks
were idle comments, or so it sounded to me, but the gentlemen's
tempers saw it differently. Or who was going to sit next to a
particular woman at a dinner could degenerate into difficulty weeks
later, particularly if the woman had seemed excessively coquettish
with a rival suitor. To avoid such problems took a lot of diplomacy,
an effort to which I gave great attention. Some of my friends seemed
to enjoy having men in contention—sometimes physical—over
their affections. I never felt that way and went out of my way to

avoid confrontations between my gentleman callers. Platonic friends were my most treasured. Clark Howell and Joseph E. Brown were certainly two of my favorites. They were like the brothers I had always wanted but never had. We could do anything together and have a wonderful time. No one thought there was more to it than honest enjoyment of each other . . . or so I thought.

One evening, I was talking with Rose Anne Martin, with whom I often attended parties. I was mentioning what fun Clark and I had had on a recent outing to the river. Rose Anne listened for a moment then asked if he has kissed me goodnight. "Of course not. Clark has *no* interest in me. We're just wonderful friends."

Rose Anne, whom I trusted as honest, cocked an eyebrow. "Oh, Sallie, you *do* live in a dream world, sometimes."

"What do you mean?" I thought I was the only one who was trying to live in the real world.

"My mother was over at the Howell's for tea last week and Mrs. Howell went on and on about how much she wanted Clark to marry you. While they were visiting, Clark happened by and his mother kept talking just like he wasn't there, telling Mother about the things she had told him to do to get your attention. The trip to the Chattahoochee was one of them. Finally Clark said, 'Mother, I've told you a thousand times I could never love Sallie as a sweetheart. She's like my sister.' Mrs. Howell told him that made no difference, that he could learn to love you if he would just put his mind to it. Then she told Clark, 'I know Dr. Johnson will make Sallie marry you. All you have to do is ask.' Mother said Clark finally stalked off in a huff. All the mothers, not just Mrs. Howell, are trying to get their darling sons married to someone of whom they approve. When you look around at our friends who are married, you can certainly see that happening. There's hardly a couple I know that didn't get pushed toward, if not into, marriage by the man's mother."

I was stunned at all that was going on behind my back. I only half-believed it, although I never knew Rose Anne to gossip. Several months later, I was coming out of Harper's Mercantile and bumped right into Clark. Before I could say, "Good morning," he blurted out, "Sally, will you marry me?" He even had his hat in his hand.

"Are you crazy? I wouldn't marry you to save your life!"

He gave his hat a little toss, caught it, and plopped it on the back of his head. "Thank God! Now I can tell mother I've done my best and maybe she'll leave me alone!" He laughed and so did I.

"You know I *do* love you, Clark, and you love me. I just don't think our parents quite understand that doesn't mean we want to get married." I hugged him and told him to run right home and tell his mother about the callous rejection he had gotten.

"I can hardly wait," he said, literally skipping off toward Peachtree.

But there was a serious side to all the courting, one that sometimes teetered on the verge of tragedy. Tradition in those days still trailed the mockingbird in the moonlight. Women were "ladies" and men were "cavaliers." The duel was still in vogue. To have a man prepare to literally die for his lady's honor was a heady, although horrifying, experience.

In the summer, we often went to Mt. Airy, in the mountains of North Georgia. Compared to the mountains of Western North Carolina or the West, these were little more than foothills, but to us they seemed majestic. There were many summer homes settled into the coves and valleys giving the area a sense of isolation that made it all the more appealing. Our family had one of the smaller cabins, although it was quite nice—much more than the word "cabin" would suggest. During the week, we would visit back and forth with the neighbors, all of whom we had known for years in Atlanta or Athens, but the real entertainment came on the weekends. A special train, The Accommodation, ran from Atlanta to the tiny Mt. Airy station every Friday afternoon. It would be loaded with fathers, husbands, and most importantly from our standpoint, with young men coming to pay call.

The railroad spur terminated at the station, and just down the street stood an old hotel. Even in 1885, it looked as though it had been there for decades. There was a veranda that ran the entire width of the building. The gingerbread of the gables and the roof lines gave it an elegance that hadn't faded with years. In the moonlight it had the appearance of a house draped in lace. Our cottage was just across the road from the hotel. Lamar and I enjoyed the afternoons sitting on our porch watching the guests arrive for the weekend. At five o'clock sharp we could hear the whistle down the valley with the engine straining up grade for the last mile or so. As The Accommodation rounded the last curve and with a great sigh of steam heaved itself into the station, Lamar and I would stand by the railing and wait for the suitors to disembark. If they could have heard some of the comments Lamar made, they would have gotten back on the train and sat there until it left on Sunday after dinner. I told her we should be pleasant to all of them, regardless if she thought they were crashing bores; they had traveled a long way to see us and the least we could do would be gracious. And gracious she always was. The very man whose nose she had compared to a pickled pepper as he waved from the station she treated with consummate charm and wit. Mr. Pepper, as Lamar called him, behind his back, would return to Atlanta basking in the mistaken notion that he was the swain of the beautiful Miss Rutherford.

Shortly after the gentlemen had checked into the hotel the baskets of fruits and flowers would begin to arrive. Whenever I received more than Lamar I would comment that it was my "beautiful nose that attracted men." We would both laugh, remembering our beauty contest in front of her mirror a decade earlier. "Just think how far you could go if you had a *really* cute turned-up nose like mine!" Lamar pushed my nose into a little button. The love we had for each other assured me my "rainbow wish" the first time I had visited Athens was coming true.

When the callers would begin to arrive, Lamar would station herself at one end of the porch and I at the other. Those nights were such fun. The gentlemen were probably no more serious about us than we were about them, but good conversation, good humor, and good food make those summer evenings a delight to recall. They were a delight when they were actually happening, but one night in August, we had an event that really put a different light on the whole business.

I was sitting with three or four gentlemen and we were enjoying our after-dinner refreshments. I looked across the road to the hotel and saw George Jackson standing on the veranda looking at us. We were being noisy and full of laughter but not creating any disturbance. Mr. Jackson had been to visit me several times. He was older than most of the others and quite wealthy. I think I knew that he wasn't coming to Mt. Airy just for the conviviality of the weekend, but until that night, I didn't understand how quickly a serious turn could be taken.

After watching us for several minutes with what appeared to be a look of disapproval, he started across the street and up the walk to our house, his steps very deliberate and measured. There were some gentlemen seated on the steps to the porch and there was no place for him to sit. He stood in front of the assembled crowd, the look of disapproval now quite obvious.

"Miss Johnson, I wish to see you." It wasn't a request, but more like a summons.

"Certainly, Mr. Jackson," I said, standing and giving a little twirl, then posing behind my fan. It was just the sort of thing my cousin Lucy, the manners mentor, would have loved.

Everyone laughed. "She's something to see, no doubt about that," Clark Howell called out from Lamar's station. More laughter. But not from Mr. Jackson. He was not a man to be taken lightly, particularly by men whom he definitely considered his juniors. He was furious.

"But I wish to speak with you." His tone was solemn and the crowd suddenly became quiet.

"I'm terribly sorry, but I'm crowded in this little corner. I'm sure one of the gentlemen on the steps will make a seat for you and we will all be interested in what you have to say." I wasn't trying to be rude, but I didn't know what else to do.

He didn't sit down, but stood with great dignity as if he were about to address the House of Representatives. "Miss Johnson, I wish you to come privately into the parlor where I can see you alone—you understand—alone."

Now, I was getting irritated. I resented his command, especially in the presence of others who, according to Lucy's teachings, felt themselves favored by me. I quietly, but decisively, replied, "Sir, I regret not being able to see you this evening."

He stood there for a long moment, replaced his hat with a little bow, turned as if on a parade ground and walked back to the hotel without looking back. Everyone was quiet, then my old friend, Clark said, "That may have been a mistake, Sallie. He was probably going to offer to marry you and make you wealthy."

I laughed it off. "I'm already wealthy—with friends, if not with money. I would take the former over the latter."

The tenor of the evening was changed. We all knew that something had happened which we didn't quite understand. When the gentlemen returned to their quarters later in the evening, there was much conversation about Mr. Jackson's behavior. Unfortunately, the men, who had a julep or two by then, did not take into account that the walls of the hotel were paper thin. They might as well have been talking directly to Mr. Jackson. It's probably just as well that I didn't hear what they were saying—and unjustly—about Mr. Jackson. It would have been better if I *had* been the one who heard it, rather than Mr. Jackson himself, which is exactly what happened. St. Julian Ravenel made the final comment which brought Mr. Jackson right into the room where the revelers were holding forth.

Before anyone could move or make some effort toward amends, Mr. Jackson fetched the man nearest the door a smart rap with his cane, and when St. Julian went to his aid, Mr. Jackson dispatched him with a single blow to the face. A general melee then broke out leaving most of the gentlemen, save Mr. Jackson, bloodied and bruised.

"That will teach you to make light of a soldier, young sirs!" he said. "I will extract formal satisfaction from you on the field at Talullah Gorge in the morning." To whom the challenge was issued, no one was sure. From what had just happened they must have wondered if he was suggesting a duel against the lot of them. He had acquitted himself in such a way as to suggest he might be up for that.

I knew nothing of the fracas until the next morning when

Mother came into my room at five o'clock. "Get up, Sallie. You've caused a fine mess. Mr. Jackson is in the parlor and he demands to see you."

"At this hour?" I moaned. "I never receive before ten o'clock."

"Well, I advise you to receive him—and right now. There's to be a duel fought shortly and all because of the scene on the porch last night."

I was awake now. "A duel!? What in heaven's name for? No one's honor was besmirched."

Mother explained what had happened. St. Julian had given her a full report as soon as the fight was over, and now Mr. Jackson was in the parlor wanting to speak to me. "What in the world does he want to see me for? He brought all of this on himself." I was becoming more exasperated by the moment while trying to dress.

"Yes, he did, but you had a part in it. Had you been more gracious and not demeaned him in front of your young friends, I doubt this would have happened."

"I never intended to demean him, Mother. He was unconscionably rude about the whole thing."

"Be that as it may, he's downstairs and has given me a copy of his will." She held out a piece of expensive-looking stationery. I hastily read it and was astounded to see that, in the event of his death in the duel, he had left everything to me. I was horrified.

"This has gone too far. I'll put a stop to it immediately. Where is St. Julian Ravenel? This is madness."

"And so it is, my sweet thing, but your little St. Julian is powerless to do anything. He's the one Mr. Jackson named and the poor boy can't refuse to meet him. You must talk to George Jackson. Apologize, beg, do whatever you have to except marry him, to get this insanity stopped."

I was dressed, more or less, by then and went down to the parlor. Mr. Jackson was standing in front of the bay window looking out across the lawn. He was dressed in a morning coat with riding boots that gleamed like oiled ebony. In his hand he held the same elegant hat which he had carried the evening before. Seated in the parlor was a gentleman I did not know, but in his lap he held a polished walnut case with brass hinges. The pistols! The sun was just coming up, casting long shadows through maples, the leaves glistening with the rain that had fallen in the night. Had there not been such a pall over the morning, it would have been a glorious sight.

As I entered the parlor the gentleman acting as second rose and Mr. Jackson turned to face me. He was calm and totally placid, as if it were mid-morning and this were nothing more than a social call. He introduced the gentleman with the pistols and asked him to step to the porch. When he was gone, he closed the parlor doors.

"Miss Johnson, will you grant me an audience now, since I was unable to speak with you last evening?"

"Surely, Mr. Jackson. Please be seated." I sat on the opposite end of the couch. "Mother has told me of this terrible turn of events and I assure you . . . ."

He interrupted before I could finish. "I do beg your pardon for interrupting, Miss Johnson, but I must speak my peace and then depart. My behavior last evening was deplorable and for that I do sincerely apologize. The sight of such a beauty as yourself, a woman of such elegant charm and style in the presence of those fawning boys was more than I could bear. I will not offend you with the thoughts that went through my mind other than to say my purpose in wishing to speak to you alone was to declare my intentions to pay court when we return to Atlanta. To have done so in the presence of those young hooligans would have been unthinkable. Of course, you had no way of knowing my intentions, else you would not have treated me in such a cavalier fashion." I started to speak, but he held up his hand to continue. "Certainly, I bear you no ill will, Miss Johnson, because of the incident, but on returning to the hotel and hearing my manhood assailed publicly, I could do no other than choose this present course. Since the meeting at Talullah Gorge may prevent my true admiration for you ever finding full expression, I have taken the liberty of conveying certain assets to you in the eventuality that a melancholy event may occur later this morning. Please, along with this conveyance, accept my deepest apologies for my behavior last evening." With that, he clicked his heels ever-so-lightly and bowed slightly.

I had the feeling I was in the midst of a drawing room drama. It would have been just the type of romantic scene I would have treasured in my Waverly-Shakespearean period. But this was not a play. This was real and the possibility of someone dying because of idle jests I had made was sickeningly apparent. St. Julian Ravenel was just a boy, but he had stepped into a dangerous man's world. In my mind I had no doubt who would be lying dead in the forests of Talullah Gorge.

"Oh, Mr. Jackson," I began, "What can I possibly say, except to ask your forgiveness for my foolish, child-like behavior? St. Julian meant no harm. Of that I'm sure. They are little more than boys, and ones who had too much to drink, at that. Your apology, although certainly unnecessary, is gratefully accepted. I trust you will do me the same honor by allowing me to apologize formally for the entire episode?"

"Most humbly accepted, Miss Johnson. But that does not address the insult at the hand of Mr. Ravenel which is, of course, the only reason for the meeting on the field of honor."

"If I am able to persuade him to offer an apology, might not you consider that a more civilized form of redress?" He looked thoughtful, but did not reply.

We chatted, rather amiably, for some time and I was surprised to find that Mr. Jackson was indeed a charming gentleman. He finally rose and excused himself. I still did not know what his intentions were, but I could only assume that he planned to carry out his plan. I ran through the house looking for Mother, but she was nowhere to be found. Lamar appeared at the top of the steps and I started to explain.

"I heard every word. I was lying on the floor right above the parlor. What are you going to do?" Then, answering her own question, she said, "You've got to find Ravenel and knock some sense into his head. Jackson will kill him where he stands. I have the feeling this isn't the first time he's fought for a lady's honor."

"There's nothing about a 'lady's honor' in this, Lamar. It's all about men and their silly pride, about loud-mouthed children, and I'm feeling very much like one of the latter." I thought about Mammy Sophy's prediction about how her menfolks would kill each other before the week was out if colored girls behaved the way I did. It turned out we weren't so different after all.

As I was sitting in the parlor wondering where Mother was when I needed her, in came St. Julian Ravenel, Clark Howell, and the rest of the group. I was shocked at their appearance. Mr. Jackson had looked as though he were on the way to a reception for the President; these looked like they were left over from a barroom brawl. Black eyes abounded; they looked like a pack of raccoons. There were bruised foreheads and several were limping. "What in the world happened to all of you?" I asked.

"Jackson! It doesn't do to make him mad," St. Julian sighed. Then they were off with their apologies, but Ravenel seemed to have no plan of what to do other than go to Tullalah Gorge and die like a man

"Don't apologize to me. Find Mr. Jackson and tell him."

"Actually, we just came to say good-bye. Sorry if we messed up your weekend," Clark said.

"Messed up my weekend! MESSED UP MY WEEKEND!! You have no idea . . . !" I shouted. Before I could continue, the front door opened; I was afraid it might be Mr. Jackson and we would have the duel right in our parlor. I turned and was relieved to see Mother standing in the doorway. The sheriff was with her. The boys saw him and started for the door, but he blocked it. They were in no mood for yet another fight.

"That'll be enough of that, boys," he said, producing a sheet of paper. "This here is a peace warrant for the arrest of anyone who even *thinks* there's going to be duel. Each and every one of you is going to sign this thing right now, then I'm marching the whole bunch of you down to The Accommodation and you're going back to Atlanta."

"But the train won't leave till this afternoon," I reminded him.

"The train leaves when I tell it to, Miss Sallie, and the engineer is down there stoking the fire right now." As if on cue, the engine whistle blew three long blasts. "Now, each of you sit down at this table, one by one, and sign my paper, else you're going to spend the week in my jail. And I can tell you," he added as an afterthought, "I don't serve no afternoon tea."

St. Julian stepped forward and sat down. "But what about Mr. Jackson. He'll tell everyone in Georgia I'm a coward." He looked up at the sheriff.

"No, he won't. He *knows* you're a fool and a loud mouth but he won't have to tell anyone. Unless you grow up, sonny boy, everybody will figure it out for hisself. I spoke to him and the last thing he wants to do is kill a defenseless boy but, mark me, he'll do it if you push him." He looked around the room at all the black eyes. "And I would agree with him, you're all pretty defenseless." He turned back to St. Julian. "When you get back to your high-falootin' house on Peachtree, get your mama to help you write Mr. Jackson a note of apology."

They were a sad looking bunch as they signed the peace warrant, but when the train whistle blew again, the sheriff ushered them out the door. Mother, Lamar and I stood on the porch and watched them go. As they approached the day coach, Mr. Jackson appeared from the station and the boys stood aside to let him board first. He smiled, then said to St. Julian in a voice we could easily hear, "After you, son." Then he tipped his hat to me and boarded.

As the train pulled out of the station, Mother smiled in relief. She had averted a tragedy at Talullah Gorge when she went to fetch the sheriff. No one ever suspected she had done it, but I was forever grateful.

News of the weekend events spread rapidly, and the whole story took on mythic proportions as it was passed from person to person. I was growing alarmed at all the exaggerations being added to the facts. One evening, not long after, a group of us were sitting in the salon of Henry Grady and his wife, Julia. They were neighborhood favorites. Both Henry and Julia had grown up in Athens. They were great friends of the Cobb family and the Rutherfords, so we considered ourselves practically cousins. Henry's father had been killed in the battle of Petersburg, so Henry had become the man of his family when he was little more than a boy himself. The family had been prosperous, but Henry, in some ways, never grew up. I suppose that's one reason I liked him so much. Even though he was fifteen years older than I, he never lost his sense of boyishness. He loved a good prank as much as I.

After he heard the true story of what had become known as "The Duel That Didn't," he laughed and said, "What you needed was a good reporter to get the facts straight!"

And if there was ever a good reporter, it was Henry Woodfin Grady. In his early work in the newspaper business, I suspect that his progress was slowed by his pranks and the lack of understanding by some of his stodgy bosses. After having presided over the bankruptcy of a small newspaper in Rome, as well as the ill-fated *Atlanta Herald,* he moved to New York, then was assigned to Atlanta as a special reporter for *The New York Herald.* Despite those hard years when he had run through most of his family money, he soon established himself as a first-rate reporter with an unerring sense for news. He was a natural-born journalist as well as orator, but he hated the exact sciences. In those three categories we definitely saw eye to eye. He borrowed $20,000 from Cyrus Field whom he had met through his friend General John B. Gordon and bought one-quarter interest in *The Atlanta Constitution.* By the time I was a teenager, he had become quite well known for his outspoken, but well-reasoned editorials. The responsibilities of *The Constitution* calmed some of his boyish ways and gave him a great forum for his ideas. And it was his ideas that appealed to all of us.

Everyone, North and South, was exhausted by the post-bellum animosity that still existed. The question of what would become of the Negroes was on everyone's mind, but no one had any solution. Manufacturing in the South had become non-existent because of the wholesale destruction by the Union army. And the only crops we seemed to know how to grow were cotton and tobacco, both of which seemed to be damaging the soil so much each year, the crop yields became lower and lower. Henry addressed all of those problems and he did it in such a way that it immediately caught the attention of everyone. Many didn't agree with his solutions which were bold and far-sighted, but the respect he garnered was immense. Even with all this, he was a charming man, one with whom everyone, regardless of station, felt welcomed and comfortable. To be able to visit so freely with such a person was a true gift.

After we had finished with "The Duel That Didn't," someone of prominence—it may have been the governor—commented, "Henry, you surely have the gift of gab."

He laughed. "Why shouldn't I? My father was an Irishman and my mother was a woman. But putting that aside, I want to use my ability to speak, to write, to impress on you statesmen that our Southern people cannot live to ourselves. The North needs us and we need them. If we are ever to progress or find success, we must get together again."

The politicians who were there began to discuss what could be done and how impossible it all seemed. At every juncture, just when all seemed ready to throw their hands up in defeat, Henry would bring up a point they had overlooked and they were back at it again. As a young woman, I took little part in the discussion, although I had had some experience in the North, an advantage lacking most of the Southerners. They listened to my accounts of what a gentleman General Sherman was with great skepticism.

"Sallie is right, gentleman," Henry agreed. "Judge a man only by what you hear and I can guarantee you will do yourselves as well as him a disservice. We *must* find a way to reach out to the North, or others will be having this same discussion a hundred years from now!"

In the midst of the debate, the telephone rang. It was the editorial office at the paper reminding Henry that he had forgotten to write an editorial for the morning's paper. "All right," he sighed. "Get a pencil and paper. I'll dictate it to you."

We all sat there, mouths agape, as Henry Grady took what had been discussed that evening and distilled it into a work of art, an editorial that was picked up by all the major newspapers in the country. Who would have thought that the innocent evening which started off discussing the vagaries of young men and their romantic passions would have ended in such an instrument? That editorial was the beginning of Henry Grady's fame, which was very soon to become nationwide. It was out of that editorial that Henry received an invitation to speak to *The New England Society* in New York City. It was, he told me afterwards, the opportunity of a lifetime. In the midst of the most formidable minds of America, he would be allowed to speak his views on reconciliation, on the rising of The New South. His anticipation of the event and its importance led him to devote almost all of his time to preparation of the speech. He knew a good speech when he wrote one and this was one the best—or so he thought.

Several days before leaving for New York, he began to have the feeling that this speech would never be delivered. It was a ridiculous thought, he told me. It was well-crafted, reasoned beyond refutation and said all the things that he so fervently believed about the importance of the South in the future of the country. Why in the world did he have doubts that it would be delivered? He had no answer, but he believed in psychic influences enough to tell Clark Howell, the non-duelist from Tullulah Gorge and night editor of *The Constitution*, not to print the speech in the morning edition until he had heard from Henry that it had, in fact, been delivered. Clark was nonplused, but he knew enough to listen to Mr. Grady and follow instructions. Happily, he was a more reliable newspaper man than he was a suitor.

The evening *The New England Society* met, Clark set the proposed speech in type, but did not print it. He fully expected to receive word, no later than ten o'clock, to go to press with it. As he sat in the editor's office, no phone call came, no wire was received. By midnight, he became concerned. What could have happened? Had there been an accident? Had the speech evoked a riot? If Clark Howell, if any of us could have been there, we would have been witness to one of the greatest speeches ever delivered in America.

My old friend General Sherman would be there. What would be his response to the spokesman of the city he had left in ashes? Dr. T. De Witt Talmadge was the speaker before Henry. To follow such an orator would be a daunting task for anyone. Dr. Talmadge, a minister, was the pastor of The Central Presbyterian Church of Brooklyn, the largest congregation in the country. He was a tall man, Patrician in bearing and elegant in every detail. Beyond that, he was well-educated and had a sense of stage presence that could have won him a place of fame in any theater. Some thought him overly demonstrative, histrionic and very much concerned with the reception he would receive. All of that may have been true, but no one could doubt his prowess as a speaker. His sermons were published in 3500 newspapers across the country. That night, he did not disappoint them. His was a stirring speech detailing the triumphant return of the Union soldiers to their homes. The picture he drew, "with a master's hand," as Henry was to quote in his following speech, was "of returning armies marching with proud and victorious tread, reading their glory in the nation's eyes."

Grady drank in every word of the speech, and with it the memories of his father dying in the Battle of Petersburg. He saw the desolation of his mother, the tragedy and misery of his beloved South. When it was his turn to speak, the prepared text remained in his coat pocket. Later, he told us of his feelings, as he stood following his introduction.

"When I found myself on my feet, every nerve in my body was strung as tight as a fiddle string and tingling. As soon as I opened my mouth, my emotions came rushing out."

The effect of the speech was sensational, and Henry's oratorical fame, hitherto largely sectional, became nationwide overnight. The speech was laced with humor and good-natured fun that was so typical of him, but the substance of his remarks was unmistakable. The Old South, the South of slavery and secession was dead; The New South of union and freedom was living, breathing and growing every hour. He countered Dr. Talmadge's remarks with a tribute to the courage and bravery of the Confederate troops. He painted a gripping picture of what the soldiers had left—prosperity and graceful living in a land where some were slaves. A war in which God had, thankfully, seen the South lose. He told of the soldiers returning to the rubble of their homes, the total destruction of society. They were foot-sore and weary, half-starved and dressed in tatters. They found their houses in ashes, their barns burned, their livestock stolen or killed, their money worthless, living in a land, once theirs, now without legal status and no laws. But did they sulk and become dejected by what had happened to them? No, they set about to build a new society, one that would include the Negroes, one that would found new industry. He then went on to discuss the importance of the North and South in joining together to help each other, to put aside animosity and bitterness, to work together to find the rightful place for the Negro in American society. It was the first major address to recognize the problems of the freed slaves, problems that must be dealt with, and done fairly, with a genuine concern for their welfare. The speech went beyond the passion of victory, the glory of a lost cause, and concentrated on the union of the spirit between North and South. It was the beginning of reconciliation, a process that continues even today, but my friend and neighbor Henry Grady sowed the first seeds that winter evening in New York City.

When we read the text of the speech (which Clark finally did get published) it was almost as though we had been there. It was a perfect balance of humor and seriousness, of high-minded thought and raucousness. I had wondered what, if anything, he might have to say about General Sherman. I laughed aloud when I read those comments: "I want to say to General Sherman—who is considered an able man in our hearts, though some people think him as kind of a careless man with fire—that from the ashes he left us in 1864, we have raised a brave and beautiful city; that somehow or other we have caught the sunshine in the bricks and mortar of our homes and have bundled therein not one ignoble prejudice or animosity." That was so much like Henry—gracious and inspiring, as well as humorous, all in one sentence. There was another anecdote that I wonder, knowing Henry, if he didn't perpetrate. He told the story of an old preacher who told his boys he was going to read them the story of Noah the next day. The boys (Henry, perhaps?) got his Bible and glued the pages together. When the old man started to read, he said, starting at the bottom of one page, "When Noah was one-hundred and twenty-years-old he took unto himself a wife, who was . . ." here he turned the page and continued, " . . . one hundred-forty cubits long, forty cubits wide, made of gopher wood and covered inside and out with pitch." The minister paused, checked to see he had read it correctly, then said, "I never encountered that passage before, but in faith, I take it to mean that we are fearfully and wonderfully made." Henry then asked his audience for that same unwavering faith in the message he was about to deliver. His ability to tie the ridiculous to the sublime was unmatched. I have often wondered where that speech might have led. I wondered if Henry Grady was destined to be a true healer for the nation, but we never found out. His speaking schedule was rigorous. He believed so passionately in his vision of The New South that he would travel anywhere people would gather to listen. He drove himself unmercifully, sleeping on trains more than in his own home and trying to see that *The Constitution* was publishing in a responsible way. He returned from just such a trip in the winter of 1889. He didn't look well. He was pale, tired, and seemed to be having trouble getting his breath. Although he tried to make light of his symptoms, he knew he was ill with pneumonia, and just a few days before Christmas he was dead . . . at the age of 39. If he had lived, what all might he have accomplished, but then how much he did accomplish in his short life. I was 24 when he died. Much of what motivated me in my later years was nurtured by the memory of Henry Grady.

# CHAPTER VI

A new problem surfaced. It actually was an old problem, but one that we had lived with but now was changing everything. My father's health was failing. He was born in 1810, Twenty-five years before my mother. When his first wife died in 1863, he was working at the post surgeon in Atlanta, having just been assigned that position. Immediately before the war he had been a candidate for governor of Kentucky, but medicine was his real love and his taste for politics was born of the urging of his friends. His office when he first came to Atlanta was in the second story of Magnum & Hightower, a drug store on the corner of Decatur and Peachtree Streets. When I was born in 1865, my father was fifty-five years old, old enough to be my grandfather. He *did* spoil me, of that I'm sure, and it hurt me to see him failing physically. He gave up his practice in 1882 because he just wasn't strong enough to carry it out. He would never turn away the poor or the disadvantaged and often took no money for his services. I remember sitting in his office one afternoon and someone came in with a sack full of change. He took it, thanked the man, then said, "Your account is fully settled. Now go by some food for your family," and he handed the money back to the man. Often, when he attended a poor family, he would take me on his rounds to check up on their progress. Into the house he would go with his black satchel in one hand and a basket of vegetables in the other. My job was to attend the buggy and horse while he was inside. I could tell when the some of the family would walk him out to the carriage, his vegetable basket empty, there was real love in their eyes. Once, a prominent man in the community came by the house in the middle of the night, asking him to come see his sick daughter. My father excused himself and suggested the name of a colleague. It was a terrible night of ice and wind and I didn't blame him for not going out, but shortly a ragged man showed up at the door with a sick wife at home. Immediately, he was up and out the door to see the woman. I asked him later about that.

"Why did you turn down the first man then go out for the second one."

He smiled, and said, "Any doctor in town would be pleased and honored to see the Colonel's daughter, but finding someone to see a poor woman, now that's another matter. I like to work where no one else will go."

As he weakened, the love in which he was held became apparent. Many families came by the house. Often they would bring things that we knew they couldn't spare, things that we really didn't need, but Mother always accepted them as great gifts with many thanks. "Your father has worked so hard for them, they all want a chance to do something for him. We need to honor them by accepting all they bring."

For the last month, he was too weak to get up. Teams of doctors consulted, led by Dr. A.J. Woodward, but nothing could be done for his failing heart. He lay, as if asleep for the last four days, and at 11:15 on the bright, spring morning of May 19, 1886, he died. The funeral notice in *The Constitution* was lengthy and filled with praise. The part that would have pleased him the most was the section which was entitled, "He Did His Duty."

I was heart-broken by his death. He had meant so much to me. No father could have been more loving, more giving that he. Mother, who had lost her second husband, was more resolute than I. She had a life before him, and although she loved him dearly, she knew that she would have a life beyond.

I was surprised that life did go on after his death. People still were talking about the problems the South faced. There was still widespread interest in the ideas that were being put forth. Henry Grady was becoming better known by the day. But the idea that the North and South must remain forever different and distinct was a notion that had a life of its own. The concern about Southern women marrying Northern gentleman had abated only slightly. I was certainly of the age where marriage was in the front of everyone's mind. In fact, I was bordering on spinsterhood to hear Lucy Hill tell it.

"Merciful heavens, Sallie," Lucy said, "You're almost twenty-one years old. Pretty soon you'll be so old that no man with any self-respect would want to take a chance on marrying you. He would just assume there was . . . there was . . . something . . . wrong with you."

"Don't be absurd, Lucy. There's nothing wrong with me! Men aren't the fools you seem to think they are. The older I get, the more I learn, the more I can bring to a marriage. When I think about Margaret Jackson and girls like that who married before they had any idea what it was like to be a woman, let alone a wife and a mother, I know I haven't made a mistake. They're the ones that are getting old before their times—all wrinkled and their bellies pouched out from a pregnancy every year. I'll bet any one of them would trade places with me in a minute."

She stalked off, but I was giving thought to what Lucy had said. Father's death had left a huge void in my life. He was such a kind and loving man, but he was much older than mother. How realistic was I to think that I could find a man my age who had the same sense of dignity and character, the same love and tenderness that he had shown to my mother and to me? By the time my mother was not yet sixty, she had lost two husbands, and they had both been wonderful men, but both her senior by fifteen years or more. She was still a beautiful woman and certainly one of the smartest women I knew. I wondered if she would remarry. Certainly, there were men who would have been delighted to have become her husband. I asked her about that several months after Father's death.

"I certainly don't think so, Sallie. I've had a good life. Frank was a good husband. He gave me a wonderful few years, far better than I would have ever dreamed when I agreed to marry him. I often wonder what would have happened if I had insisted on marrying John Lamar instead of bowing to the family wishes. We would have had seven years together before the war. There would have been children. I would have had to raise them by myself. And I ended up having to do that anyway after Frank died. I don't think I ever loved anyone quite the way I loved John, but then that kind of love comes only with youth and seldom again. I found a stability and a steadiness in both Frank and your father—what a grand man he was—that was far more enduring than the passion John and I felt. You need to look for the same type of life for yourself."

"Well, I'm not looking for anything in a man at the moment. Since father died, I've found the most comfort in books and music, not in the company of men." It was true. My enjoyment of the social scene had waned since his death, but even so, I was interested in going to New York City for a visit with friends and family. Lucy, as usual, was aghast.

"Mother, you simply *must* forbid this trip," she told Mother when she first heard of it. "You know how Sallie is. She'll get up there in New York City and be dazzled by those smooth talking Yankees and the first thing you know, she'll be married and we'll have some little runt-faced boy running around here with buck teeth and talking through his nose."

And Lucy wasn't the only one. Poor Mother got the same speech from a lot of her friends. The James Swann's, from whom the invitation had come, were Southerners, Mother pointed out. That was true, but they lived in a fashionable section of New York and were surrounded, my mother was told by her friends, by foreigners. I think the thing that really upset them was my plan to visit Captain and Mrs. Williams who were stationed at West Point. No matter that Lizzie Williams was from Atlanta. "She married that Yankee out at Ft. McPherson and hasn't been seen since. She ought to ashamed of herself, inviting Sallie in to that hotbed of Union soldiers at West Point, all of them looking for a Southern Belle to despoil," they all chorused.

Mother reminded them that it was Lizzie's uncle, General John B. Gordon, who had intervened and convinced her parents that if she truly loved Lieutenant Williams that she should be allowed to marry him. That had been almost twenty years ago and their marriage had been very happy.

Henry Grady saved the day. He had heard all the conversation one evening at whist and finally could stand it no more. "Mary Willis, you're entirely too intelligent to let such conversation frighten you. First of all, none of it is true. The gentleman of the North are just as well-bred, just as intelligent as Clark Howell or any of our fine young men you care to name. Beyond that, Sallie is a bright and intelligent woman. She's not a child. She will make her own decisions—something she seems to have been doing since she was about three, so far as I can tell."

Mother laughed. "That's certainly true. And most of the time, it has worked out well. I know that was one of the things that John loved so about her. Of all the children he had, Sallie certainly has been the most spirited and the most adventurous."

"And a visit to New York City is an adventure she is more than capable of handling," Henry argued. "It will broaden her perspective, it will introduce her to a type of society that it vital for her to understand, for all of you," he gestured around the room, "to understand. The New South will be born one citizen at a time, and Sallie is certainly a prime example of our hope in the future. What we are all saying is there should be no North, no South, just Americans. If we can't learn that lesson then we will have gone through all this struggle in vain." He paused and looked around the room. Everyone respected his opinions, but they still had grave misgivings.

Mother joined in, "I understand how you all feel, but think about her trip to St. Paul. I heard the same arguments then, but when Sallie came home, she was a different person. She went away a little girl, but returned a young woman. Nothing bad happened. She learned more in those months with her Uncle Dick than half a life time of trailing around Southern traditions and prejudices."

Lucy was listening, but not convinced. "I don't know. If Daddy were alive . . . ."

Mother brought her up short. "He *is* alive! He's alive in you, Lucy, in your brother, and he's alive in Sallie. I know one thing for certain: John Johnson always trusted Sallie's intuition and her good sense, sometimes when, I have to say, I wasn't too sure of her myself. I will honor his memory and his love for all of us by agreeing Sallie should make the trip."

Between Henry and my mother, the family and friends were won over. The long faces and the dire predictions gradually disappeared, but they will weren't above giving me warnings, especially Lucy, right to the time I boarded the train, bound for the capitol of the North.

I had thought that St. Paul was a large city, and by the standards of Atlanta, it was, but it certainly couldn't compare with New York. As the train pulled into the station, I felt as though I had entered another world. The streets were packed with wagons drawn by oxen, elegant carriages with high-stepping horses, their coats gleaming like polished walnut in the morning sun, people on foot, dodging between the constant river of traffic and every other kind of conveyance you can imagine. As Janie Swann took me to her waiting buggy, I felt as though I had to stand and take it all in at one time, but that was impossible. On every hand there were buildings larger than I had ever seen; there were people of every background and dress. It seemed like a foreign country. "Come along, Sallie," Janie called. "We need to go to the market on the way home."

The open air market was filled with foods of all types, many I had never seen and some that looked positively dangerous. Janie quickly sorted through the fresh vegetables she wanted, selected a monstrous and mean-looking fish from a barrel filled with ice; a sturgeon, she told me. It certainly was not like anything I had ever seen. Soon, we were riding through what appeared to be countryside, surrounded by the city. In those days, Central Park seemed larger than the whole of Atlanta. The thing that impressed me the most about New York wasn't its size, but the air of expectancy. I felt as though anything could happen here. If the sky opened up and chariots came down to earth, this looked like the place it would happen. The museums, the concerts, the art galleries, the lecture halls—all of them held an allure which I had not imagined possible. In Atlanta, buildings and activities of that sort were just beginning to be available, but on the grand scale of New York, it would be after my lifetime that such sophistication would come to the South, I felt sure.

Janie had quite a tour laid out for me. In the morning we would go to a museum, a library, or a special garden. After lunch, we would pick up right where we left off. The evenings were filled with sumptuous dinners, lectures and concerts and, as I had been warned, with many suitors. It was amazing. There were young ones and old ones; there were rich ones and poor ones. The latter group were all from the South. Many of them had come from wealthy families, who like most southerners, had lost everything. They had come to New York to start over, to found new businesses. They all shared one trait—other than their lack of money—they all looked tired and old beyond their years. As I got to know some of them, I understood the struggle they were going through, but I was surprised to find how little understanding the rich young men from the old, fine New York families understood what a gift they had received from their heritage, and not one they had deserved anymore than my poor friends from the South.

If I thought the food that Janie bought at the market on my first trip there was exotic, I was mistaken. Many of the epicurean bachelors had dinner parties for me and the array of food was beyond anything I could imagine. In St. Paul, I had learned some of the art of subtle inquiry. Rather than blurting out, "What is this?" when presented with an usual looking or odd tasting morsel, I would say, "Are these grown locally?" or something equally innocuous. One of my hosts did laugh and said to his amused guests, "Well, there's not much we can't produce around here, but I've never seen a local octopus." It was rather chewy with a faintly fish-like taste. My squeamishness reared its head when one evening we had escargot from France, but I remembered my sherry maneuver at the parties when confronted with raw oysters and I enjoyed it all. There were foods that I had to be shown how to eat. Lobsters, long thought to be poisonous had been discovered to be a delicacy, but how to eat one is not something you can figure out yourself. I was not above asking my escort if he would mind opening it for me. Judging from their performance some of them, while feigning great urbanity, were doing it for the first time.

Within the group of young men I met were a few gentleman who had no means of support so far as I could determine. They usually had some mysterious story about a lost fortune in Europe which they expected to reclaim in the immediate future. Somehow, I had arrived with the reputation of a rich young woman from the South, a worthy catch for anyone who was in financial difficulties. The fortune hunters had a little network of their own. I overheard conversations that detailed their plans for other young women whom they thought to be wealthy. As soon as I asked one of them if he could lend me ten dollars so I could buy my ticket back to Atlanta, they all disappeared.

After ten hectic and fun-filled days, Lizzie Williams arrived from West Point to take me home with her, but Janie would not hear of it. "It's out of the question, Lizzie. Sallie hasn't even gotten her feet wet in New York and you want to take her up to the God-forsaken fort at West Point. She will simply die of boredom. She must stay in the city and complete her visit with me."

Lizzie's eyes brimmed. Mrs. Swann was a formidable woman and not one to be taken lightly. "Oh, Janie. You're right about one thing. It *is* a God-forsaken place when you're looking for someone from the South. The Army has cut me off from all my people and with Sallie, I'll have a chance for a little visit back home. I'm so homesick for news of all my people. Please let me have Sallie. I promise to have her back in two weeks to the minute!"

I felt like a valuable commodity. I was having a marvelous time in New York, but I did long for some time with Lizzie. I wondered what was really behind Janie's resistance. I knew she had gone to a great deal of trouble to arrange the introductions, schedule the events, and guide me through all the entertaining. Janie finally relented and it was agreed that we would leave for West Point on the morning train. As we were walking to the carriage, Janie called out, "Sallie don't you forget about the young doctor."

"Young doctor?" Lizzie asked, after we were on our way, "What young doctor? I'll bet Janie Swan has already got one picked out for you to marry. Knowing her, she's probably already chosen the church and talked to the minister. Forget about all these New York men, that's my advice to you. I'm going to show you some *real* men. I have no intention of letting you marry outside the Army. Look what a row my family kicked up over my marriage and look how happy we've been. The Army life is the place for you, Sallie."

Maybe all the family and friends in Atlanta had been right: This was a trip to secure a husband. It would have been nice if they had asked me if I wanted to get married. I suppose they assumed that I did and in fact, I was interested in settling down, but I had never been so intentional as to think the trip to New York was to parade myself in front of a bunch a eligible men and select the highest bidder. Yet, there was, as Janie had guessed, the matter of the young doctor. Saying good-bye to Hugh Hagan had been difficult. He was a kind and gentle man, studying medicine at The College of Physicians and Surgeons. As the train rolled along the banks of the Hudson, I looked out the window watching the scenery glide by. It was a lulling time, a time of feeling sentimental, a special kind of longing that I hadn't felt since my school days when the charm of young men first began to catch my consciousness. Hugh Hagan. What an interesting name—short and to the point, no nonsense. None of your J. Worthington van Rensselaer, IV or anything so pretentious. Just Hugh Hagan. What an interesting man! As much as I wanted to be with Lizzie and to meet her friends at West Point, the idea of not seeing Hugh again was depressing.

I had never considered myself a fickle woman and I certainly had heard nothing from young Dr. Hagan to make me feel his intentions were anything beyond cordiality and friendship, but I was unprepared to be so taken with the young men of West Point. I had assumed that Captain Williams would meet us on arrival, but no, at a stop an hour before we were to arrive, Captain Francis Brown and Lieutenant John L. Chamberlain boarded the train. At first, I thought they had been off on some official mission and were simply returning to the Point, but they left the impression they had come down line, at the request of Captain Williams, to join us and make sure my baggage was properly handled. Try as I might, I could not find out what the truth was, but both men were so charming and clever, so full of repartee, it took my full attention to keep up with them. By the time we reached West Point they had so thoroughly engaged my mind that the thoughts of the handsome Hugh Hagan were fading rapidly.

Why I should have been paid such attention was a mystery to me, but the entire time I was in Lizzie's home, I seldom had a moment to myself. The young officers, who I am sure had multiple duties to which they normally would attend, seemed to have no shortage of time to spend with me. The weather was fabulous and as different from the indolent winters of Georgia as one could possibly imagine. A sprinkling of snow in Atlanta was a cause of wonderment, but here, it was a daily occurrence. In the mornings, I would look out my window and see the trees, newly draped in lace from the latest snowfall. The Hudson, just down the hillside, flowed like liquid sapphire in the morning sun. Could the brick-red water of the Chattahoochee be the same element as this elegant river? It was a Wonderland and I was Alice. In the morning, there would be strolls along the water's edge, John Chamberlain graciously helping me across the slippery spots. In the afternoon, there would be tobogganing down the rolling hills, a fire at the bottom with gallons of steaming tea and warm muffins. In the evening, there were dances and strolls down Flirtation Walk with the cadets. The idea that these were sons of the men who had destroyed the South was the furthest thing from my mind. They were courteous and gentlemanly in every respect. Obviously, some had romantic interests and I found that appealing, but they also were intelligent and well-informed. They expressed a genuine interest in learning about the South, about the all we had been through in Reconstruction and what our vision for the New South included. It was the conversation that I enjoyed the most. The parties, the festivities were wonderfully grand, but the men that I met confirmed an opinion that I had formed in St. Paul: Where you come from and from what roots you rise is not what's important; the thing that matters is the type of person you are.

Lizzie had promised Janie Swann that she would have me back in New York in two weeks—to the minute. The time was almost up, but Lizzie walked into my room one morning with a letter in her hand.

"You won't believe what Janie Swann has done! She wrote your mother and made it sound as though I had positively abducted you from New York. This is a letter from cousin Mary Willis— your mother—telling me to get you back to New York City immediately I can't believe it! You're my cousin and I need you here more than Janie Swann and all her snooty friends could ever imagine."

I looked at the letter and knew that my time at West Point, at least for this visit, was over. "Lizzie, I promise on my next trip, I will spend the entire time with you and all your wonderful friends. I can't thank you enough for all you have done for me. And the gentlemen of the Corps . . . what a wonderful group they are. Please tell them I'm sorry to leave in such a rush, but I will be back."

My trunk was packed and I was on the afternoon train back to the city. On the way up to West Point I had been thinking of Hugh Hagan. On the way back to the city my mind was filled with Lieutenant Chamberlain, of the moonlight sleigh rides, his high-stepping quarter horse with hooves thumping across the snow-covered fields and the bells ringing, the conversations that flowed between us like we had known each other for years.

I had only been back in New York for a week or so when who should appear at the front door but Lizzie with Lieutenant Chamberlain. Between the two of them, they managed to convince Janie that I *must* return to The Point with them on the afternoon train. I had my bag packed and we were off to the station before Janie could mount a reasonable objection. It was the best of both worlds, because Hugh Hagan was always waiting in the city for my return. He was most attentive. Flowers would arrive at West Point simply signed, "From an admirer in the City." When I returned from West Point, he was at the station to meet me and had arranged a special carriage for the trip across the Park. Although Lieutenant Chamberlain and I had many lengthy and platonic conversations, when I felt the talk was about to take a serious turn, I would change the subject. Quite the opposite was true with Hugh Hagan.

I stayed on through the winter in New York with my trips to West Point being frequent. Each time I would return, I felt sure that Hugh would declare his intentions and I was quite prepared to toss Cousin Lucy's advice about always keeping a man dangling right out the window. When Hugh Hagan asked me to marry him, I was certainly going to tell him that I would.

One particular night, I knew it would happen. We had had an excellent meal at the Waldorf, then gone to the opera. Although it was still very early spring, the air had a different feel to it. The biting edge of winter had softened into the promise of something more gentle. As we were riding across the Park, I gave him every opportunity to say how he felt, to ask me to be a part of his life. When we arrived back at the Swanns', Hugh took my hand, kissed it lightly and said—as he always did—"Good night, Miss Johnson."

I was furious! Did the man have half a mind about him? Maybe Lucy's commandments were correct. Maybe I had made a fool of myself, allowing feelings for a man to overtake good judgment. I decided that I would marry John Chamberlain (not that he had asked me). If he didn't propose, then I would marry the most eligible of my suitors. There was always Mr. George Jackson; he'd been willing to *die* for me! Then I decided I would marry no one; I would be an old maid. I spent a fretful night, alternately crying out of frustration and being angry with the men in general. The next morning, I decided I needed to go back to Atlanta; I wasn't thinking very clearly in the North. I sat down to compose a letter to Mother, telling her to send for me, and hoping that I could just put my head in her lap and cry for a month. As I was writing, the maid brought in a box of a dozen roses with a card signed, Dr. Hugh Hagan. Was this a Northerner's idea of charm? If he cared enough to send me flowers, why didn't he say something for himself, I wondered.

But Hugh Hagan *wasn't* a Northerner. He was from Richmond, the capitol of the confederacy. His background was so different from mine. Maybe that was part of the attraction, maybe it was part of the problem. I was expecting him to act as the Southern gentlemen I knew, but they had all come from families that had, at one time, been major land owners, the plantation class. Those days were over, and the money they had once known had long since disappeared but like my family, their traditions remained. None of that was in Hugh's background. His mother and father, both children of Irish immigrants, and had not been able to marry because of lack of funds. Two of his uncles, John and Alexander, apparently got tired of living on next to nothing and moved to New Orleans. Hugh didn't talk much about them but whatever it was they did in Louisiana, they apparently did it very well. He did say they were involved in shipping. Maybe it was cotton and tobacco. I suspected it might be something less acceptable but didn't ask. When John and Alexander died, there was a lot of confusion about their estates. Neither had married, so Hugh's father moved to a hotel in New Orleans to settle the estate of his brothers, who left all their money to him his mother and a sister. It wasn't until this veritable fortune came to Hugh's father that he could afford to marry. Hugh was born in 1863, just two years before I was. How they managed to keep their money through the war, I have no idea, but eventually, Hugh moved to New York to study medicine. Given that background, maybe I was expecting too much of him. All I was certain of was that I cared deeply about him.

As I was sitting on the couch thinking about going back to Georgia, thinking about Hugh, I got out the letter I had received from Lieutenant Chamberlain.

> Dear Miss Johnson:
>     I am relieved to hear from your own dear self that you have recovered from the shock which you experienced in leaving me (Ha-Ha!). I feared that serious results my follow

(Ha-Ha!). I send by express today the rest of the stolen property.

If possible, I will come to see you Saturday and, if you wish we can go to the theater. Sunday, let us go to St. Thomas' where I can doubtless show you the widow whom you have so often expressed a desire to see. Excuse this paper. I am in my section room and have no other writing materials. The cadets are coming so I will close and make the boys as miserable as I can for a couple of hours.

Oh, my, such sleighing and tobogganing. I wish you were here to take a hand.

Sincerely,
John L. Chamberlain

It was an odd letter. I didn't know what he meant by several references, but it was clear that he was thinking about me, he was coming to see me in New York and he wished I was back in West Point. At least he made himself plain on those accounts, much more than I could say for the close-mouthed Dr. Hagan. I began pacing the floor, wishing I were back at West Point. On the other hand, I was glad to be away from the keen eyes of cousin Lizzie. I was tired of other woman planning my life. I would be going to the theater that night with Hugh. Maybe he would saying something then. Maybe the flowers were a preamble to a proposal. The next night Lieutenant Chamberlain would be arriving. He was diverting and amusing. I enjoyed his company, but I began thinking about the eligibles back in Atlanta. George Jackson, courtly though he was, did not seem a man with whom I could be comfortable. I was looking for a companion; I did not want to become an addition to an already established household. That would certainly be the case with Mr. Jackson. I picked up my portfolio to finish the letter to Mother and a little envelop fell out. It was a poem from John Fulton written for me just before I left for New York. He had given it to me at the train and I had stuck it in my stationery case and forgotten about it.

## To Miss Sallie

She stood erect, a perfect queen and every move was grace,
I thought I had seen, but ne'er beheld, the goddess of her
race.
And as I looked upon this queen, I wondered in my soul
Why Christ did a man seem and not of woman's mold.

For man could bow before this shrine and daily ask for love
And praise God for mercy kind when He called her above.
Beautiful Angel, what is the task to you on earth now given,
If not to make a Paradise and charm some soul to Heaven?

Well, *that* was certainly to the point! Why couldn't the good doctor put something like that in the box of roses? The curt, little card he had sent still irritated me.

John Fulton. Now that was a thought. He was handsome, tall and elegant with a crooked little smile that suggested he knew a secret and wasn't going to share it with anyone but me. His family were well known in Atlanta, prominent in politics and the law, which John was practicing with an ever-growing reputation. I would marry John Fulton. I didn't love him, that was true, but my mother hadn't loved Frank Erwin, but they had a wonderful marriage. I respected John and he obviously was wearing his heart on his sleeve with that poem. "Mrs. John Rutledge Fulton." It had a nice ring to it. That would show the whole bunch of them I was in charge of my own life. I began to think about walking down the aisle, John, splendid in his morning coat waiting at the altar. When I got to the fatal part about "I do," I came to my senses. John would never do. If I couldn't marry for love, then I wouldn't marry at all.

The diversions of the next two nights failed to ease my ill-temper. Dr. Hagan, ever the gentleman, failed miserably in showing any interest in knowing what my feelings for him were, let alone expressing his. When Lieutenant Chamberlain arrived, I told him that I was soon returning to Atlanta and would be beginning a new life there. I had no idea what the new life was, nor did he ask. I assume he thought I had accepted an offer of marriage and he made no further inquiry. He simply gave a little nod and said, "I see." Well, I saw, too. If that's all he could say, his feelings for me weren't very deep. For the last week of my visit, I puttered around the house and Janie left me to my own devices. To her credit, she could see I was troubled and I suspect she knew why, but she did not ask and I appreciated her respecting my privacy.

Two days before I was to return to Atlanta, Lizzie appeared at the door announcing that she was taking me back to West Point for one final farewell. I was so restless in New York that I agreed to go, but as soon as I was on the train, I wished I hadn't. We had scarcely left the city when she revealed her plan. Lieutenant Chamberlain apparently had told her that I had matrimonial plans on my return and she was having none of it. She had apparently been dead serious when she said she planned for me to marry an Army officer. I don't know why that was so important to her; maybe it was a final vindication that her own marriage to a Yankee officer had been a good thing. "See, even Sallie Johnson married one," she could say. If that were the case after all the years she had been married, I knew my making the same mistake would not rebuild any bridges with her family.

To my surprise, it was not John Chamberlain she was promoting, but a Lieutenant James Alexander. "He's the only office I know who can compare with my husband in terms of character, charm and wit," she confided as we pulled into the station. Why she had held him in reserve until the eleventh hour, I could not understand nor did she bother to explain. As soon as we stepped from the train, there he stood and quite a sight he was, at that.

He was tall and lithe as a willow, but gave the appearance of great strength. His beard was full and neatly trimmed, a shade lighter than his sandy hair. He took my hand as I stepped from the coach and as he helped me down, his eyes seemed to look right into my soul. The only time I had seen eyes like that were those of General Sherman. His conversation was smooth and urbane. He seemed to have a level of maturity that I had not seen in John

Chamberlain. In five minutes I felt as though I knew him better than I had gotten to know Hugh Hagan in four months. The sense of who he was seemed evident but he never gave the impression that he thought highly of himself. Maybe this final trip up the Hudson wasn't a bad idea after all.

When we arrived at the Williams' home, Lizzie showed us into side parlor. She was amazingly frontal about her approach. After extolling Lieutenant Alexander's virtues for what seemed an interminable time, I wondered what he must be thinking, just sitting there and have this woman plead his case. I felt like we were Priscilla and Miles Standish. Couldn't he speak for himself? Finally, Lizzie, finished her oration. "Now then, Sallie. Tell him you will marry him. Tell him!"

"Lizzie, this is beyond belief! Why is everyone so anxious to get me married? This gentlemen is . . . ," I paused, wondering if I should apologize to him, but Lizzie had caught her breath and started in again.

"Time is of the essence. The guests will be arriving for your farewell party and all will be lost. Tell him, Sallie. Go on and tell him you will be engaged to him." She was insistent and repeated her demand several times.

I stated the obvious. "Lieutenant Alexander doesn't know me from Adam's cat. He doesn't want to be engaged to a woman who doesn't love him."

Lizzie looked at me through her eyelashes, a little habit she used when she was about to make an important point. "Oh, yes he does, Sallie."

The lieutenant found his voice. "Oh, yes he does, Miss Sallie," he echoed.

The guests were arriving. I wondered if John Chamberlain was aware of all this? He had been far more attentive than anyone else at the Point, had made several trips to New York, ostensibly on business, but I knew he had really come to see me. He was a fine looking man with a wonderful sense of humor that I appreciated. Why wasn't he the one Lizzie had chosen to insist I marry. When I thought of the serious Hugh, I wondered if either one of these lieutenants wouldn't be a better choice. That's what my head was saying, but my heart was singing quite another song.

As the evening progressed my mind wandered and I had trouble really listening to what was said. I was thinking back to all the conversation in Atlanta before I had come to New York. Obviously, everyone but me knew this was an expedition to find a husband. Janie and Mother must have worked the plan out and Lizzie was serving as a backup match-maker. The whole escapade suggested I didn't have a brain in my head. It made me so mad that I thought I should leave the party, catch the midnight train to New York, get my belongings, move to San Francisco and marry a gold miner. That would serve them right!

After a glass or two of sherry, I began to calm down. Running off on some tangent would solve nothing. Marrying someone about whom I knew nothing and didn't love would be even a greater mistake. If I went back to Atlanta empty-handed, then there would be all sorts of talk. I would end up having to marry some buffoon from Birmingham and that would be a life sentence for certain. And behind it all was the silent, mysterious attention of Hugh Hagan. He could have made this *so* simple!

As the evening was winding down, I realized I had missed a good party. The pheasant was dispatched down to the bone, the smoked salmon looked like something the cat had visited, the *pate foie de gras* had long since vanished and people were saying their good-byes, hoping they would see me again soon. Lizzie and her friends had been truly gracious and I had acted quite removed from the whole scene. But who could blame me? A lot to think about.

Out of all of that came a reasonable alternative. Lieutenant Alexander was obviously a wonderful man. Maybe something would develop there, but I was certain he would settle for less than acceptance of the proposal Lizzie had delivered. If I agreed to an a tentative understanding, not a binding engagement, it might prove to everyone's advantage. It would get me back to Atlanta with something to show for my trip. Lieutenant Alexander would be happy since he seemed to have a genuine affection for me. I was certainly attracted to him and in time, might grow to love him.

The two of us were sitting by the fire after everyone else had left. Lizzie was fussing around the salon, calling for extra logs and looking as though she was going to settle in for the evening with us until things were resolved to her satisfaction. It was time to take charge of my plans.

"Lizzie, it was a wonderful party. I know you must be exhausted . . ."

"Oh, no! I'm just tidying up a bit before we all sit down and talk."

"Tidy up tomorrow, Lizzie. Go to bed, or at least leave the Lieutenant and me alone so we can talk. We are quite capable of working out our future without guidance from you." As soon as I said it, I realized it sounded more harsh than I had intended.

Lizzie looked startled, then she smiled. "Well, of course you are. I just thought . . . ." her voice trailed off. She picked up a poker, gave the logs a few jabs and the sparks flew up like orange confetti. "I'll just bring you the sherry and I'll be off." She crossed the room, picked up the crystal decanter and set in on the table between us. "Well!" she sighed, "I guess I've done all I can do," and she left the room.

"Thank you, cousin Lizzie. Rest well. I'll be up shortly," I called after her. "This must be the most extraordinary evening either of us has have had, James. Can you imagine the brass of Lizzie suggesting such a thing as marriage?" I shook my head.

"You mustn't be too hard on her, Sallie. It is all right that I call you 'Sallie' isn't it?" He didn't wait for an answer. "John Chamberlain is my superior officer . . . this is difficult for me, Sallie . . . and I respect him a great deal. He has talked with me about you ever since he first met and he was quite smitten. When you told him last week that you were returning to Atlanta to 'start a new life,' I believe is the way he put it, he was devastated. I, of course, had seen and admired you from afar since your first visit to the Point, but because of John's interest, there was nothing I could do or say. Last week, Mrs. Williams and I were talking and I let slip how much I was attracted to you and she immediately hit upon the idea of the farewell party. I must say, I didn't think she would get down to brass tacks so quickly. I guess she knew I would be too shy to speak my mind on an evening when we had just begun to get acquainted, so she took the short cut of suggesting you marry me." He laughed and looked at me with an expression of wonderment.

His candor was impressive and the whole affair made a bit more sense now. I wondered what might have happened had he declared himself, chain of command notwithstanding, when I first came to West Point almost two months ago?

"I would never presume," James continued, "to ask you to marry me. I realize we know little of each other, but I do know that I'm attracted to you in a way that I have never felt before. To have you leave without me telling you that was unthinkable. If you laughed in my face, as well you might, then I would never see you again, although I can promise I would never forget you."

The lieutenant *could* talk. And when he did, he sounded so sincere, so kind and caring that I could feel myself being drawn toward him. "I'll be leaving here in the morning and then back to Atlanta in a few days, James. That gives us no time to really think this through. I live half a continent away from you, and who knows how different we might find one another once we become better acquainted."

"But that's what I suggest we do, Sallie: become better acquainted. I want you to take my West Point ring as a seal of my sincerity. There's nothing binding in your accepting it, but I hope you will invite me to Atlanta to meet your mother and then we can talk about the future.

He took my left hand in his and slid the massively ornate ring on my finger. It was handsome and reeked of tradition. I was surprised, pleased, and a bit awe-struck all at the same time. "I will accept this, James, but only as a wish for our happiness." He continued to hold my hand and those intense eyes were so filled with light they had a hypnotic effect. I could see the flames from the hearth reflected in his pupils and I was truly stirred by what was happening.

"I could certainly ask for no more than that, Sallie Johnson. You do me a great honor." He raised my hand to his lips. His moustache was soft as silk and his eyes never left mine. It left me wondering if I could still breathe.

We sat by the fire for some time, the sherry warming inwardly as the flames did the room. Little more was said and when he rose to leave, he took both my hands in his, kissed me lightly on the forehead and then said shyly, "Oh forgive me, Sallie. I should have asked before taking the liberty."

"Had you asked, I would have happily assented," I told him, as we walked to the door.

"I will see you in the morning and drive you to the station with Mrs. Williams. If, of course, that's all right with you."

"Certainly, James. I will look forward to it."

The following morning, the sky was gloomy and it matched my mood. Having had the night to think it over, I had decided taking the ring was not a good idea. Although I found him attractive and I had made myself clear (I thought) accepting the ring was only a token of friendship, I knew that I was hoping for a different message to be delivered to my friends back home. I wasn't being entirely open with James or with anyone else. I knew what was in my mind and it wasn't just this handsome lieutenant who seemed, without apparent reason, to be so taken with me.

He arrived promptly at nine with a carriage to deliver me to the station. Lizzie must have taken a cue from her dismissal the evening before and said she would say her good-byes at the house and leave me in the "gracious hands of Lieutenant Alexander," as she put it. I had already made up my mind that I should return the ring; at least that was the honest thing to do, but when he helped me in the carriage the look in eyes told me it wasn't going to be easy. I certainly didn't want to hurt him. We rode in silence to the station but he gently took my hand and looked at the ring which I had on my thumb, very handy for easy removal.

"Sallie, I can't tell you how pleased I am to see that you're wearing it. When I awoke this morning it was so gloomy and dark, but I felt like I was standing in the middle of the parade ground, the band playing, the winds blowing up from the river and glorious sunlight washing over me. You've made me immensely happy."

And he looked it. I couldn't bring myself to dim the light in those brilliant eyes. "Well, I certainly never expected to return to New York with a ring on my finger—on my *thumb,* of all places!" I said, and it was the total truth. It was the best I could do right at that moment.

When we arrived at the station, the train was just pulling in, billowing white steam in the cold air. It squeaked to a stop as the conductor swung down from the first coach, taking my bags and giving a little salute to James all in one smooth motion. "Good morning, Miss Johnson," he said. "You've become our best passenger from here to New York. Hope we'll be seeing you on the Northbound real soon." He swung the bags into the car then stepped aside for James to escort me to my seat. The coach was partly filled and as we walked down the aisle, I could feel the eyes of the passengers focused on us, particularly the older women. I wondered what they were thinking? Young lovers with a sad parting? Husband and wife, parting for a brief visit to my home? They would have never guessed the truth.

"Sallie, I will be writing you each day. I will send them to Atlanta since you'll soon be home. As soon as your mother is agreeable, I will ask for leave to come visit you. I'm anxious to meet her." He paused, then said as the conductor called, "All aboard,"

"You won't forget me, will you?"

"Of course not, James. I will be writing you as soon as I return home." Then he stood and walked briskly out of the coach, not looking back, but when he reached the platform, he stood outside my window, straight as an arrow but a faint smile on his face. I wondered what I had gotten myself into?

The trip down the Hudson was not as enjoyable as usual. The beech trees lining the tracks looked like remonstrating fingers, all about to be shaken at me. The river was slate gray and still had patches of ice. It made me cold inside just to look at it. My thoughts were a jumble remembering everything that had happened during my winter months in New York.

The morning I was leave for Atlanta, Hugh arrived at the Swann's to say good-bye. He had sent a note of his coming so I had time to wonder if he were going to confuse things even further by finally telling me his feelings. I need not have worried. He appeared at the front door exactly at 9:30, a fruit basket mixed with flowers in one hand, his hat in the other. He declined to come in, but simply said, "A little something for your trip. Good-bye, Miss Johnson." After a little bow, he turned quickly and trotted down the steps to his carriage. I considered tossing the whole basket at him. Instead, I stood there as much mystified as angered. Why in the world would he drive all the way down from Physician and Surgeons with an extravagant gift and do no more than say, "Good-bye, Miss Johnson"? It made no sense. Why didn't I ask him if he loved me? Maybe I was afraid of the answer.

Janie took me to the station later that morning. I could tell she was burning to ask questions, but I was equally determined to keep my thoughts to myself. The West Point ring was safely stowed in my purse. As the train sped south, I resigned myself to reality: Hugh Hagan was not going to be part of my world. I took the ring out and turned it over and over in my hand. When James had first given it to me, I was surprised at the warmth the gold had carried from his hand. It almost seemed alive, but now it lay cold and lifeless in my palm. There was nothing else to do. I would marry James Alexander and make the most of it. As for Hugh Hagan, I would forget him. I would never survive the rigors of an unrequited love.

The closer I came to Atlanta, the less my inclination to tell Mother and have an extended cry over the whole thing. She had borne a secret sorrow in giving up John Lamar, her true love, for a marriage that was "more convenient." That had worked well for her; I should expect the same thing. Col. Frank Erwin, Mother's first husband, was a good man by all accounts and she had learned to love him in her own way. Lieutenant Alexander was much more appealing than Col Erwin had sounded. I would never find a nobler man than James. By the time we pulled into Union Station, I had decided to tell Mother and Lucy at the first opportunity.

"*NEVER!*" they exclaimed in unison throwing their hands up in horror.

I was dumbfounded at their adamant stance. I had decided that marriage was the real reason they had sent me to New York. I thought all of the talk about marrying a Yankee was just posturing, a view expected of them but not what they really thought. If I found a suitable gentleman, they would respect my judgment. That was what I had told myself.

Lucy appeared on the verge of apoplexy. "I told you, Mother! Didn't I tell you this would happen? I most certainly did!" Then she turned her attention to me. "Have you not learned a single thing I have told you, Sarah Johnson?" I knew when she called me "Sarah" that I had made a serious miscalculation

"In the Army! At West Point! That's enough right there to condemn him," Mother sputtered.

I tried to mollify them with a detailed account of his good qualities. I confessed that I did not love him, but there was much else to commend him.

"That's like commending small pox as a good reason to take a rest," Lucy shrieked. "If you do this thing, it will break all of our hearts."

It was useless to try convincing them. I was upset with myself for having underestimated their true opposition to marriage outside of the South. Had I told them there was a handsome young doctor from Richmond for whom I did have a deep affection, but was not going to pursue that, then I think they would have throttled me on the spot. I had the good sense to remain quiet on the subject of Hugh Hagan.

Lizzie, ever the busybody, was quick to write all her friends and relatives in the entire state of Georgia about my Yankee alliance. The innuendo of a deeply involved relationship soon was coming back to the house from every quarter. Along with the horror of everyone who heard about James Alexander came a list of "wonderful young Georgian men who would love to become my husband."

Not a one of them would I have had on a silver platter with an apple in his mouth. Even my staunch ally, Henry Grady, reversed his view. His idea of The New South did not, apparently, include a Yankee husband for me. He had his own favorite candidate, Jefferson Bohart, my childhood sweetheart from Athens. He was one of the circle from my visits to Lamar Rutherford when I was a child. Now he was a successful journalist, but he would forever be in my mind the freckle-faced little boy who couldn't keep his trousers hitched-up because he was so skinny.

Just as the furor began to subside, I received a letter from James announcing he would be in Atlanta the next week—on military business, he said—and would be seeing my mother for a formal introduction. There was nothing I could do but sit back and let them fight it out. I would warn James, if I got the chance, that he was stepping into The Second Battle of Atlanta.

When the carriage pulled up to the house, I was standing on the upstairs porch. As he got out and paid the driver, my fears of what might happen to him evaporated. He was wearing his dress uniform with the left side of his tunic heavily decorated with medals and ribbons. His sword sparkled in the sun bright as a winter icicle. His boots were a black mirror. As he started up the walk he saw me standing on the porch and stopped. He saluted, then flashed that smile. There would be no surviving the charm that was so much a part of him. Mother had been fluttering about the house all morning, muttering under her breath and invoking the wisdom of my father. She had not mellowed with the passage of time, but I knew she had met her match in James. Her plan was to receive him in the parlor and then instantly dismiss him. Had she actually been able to do that, it would not have mattered. I had had quite enough of everyone planning my life and I was determined to marry James Alexander and the devil take the hindmost.

It was quite a scene. When Mammy Sophy showed him into the parlor, Mother had her back to the doorway. When she deigned to turn and face him, her mouth open for her little speech, she stopped like a wind-up doll on a music box when the spring had snapped.

"Madam," said James, "Please forgive me for not giving you more notice, but my orders arrived quite suddenly. You're most gracious to receive me." Then he handed her a single, brilliant, long-stemmed rose. Her mouth was still open and when her eyes met his, I knew she was as disarmed as a trooper who had left his sword in the armory.

She reached out and took the rose, then gestured toward the wingback chair opposite the sofa where she gingerly seated herself. I took a seat on the settee by James' chair. His remarks flowed with such precision it sounded as though he had been rehearsing them for days, but at the same time it was apparent he was speaking with total spontaneity. He outlined his hopes and dreams for us; he told of his great affection and devotion to me. He sounded so convincing, so sincere that my mother was in a condition rarely seen: She was speechless. I don't know what she expected—maybe a dirty uniform, splotched with mud and grime, but what she saw was resplendence standing before her.

She soon recovered, though, and began her litany of concerns about the uncertainty of military life, the hardship of such a "delicate creature" as I living with savages in the far West. Unlike the smooth presentation he had made, she was sputtering and floundering through her objections while James listened patiently, then with infinite gentleness, defused every one of them.

I sat quietly by, a total spectator, as these two jockeyed for my future as though I were a piece of pasture ready for cultivation. I was willing to let them have their little say, but I was definitely going to be the one who made my own decision; they could talk till the river ran dry, but I was certain of myself.

Mother saw that she was no match for the Lieutenant. I'm sure she wished Lucy were there to bolster her arguments, but it would have made no difference. James was in total control of himself and of Mother, too. Finally, she capitulated.

"Captain," she began, having promoted him in her frustration, "If you will call off this . . . this 'understanding' for a year, I will withdraw my opposition."

Mother had the good graces to invite him to return for dinner, which I though signaled a major triumph. From my seat next to James, I could see the servants making unnecessary trips back and forth by the open parlor door and stealing a glance at the Yankee General (that was the rank they assigned him). After our visit with Mother was concluded, I said to James, "You must come with me and let me introduce you to quaintest trio you'll ever meet." I took his hand and led him to the back porch where Mammy Sophy, Mammy Phyllis and Kitty had hastily retreated when they realized we were leaving the parlor.

"Here, Mammy Sophy, I want you all to meet my friend, Mr. Alexander." I thought that a better title than a military rank.

"How do you do, suh?: they chorused and curtsied like they were a stage show.

"Mr. Alexander came all the way down here from New York to see what kind of girl I am," I teased. He smiled pleasantly and bowed slightly to the three wide-eyed women.

"Lawd d'murcy," Mammy Sophy exclaimed. "Couldn't he see dat wid his eyes up yonder? Eberbody know what Miss Sallie's like, eben when dey don' see her." Mammy Phyliss and Kitty wagged their heads in agreement.

"I saw her so well in New York that I had to come all the way down here to make sure my eyes hadn't deceived me. They surely haven't so I've asked Mrs. Johnson for Miss Sallie's hand."

The three of them looked at each other, then at my hands. "What'cha gon' do wid dat chile's hand," Mammy Sophy asked, taking a step between James and me.

He laughed and touched her on the shoulder. "I mean I want to . . . marry her."

Kitty spoke up. "Dat's different, but whereabouts does you live?"

"I live at West Point in New York. I'm in the army. My next post will be out West."

That did it. "Out West?" Mammy Phyliss demanded. "You gon' take dis chile out dere where de injuns is? No, sireee, General. We ain' gwine have none of dat foolishness." There seem to be no end of my caretakers.

"It won't be anything like that, I'm sure, Mammy. Lieutenant Alexander will go where the army sends him and I would go with him."

They took another tack. "You in de army? Does you know our General Lee and General Cobb? He was Miss Sallie's uncle."

"No, he's too young to be been in the Confederate army," I explained.

"Den what army you talkin' 'bout?" Mammy Sophy asked, her eyes getting narrow. "You ain' hitched up wid dem Billy Yanks, is you?"

"Oh, Mammy! Stop being so hard on Lt. Alexander. He's not a Yankee. He was born in Kentucky."

"Shucks! Dat don' make a dime's worth of difference. Yo' Uncle Dick, he born in Kentuck and he wuz in da Yankee army. I tell you what's a fact, mister. You best skedaddle but up da road and fine yo'self 'nother woman. We ain' gon' let Miss Sallie marry no Yankee." She shook her head in emphasis, looking at Mammy Phyllis and Kitty for support. They nodded solemnly.

I gathered them all up and hugged the whole group. "James, was I right? Did you ever see such a trio?" All three of them looked at me, expectantly. I guess they were hoping I would set the dogs on him but I said to all of them, "You'll never meet a finer gentleman than Lieutenant Alexander. I know you'll come to love him, too."

"'Bout da time the Chattahoochee runs clear—dat's when we be lovin' Yankees," Mammy Phyliss said, but she winked at me as they started back toward their cabin.

As we sat down on the porch swing, James said, "The people who haven't lived in the South don't understand the love that Negroes have for their families. I know it's not always true, but anyone can see how much those ladies love you . . . and how much you and your family care for them. If I had taken a step to hurt you, they would have killed me on the spot. I'd rather face a band of wild Indians any day than have one of those mammies go on the warpath."

By dinner time, Mother had collected herself. James and I had agreed that we would not have an immediate wedding and that seemed to mollify her. As Kitty was serving dessert, I could tell she had been won over by his politeness to her. Every time he was served, James turned to thank her. That was not attention that she often received from Southern gentleman.

When his carriage pulled away, I felt more calm about the situation. Maybe I was doing the proper thing. Time would tell.

Time wasn't long in telling. The next morning, Mother announced that we were catching The Accommodation for Mt. Airy. "This whole thing has made a nervous wreck of me. We need to get away to our little mountain hideaway where we can both get some rest."

The ride to Mt. Airy was anything but restful, the was train slower that usual and the first hot weather of spring made the trip seem interminable. After we settled in Mother's idea of rest changed to having more talks about the rigors of army life and long sessions with her prayer book all aimed at hoping her child would come to her senses and marry some splendid Georgian. I remained quiet about the whole thing. I decided it would blow over just as the marriage of Lizzie to her "Yankee Lieutenant" had done so many years before.

After dinner one evening we were sitting on the veranda, the night noises of early spring just beginning to fill the air. In the distance the cow bells were tinkling as the cattle were coming in for milking. The breeze blowing up from Tullulah Gorge was soft and cooling. It was a tranquil time. Mother had been less vocal about her problem but was being unusually silent. From across the road I saw Mr. Wiggins, the station master come out of his office and start toward our house. He frequently came by for a brief visit on his way home, so I thought nothing of it, but when he arrived on the steps, he said, "A telegram for you, Miss Sallie." He tipped his hat and was off.

"Who in the world . . . ," I wondered as I opened it.

My Dear Miss Johnson Stop I will be arriving Mt Airy
Friday evening Stop I look forward to seeing you again Stop
Sincerely Hugh Hagan Stop

"Merciful heavens!" Mother shrieked. "There's another one coming? I should have listened to Lucy and none of this would have happened."

"Calm down, Mother. Hugh Hagan has not one vestige of sentiment in his entire body." I decided to explain my feelings to her and how he had failed to indicate the slightest interest in me.

"You truly *are* a child, Sallie. He sent you flowers and fruits— how many times—a dozen or more? And he took you to the finest restaurants in New York, the opera, the theater several times a week for nearly three months. And now he just decided to make a trip of a thousand miles because he hasn't the slightest interest in you? Where is your brain, woman?"

"But the 'Miss Johnson this, the Miss Johnson that,' if he was attracted to me, surely he would have shown some sign of it."

"He did everything by wave a flag with his intentions on it right in your face. Not every man is expressive in the ways you seem to expect." She sighed monstrously. "Another damn Yankee, pardon my French. If your father were alive . . ."

"But he isn't a Yankee, Mother," I interrupted. He's from Richmond. His uncles lived in New Orleans. He's a Southern gentleman."

"Then what's he doing in New York? You know all the Southerners up there are poor as church mice. Why didn't you tell me about him in the first place?"

"I didn't want to tell anyone how I felt about him because it was apparently so one-sided. And he's a doctor at Physicians and Surgeons."

"Well, that something in his favor, at least."

"What? That he's a doctor?"

"Oh, heavens no, Sallie. So long as he's a gentleman, I don't care a fig what he does for a living. He's from Richmond. That might count for something."

So much conversation had gone back and forth about my pre-marital plans that I was almost hoping that Dr. Hagan would arrive, the ubiquitous basket of fruit and flowers in hand, would say, "I just wanted to deliver these to you, Miss Johnson. I do hope you enjoy them. Good-bye." and get back on the train. As restrained as his behavior had been that didn't seem totally out of the question. If, however, Mother was right and he was coming with a more serious purpose in mind, then I was caught in a serious dilemma. My feelings for James had certainly grown; how could they not, given his charm. I had repressed my affection for Hugh believing that nothing would ever come of it. Now that he was soon to be on the scene, I would have to get those feelings out, dust them off and see if there was anything left.

The afternoon of his arrival began with violent thunderstorm. Clouds boiled up over the mountains soon followed by a torrential downpour. It was at its peak when I heard the whistle of The Accommodation just coming out of The Gorge. As the engine hove into sight, the boiler looked as though it was on fire, the cold rain hissing into instant steam. No one got off the train until the rain had begun to abate. Most of the passengers had disembarked and there was no sign of Dr. Hagan. I gave a little sigh. The conductor got off carrying a basket of fruit and flowers. Maybe he had just sent his usual gift and decided to stay in Atlanta, I thought, smiling at how worked up I had gotten over this visit. He had treated me with such coolness, I certainly had no intention of flying down to the station simply to have my hand shook—if he was even on the train. The conductor disappeared into the station and I was about to go in the house when I saw him. He stepped from the coach and looked around the platform. He was carrying his baggage and dressed in a brown, tweedy-looking suit that must have been frightfully hot. The rain had stopped and steam was rising from the brick walkway. He walked along with a brisk step, entered the station and re-emerged with the flowers. He looked across the tracks and saw me standing on the porch. I began to feel self-conscious. I had not dressed especially for the occasion and wondered if he might think I was being too casual. He was getting what he deserved, I thought. He set the basket down and waved with both arms. I waved back to him, tentatively at first, but then he started running toward me, leaving the flowers and bag behind. I went down the steps and met him at the front gate. "Good afternoon, Dr. Hagan," I said with much formality. "It's nice to see you," I added. He took both hands in his and smiled shyly.

"Yes, Miss Johnson. It is good to *be* seen in your company." He paused, then stepping back, he continued. "Let me look at you, Sallie." He did actually know my first name, I was pleased to note. "My memory has failed me. I assured myself I remembered actually how beautiful you are, but I see that I was mistaken. Far lovelier than I remembered."

"And you seem . . . you seem . . ." I couldn't think of the right phrase . . ."to have regained consciousness," came to mind but instead, I said "Very glad to see me. And I'm glad to see you, Hugh." He was still holding my hands as we turned to the house. Mother was standing on the porch and he suddenly remembered his luggage and started back to the station. "Don't worry about that. Mammy Sophy will get them," I told him.

"No, indeed. I always carry my own luggage and I wouldn't trust those flowers to anyone. They have set in the seat beside me ever since I left Atlanta." He ran back to the platform and was back in the yard before I had time to speak to Mother. When he bounded up the steps, he set his luggage down, removed his hat and spoke directly to Mother.

"Mrs. Johnson, I'm Hugh Hagan. You're kind to allow me to interrupt your vacation, but my schedule didn't permit me to plan further in advance. I have heard so much about you and your family. It's a genuine pleasure to meet you," he said, handing her the gift basket. "I brought these for you."

Mother nodded, and with a smile, extended her hand, which he took and bowed slightly. In three minutes, this was more animation from him than I had seen in the three months I had spent in New York. And that was just the beginning. Mother was in love with him before he ever got into the parlor. And the feelings that I had stored in the back corners of my mind were not dusty, but vibrant and springing to life, like morning glories on a summer fence.

The rest of the afternoon was spent in tea, in gentle conversation.

I remembered why I had been so taken with him. His manner was sincere and understated, his knowledge of any subject under discussion was impressive and his manners beyond reproach. He had none of the ebullience of James Alexander, but there was something about him that was undeniably appealing. When he returned to the hotel to check in and dress for dinner, Mother had already made up her mind.

"Marry him, Sallie. He's everything any woman could ever want."

"And, of course, he *is* from Richmond," I added with a laugh.

Mother smiled. "Well, that doesn't hurt his chances any, but I think I would love him if he came from Yonkers."

Mammy Sophy was the only servant we had brought with us and she was right on duty, making an assessment which she would report in detail to Mammy Phyliss and the others when we returned to Atlanta. Hugh won her instantly, too.

"And you're surely Mammy Sophy, aren't you? I've heard so much about you and have been anxious to meet you. Miss Sallie has told me how important you have been to the whole family."

"Yassir. I'm Mammy Sophy and I knows dis here fambly is important to me. An' I'll tell you what'sa fact, Doctor, Miss Sallie here is . . ."

I had no idea what she was going to say, but I cut her off. "Now, Mammy, don't you go telling all my bad secrets. Dr. Hagan will be right back on the train before you can serve him your good country ham and red eye gravy."

"I won't gon' tell him no secrets, I was jes' gwine tell him I likes him a heap sight better than dat General you been sportin' with."

I threw up my hands. "Hugh, you'll just have to get used to the idea of having no privacy around here. Mammy and her friends are a regular news agency." He didn't respond and I didn't offer any information about my "sportin' General."

Dinner and the evening were pleasant, but Mother acted as though she were the reason for Hugh's visit and stayed with us until it was time to retire. She initiated much conversation about our family but slipped in little details here and there about what a desirable wife I would be. I had to smile at her lack of subtlety, particularly when she thought she was being so clever. I could tell that Hugh was amused, too, but he treated her performance as though he was attending to every word.

The next morning, we took a carriage ride down to The Falls and when we got back, we sat down on the porch. The sun was sizzling. I was about to tell him we should go into the house where it was cooler, but as I started to speak, her blurted out, "Miss Johnson, I love you! Will you marry me?"

I was so stunned, I laughed hysterically. "Miss Johnson!? Surely, you can say 'Sallie, will you marry me?' Why in the name of heaven haven't you said anything before now? You've driven me half crazy with all your handshaking and "Miss Johnsons."

"Oh, I tried to! I used to stand in front of the mirror in the hospital dressing room and practice what I was going to say to you, but when the time came, my tongue just wouldn't work. I thought if I made the long trip down here, I would find the courage to tell you. I love you, Sallie. You're the only girl I've ever loved. Ever could love. Until now, I just couldn't get the words out."

He wanted to speak to Mother right away and she was delighted, as was Mammy Sophy who was conveniently dusting the hall tables when he spoke with Mother. It was quickly settled. We would have a fall wedding in Atlanta. How I would deal with all the gossip when the word got around that I was engaged to two men was something I would have to consider later.

Writing to James and returning his ring was the hardest thing I ever had to do. I had come to care for him, but the sense of love that I had for Hugh was so much more compelling, so much deeper. I hoped that I wouldn't hear from James then I could imagine that he had accepted it without pain. I came to find out later through Lizzie that had certainly not been the case. After getting the letter, he had immediately requested a transfer to Indian Territory in Oklahoma and it was granted.

Much of the prattle in Atlanta contained warnings to Hugh to, "Watch out. Sallie is very unpredictable when it comes to men."

I didn't realize how far the talk had gone until in early October, only ten days before the wedding, I was at a reception for President and Mrs. Cleveland being held at the home of the Gradys and I was placed next to Mrs. Cleveland in the receiving line. During a moment of quiet, she turned to me and said, "Well, Sallie, which one is it going to be: The Doctor or the Lieutenant?"

"Dr. Hagan, of course, Mrs. Cleveland. The invitations have already been delivered."

Later, I overheard her talking to Mrs. Grady. "Yes, I know the invitations are out," Julia said, "but Sallie is Sallie. She's acted so outrageously about marrying since her trip to New York that no one is sure which groom will be waiting for her at the altar."

After the reception, Mrs. Cleveland chatted with me amiably about the various candidates for my hand and said, with a laugh, "Whomever it turns out to be, the President and I would like you to stop at The White House for a visit on your marriage trip."

"That's most kind, Mrs. Cleveland. Dr. Hagan and I would be honored to visit you and the President, but we will be off to the seaside to be alone for a while. There's been much conversation about all this, but on October 26, when we marry, that will come to an end. I will be the happiest woman in the world."

# CHAPTER VII

O ne would have thought after all the conversation, consternation and, finally, the completion of my marriage plans that I would have anticipated how radically my life would change when I became Mrs. Hugh Hagan. I considered myself reasonably well-traveled and informed in the ways of the world, but I found there was much I didn't know. The honeymoon was all I had hoped it would be and more, but it didn't leave much time for consideration of how different my life would become. I felt at ease in New York, but the idea of being so far removed from Mammy Sophy and the gentle comforts of home hadn't been something about which I had been concerned. As our train bore us north, I was more and more aware my home life would never be the same. In retrospect, it seems so obvious to say that, but it was anything but apparent to me on those fall days of early November, 1886. With each passing mile, I could see the signs of winter coming soon, and with the change of seasons, I could feel the changes coming to me. No longer would there be the big, homey expanses of our house on Peachtree. There was nothing I had ever seen in New York City that reminded me of the way I had been living. No large yards opening on to unpaved streets lined with live oaks. Certainly, no cabins in the back lot where the servants lived, where many of them had lived as slaves when they were younger.

Hugh had been living on the hospital grounds most of the time he had been at Physicians and Surgeons. They did not allow the doctors in their first years of training to be married, but he had attained enough seniority that it was permitted. His salary was the privilege of being associated with the hospital. Fortunately, he had money of his own, and I have no idea how anyone without some resources could have gone into medicine as a career, however, many we came to know did just that. I remembered the kind of life where money was scarce, but I quickly realized we were more fortunate than most. Looking back, that seems to have been true in so many aspects of my life—part of a fortunate minority. Because of my parents, I had been taught that was not a position of privilege, but one of responsibility. Since we had been spared some of the hardships so common after the war, I had been taught that required us to be more vigilant in ways we could share what we had rather than simply bask in our own comfort.

Hugh, whose parents had come into money just before the war, understood better than I the need for service. I think that's one of the things that I first admired about him. Even though he had come to a level of privilege, he never seemed to take that for granted. He was generous with his time and his money, sometimes to a fault, but it was a loveable quality about him. The lack of those sensibilities was one of the things that I observed in "the fine Georgian men" who had been frequently suggested as suitors.

We would be living in a boarding house not too far from the College. I recalled Mother's stories of her life when she was about my age, living in the congressional boarding houses of Washington. There was an elegance to those places that was lacking in the home of Miss Lucille Brooke where Hugh and I began our married life. But what it lacked in elegance was more than replaced by charm and grace and in a sense of fun-loving conviviality. Miss Lucille was from Virginia. How she came to operate a boarding house in New York I never learned, but I did find out, rather quickly, she was very particular in whom she invited to share her home. Although she insisted she would take any "genteel lady or gentleman," I often thought she must do some background investigation, else she would not have had such an interesting array of characters as were our house mates.

The home was a typical brownstone of four stories, with a

living area in the basement which could be reached from steps beneath the front stoop. Miss Lucille lived in "the down quarters," as she called them, and none of us was ever invited into her section of the home. She was generally on the first floor, overseeing the cleaning and food preparation of four Negro women who were quick to tell me they had been freed long before I was born and let it be known that they regarded me as a former slave holder. It didn't take long to win them over with stories of all that Mammy Sophy and the others had done for me. I promised them that Mammy would be visiting them soon and they would find a kindred sister from the South who had always been free in spirit even before her life had been her own.

On the first floor were several parlors, each joined with an oaken archway between. On the opposite side of the main hall was the formal salon, the dining room with a large table that could seat sixteen, and the kitchen was directly behind. The meals all featured French service, a little item in which Miss Lucille took especial pride, although a gentle rebellion among the boarders took place the first months we lived there and we resorted to family style. Miss Lucille clucked and fussed about our passing food back and forth across the table like it "was some boarding house" which, of course, is exactly what it was.

The stairs led up from the central hallway, broad and interrupted by two landings. It reminded me of the stairs in Lamar Rutherford's Athens home, and there was even a crystalline chandelier that hung in the half circle created by the stairs. No sunlight ever reached it, so there were no dancing rainbows on which to make a wish as Lamar and I had done so many years earlier.

Our room was on the second floor. High-ceilinged, with windows across the front wall, in the center of which there was a bay window with a large cushioned sill. I enjoyed sitting there and sewing in the good light while I could watch the traffic heading down toward the Hudson River.

The four-poster canopy bed looked like it would have been at home in the South. I enjoyed having that touch of Peachtree so close at hand.

Hugh was at the hospital for days at a time. It was different from my father and his practice, much of which took place in our home in his later years. Hugh was gone long before daylight and home long after dark—if he came home at all. It was a situation in which a young bride could find herself very lonely. I suppose that could have happened to some women, but certainly not to me. My sense of curiosity about people and my enjoyment in hearing of their lives and adventures made me a welcome member of the boarding house family almost immediately. There were several elderly women who lived there who would rather tell stories than breathe, or so it seemed to me. Miss Lucille had heard them all a hundred times and more, so a fresh audience was a welcome occasion, particularly for Mrs. Olivia Stone.

The first time I saw her, I knew we would be friends. She was in her late seventies, I would imagine, but had a twinkle in her eye that any coquette would have envied. She walked with a cane, but it rarely touched the ground. More, it was used to shoo Rosemary, the cat, out of her way or to demonstrate a point she was trying to make. "And that's all there was to *that!*" she would say, jabbing her cane into the rug like a portable exclamation point.

Her late husband, General Pomeroy Stone, had been the chief aide to the Khedive of Egypt, who held the highest rank conferred on one not a prince of the blood. After her husband's "unfortunate death," which was the most detail I was ever able to garner about his passing, she had returned to New York to live in a state of permanent and unremitting bereavement. That was her stated goal, and she was succeeding quite well according to the other boarders. If she owned any clothing that was not black, it had never been seen. Watching her maneuver her food under her black veil was a source of never-ending curiosity, but she never spilled so much as a drop of soup. Despite her frequent pronouncements of her heartbroken estate, she still had the twinkle in her eye if you could catch the light going through her veil. Her eagerness for friendship was apparent and I loved listening to her talk. By living in the past, she avoided facing the loneliness of the present, or so she said. I thought much of her loneliness was just an excuse to have the boarders pay attention to her. I was delighted to be with her and the stories she told were enough to hold me in thrall for hours.

One morning in the winter, I was seated by the front parlor window doing some mending to Hugh's jacket. Mrs. Stone leisurely walked in and seated herself beside me.

"Would you like to hear a story as amusing as it is tragic?" Who could resist such an introduction, but she went on without waiting for a reply. "It's about Don, a wonderful animal General Stanley brought me from the jungles." She sniffed slightly, dabbed her eyes with her handkerchief. "We all adored him so."

"What kind of animal was he?" I asked, not being able to imagine a pet from the jungle.

"Wait and hear the story and you will understand why we loved him so. You remember General Stanley, of course." Mrs. Stone had a way of assuming that you were a personal friend of all the characters in her stories, and it was a mistake to tell her otherwise unless you wanted to get so far afield in relationships that dinner would be on the table without ever having gotten to the original tale.

"Of course. *The* General Stanley," I suggested.

"Then you know what wonderful friends he and my late husband, General Pomeroy Stone, were. Chums from their years at Exeter and ever since. They often were off in the field together, and one afternoon I was taking my nap when the General arrived home. Into my room he marched and tossed a young pup into bed with me. Of course, I was startled. 'What in the world are you doing, bringing a dog into my room?'" I inquired.

"General Stanley sends it to you with his compliments."

I looked at the little thing, so fuzzy and yellow. I had never seen a dog like it. "What kind of pup is it?"

"What kind do you think it is?"

I stroked its fur, soft as down. "It's not a Golden Retriever. And he's too large for a Collie. I don't know what it is."

He laughed uproariously. "It's not a dog at all. It's a lion cub!"

Mrs. Stone stopped to see if I was suitably impressed. "I was thrilled with the idea of having my own personal lion, and especially since he had come from the great General Stanley. The cub settled right into my arms and in no time at all was the favorite house pet. I decided to call him Don because his gentle nature reminded me of an Oxford don for whom I once had an affection. Such a marvelous man he was . . . but that's another story. No one had the least fear of my new little cub. Don played with the other pets in the house, frolicked in the nursery with the children and was amazingly gentle.

As the story developed, I remembered her introduction that this was a tragic tale. I began to become uneasy. Surely, the lion had not turned to his native ways and dispatched all the family pets in a fit of hunger. But she had said it was amusing, too, so my fears were quieted somewhat.

"Well, as the months went by, he attained an enormous size," she indicated with her cane from one side of the parlor to the other, "But he remained totally gentle. We did have a few problems with deliveries. The boys coming into the back of the house didn't know quite what to make of him. Off the porch he would bound, simply wanting to play with them. They would drop their parcels and head for the nearest tree which, of course, posed no problem for Don. He would climb up to where he could lick the soles of their feet until the poor child's screams would bring the servants running to put an end to the game. He came to think of himself as my 'watch lion.' Every afternoon, when I would retire for my rest, he would station himself at the door and would brook no one, including General Stone, to enter. The only way to avoid the problems that was causing for the staff was to lock him in the back lot, but more often than not he would climb a tree and spring through an open window, then stealthily creep to my closed door and take up his vigil.

"One afternoon, his guardianship came near to costing the life of a servant girl. I had a late, afternoon appointment at the Palace and had asked my maid to awaken me in time for the elaborate preparation. Don was secured in the back lot, or so I thought, but he had once again found a way into the house, and when she came up the steps to arouse me, Don assumed his ferocious expression.

The poor girl was terrified, but the idea of letting her mistress oversleep and be embarrassed by being late for a royal appointment was foremost in her mind. After a lengthy prayer, she decided to risk her life and walk right by Don. She did it boldly and with certainty that it was her duty to carry out my wishes. Fortunately, Don made such an uproar, that I was awakened. When I opened the door, he was crouched and ready to spring. 'You naughty, naughty cat,' I scolded him and gave his tail, which was writhing in the air like a golden cobra, a smart jerk. He turned and looked at me, and if you have never seen an embarrassed lion, you can't appreciate how funny it was." She paused to see if I was acquainted with embarrassed lions, and seeing that I knew nothing of such matters, she lifted her veil and gave a remarkable imitation of what the lion must have looked like. "He even blushed, he was *so* ashamed."

I could appreciate the servant girl and her terror. I was astounded that she would risk her life to keep her mistress on time, even for the Royal Highness. Mrs. Stone and her interpretation of leonine behavior was the most ridiculous of all.

"Things were never quite the same with Don after that," she sighed, heavily. "The servants would have nothing to do with him, although I assured them he was just a big pussy cat. The *coup de grace* came some months later. The General and I were entertaining a large number of potentates from Arabia with a lavish banquet. The table seated thirty-six men—the women, of course, were not allowed to dine with the men. Just as General Stone was leading the march into the dining hall, having been very careful to have the ranks properly assigned to their position in the line, who should bound into the room but Don? He took the corner of the table cloth in his mouth and dragged the entire dinner to the floor, then sat in the middle of it, licking his chops and trying to decide where to start. No one could approach him, so they had to call me from the ladies' dinner parlor. Don was abjectly sorry for disrupting the party, I could tell. I was going to explain to the potentates, but they had all disappeared.

"That was the final appearance of Don," she said, sadly. "The very next day, General Stone had him shipped off to the Paris zoo. The children were so upset, but I promised them we would stop by Paris on our next trip back to America and they could visit Don. When we did visit the following year, poor Don was in a tiny little cage and half the size he had been. He was unkempt looking and whining all the while, until he saw me and the children. Then the light came back to his eyes. He began to dance around his cage and paw the air as he did when he wanted to play with the children. The zookeeper, I must say, was most rude when I asked that he allow the children in the cage. When he refused and scoffed at me, I threatened to report him to the Prime Minister and have him thrashed if he didn't let me put my children in the lion's cage. He called the *gendarmes*. It was *not* a pleasant encounter."

The stories of Mrs. Stone and her Egyptian adventures were so memorable that I decided I would one day write a book about her. That was the first time I had seriously thought of becoming a writer. And, sad to say, that story of Don and his sorry demise never did get written.

Most of the other boarders simply tolerated Mrs. Stone and her stories, but I found them intriguing. More importantly, I recognized how hungry she was for attention. Here was a lady who had lived at the pinnacle of the diplomatic corps. In her youth, I'm sure she was strikingly handsome. Now, her looks fading into wrinkles, alone in a brownstone apartment in a city where she knew no one, it was easy to understand the "widow's weeds." She really didn't want to be seen. I tried to interest her in a new wardrobe.

"Let me take you shopping, Mrs. Stone," I offered her one day. "We can go down to the shops and find some dressy clothes for you. I know you would like that."

She drew herself up to her full height and poked me gently in the stomach with her cane. "Sallie! How could you suggest such a thing? You know I'm in mourning." Then she raised her veil and gave me a wink. She was in mourning, but not for the General. Her current sadness was over the loss of her beauty and the lack of friendship. There was nothing I could do about the former, but I was glad to supply the latter.

"Well, have it your way. I suspect the General is in heaven and I doubt that *he's* still in a state of bereavement. I'll bet he's got every lady angel listening to his stories. You should be out and about like the rest of us. That's what he would want." Eventually, she did go out with me, but only on her own terms; just for tea, never for shopping. I realized that she was taking the place of my mother and I of the daughter she never had.

Hugh's work at Physicians and Surgeons was going well. His faculty appointment arrived on schedule and his interest in diseases of the nervous system soon took him to the top of that department. One evening, we were sitting around the parlor and I noticed he was quieter than usual. I asked him what was on his mind.

He tamped the ash from his pipe and re-lit it. In the midst of an expansive cloud of smoke, he told me. "I am at the top of my section. Not to brag, but there is no one to whom I can turn when I have questions. The amount of literature in the field is limited and I have read most of it . . . several times. It's frustrating to have patients sent to me with severe problems that fit none of the categories in which we usually find help. I come home some evenings wondering if I have done any good at all."

He seemed troubled. "Of course, you have. You know all there is to be known about these problems. That you can't help them all is understandably troubling, but that's the way life is; you can't cure everyone."

"That's certainly true," he said, "but you're wrong about the first part of it. I may know as much about neurology as anyone in New York, but there are many doctors who know a great deal that I do not. It worries me that what we offer patients may not be the best that's available."

"What can you do, other than your best?" It was, I thought, a rhetorical question.

"We can go to Vienna."

He said that as casually as if he were suggesting a relocation to Brooklyn. "Vienna? As in Austria? Why in the world would you want to go there?"

"Because the most famous neurologists and specialists in

nervous disorders are associated with the University of Vienna. A whole new approach to neurology is being developed there. There's a Doctor Freud who studied with Charçot in Paris and returned to Vienna a year or two ago. His ideas may revolutionize the entire field of neurology. If I could get an appointment there, then I would be right in the center of what is happening."

Mrs. Stone had been suggesting for months that I was pregnant. I had seen no sign of it until the last months. Now, I was beginning to wonder. I didn't want to say anything to Hugh until I was sure, but if we were moving to Vienna, he needed to know. His reaction to the news was first clinical, then husbandly, and finally joyful. True to his courting-days style, it took him a while to sort through his emotions and decide which ones he would share with me. After the initial conversation about Vienna, I could see the value of what he was proposing. His drive to be the best at whatever he did was impressive. If a turkey was to be carved at dinner, he would be called upon to operate. Mrs. Stone would comment on how precise was his technique. "Why, I could read *The New York Times* through this slice, Dr. Hagan. Give me some food. This isn't surgery! This is dinner!" He would smile and give her another paper-thin slice. He wanted to be the best, even at serving a turkey. I could see that living with less than the best he could accomplish would be a goad that might sour his life, particularly if I were an obstacle to his achieving it. As my pregnancy became apparent, we made the decision that we would go to Vienna after the baby was born. I found the idea of living abroad exhilarating. A wonder of youth is the perspective that all things are possible and most can be achieved, so I approached our move with less apprehension than might have been normal. I did have enough common sense to know that help would be needed. In Atlanta, I could do anything I chose to do because there were so many people to help me. In New York, I essentially had only myself to look after and the few needs that Hugh had. Austria would be different. I spoke some German, but had no understanding of how life might be. I assumed that it might be like New York, only smaller. Not so, I was told by people who had lived there. In Austria, even in the larger cities, the level of living was much less comfortable than anything to which I had been exposed. That seemed odd since New York was a brand new city, relatively speaking, compared to Munich or Vienna.

The solution seemed obvious: We would take help with us. I would take one of the servants from Atlanta and Lamar, my beloved cousin from Athens. It would be like taking a little piece of Georgia with us.

When the time for the baby drew near, I was beside myself with excitement. A baby! A move to Austria! The most famous opera houses in Europe! The most famous doctors in the world! It was a heady time. Mrs. Stone, having lived all over the world, took it upon herself to educate me in the ways of European living. I had a difficult time getting her to understand that sheiks from Arabia would *not* be dropping by for tea, that the Khedive of Egypt would not be impressed that I was a personal friend of the widow of General Pomeroy Stone. All that aside, she did help me prepare. She became a mixture of joy and sadness. She was happy about the baby, sad about losing her "daughter." At her age, we both knew we might not meet again.

Hugh Johnson Hagan was born at Physicians and Surgeons on December 11, 1888. He was a strapping little fellow with a set of lungs that were impressive for his size. All of Hugh's colleagues came to visit me during my confinement. There was much joshing about how Hugh could have fathered such a good-looking son, and I assured them the beauty came from my side of the family and the brains from Hugh. When Hugh was three months old, we set out for Atlanta and a farewell visit with Mother and the family there. I wasn't prepared for how difficult that visit would be.

When we arrived at Union Station in Atlanta, I was surprised how small the city looked. Compared to the urban immensity of New York everything appeared quite rural. As we rode out Peachtree, old memories came flooding back. Although I had been gone only eighteen months, so much had changed in my life that it was hard to believe. The inconvenience of unpaved streets was something I had forgotten until I stepped from the carriage, Hugh in my arms, into the ankle-deep mud in front of our house. I didn't have time to be concerned about that. Mammy Sophy had been sitting at the front window since sunrise watching for us. She was waddling down the front walk, her full skirt held in her hands to avoid stepping on the hem. She had aged; . . . no one knew for certain how old she was but the years were showing.

"Lawda murcy, chile," she shrieked. "Lemme see dat baby!" She scooped Hugh from my arms, his eyes getting big at the swooping transfer. His bottom lip turned down and he was about to cry. "Dere! Dere! Little baby. Mammy got you now and ain' nuthin' bad eber gon' happen to you, sweet baby chile." She rocked him against her ample bosom. Whatever it was that lived in Mammy's heart that made children think she was special was still working. He looked up at her and reached for her bandana knotted around her head. "Lookit dat! Ain' he smart just like his mama! Miss Sallie, you was always tryin' to untie my kerchief from the time you could reach up. He just like you, I can tell."

"Well, I had a little something to do with him, Mammy. Don't I get a little credit?" Hugh laughingly asked.

"You gits some credit if you brings in der luggage, Doctor. I'm gwina take him in da house. Miss Mary Willis, she be 'bout to bust to see her gran'baby." She turned and started up the walk, humming a little tune to Hugh.

"You're in for a bad time if you think Mammy's going to let us go to Vienna without her," Hugh sighed, as we walked into the house.

Mother was waiting in the parlor. She looked thinner than I remembered her and I wondered if she were ill. As soon as she saw the baby, she brightened and seemed more like her old self. After she had thoroughly admired him, Sophy said she might let Mother hold him after his nap. Mother smiled. "You can see who still runs things around here, Sallie. Step back and let me look at you." After a moment of appraisal she said, "I think marriage and motherhood agree with you. What do you think, Hugh?"

"I couldn't agree more. Sallie and I have had a wonderful life together and it's about to become even more wonderful. Vienna and the university—it's a dream come true."

Mother's face darkened a bit. "I know that's true from a professional standpoint, but it surely is a long way from home. I hate having you and the baby on the other side of the world. I'm getting along and I might not be here when you get back."

"Oh, Mother," I interrupted. "You're only 60! That's young. And besides, we'll be back in a year or so. Then we'll all be right here together. This is where we want to settle down, isn't it Hugh?"

"It seems like a good place. I would be the first doctor in the South to have this type of training. I think we would do well here."

"Well, I hope so," Mother said with resignation. "Still, it's a long way to take a baby."

"It's not like it was when you were my age, Mother. Ships make the trip in less than two weeks now." We talked on about our plans, but after the conversation was over, I knew Mother wasn't pleased; however, it was our decision and we were happy with it. Talking with Mammy Sophy, that was going to be the hard part. I put it off for several days, but I realized that it wouldn't be any easier if I waited longer.

Later in the week Lamar arrived from Athens. When they carried in all of her trunks, I was dumbfounded. "My heavens, Lamar! We not moving there for the rest of our lives. It looks as though you brought everything you own."

She smiled politely, just as she always did when she knew she was going to get her way. "That's easy for you to say, Sallie. You'll be spending all of your time looking after little Hugh. I'll be off skiing in the Alps or going to parties on the Danube. You wouldn't expect me not to have all the proper clothes, would you?"

"Well, one thing's for certain: Belle won't have to wash any clothes. You've got a daily change for a year." I was delighted to have her along, no matter how much the luggage. Our lives had been so close all the years, the idea of being that far apart for such a long time was harder than the thought of leaving Mother and Mammy.

After breakfast one morning, I went out to the cabin where Mammy Sophy was doing some mending. She looked up and smiled. "Dat sho' is one fine baby, Miss Sallie. Last night when I put him to bed he look up at me and say 'Mammy' jes' as plain as day."

"There's something I have to tell you, Mammy. Doctor Hagan and I are going to take Belle with us to Vienna. She'll be a wonderful help and . . ."

"What'chu talkin' 'bout, Miss Sallie. You can't take Belle wid us. Miss Mary Willis need her here."

"Oh, Mammy," I said, sitting down and taking her hands in mine. "You'll be here. You'll take good care of Mother."

That was probably the only time I ever saw Mammy speechless. Tears started rolling down her cheeks. "You mean, I ain' gwina git to go wid you and da baby?" she finally asked.

"No, Mammy. You need to stay here. The ocean trip will be long and hard. You're too old for all you would have to go through." It sounded so lame when I said it.

"Too old!" she shouted. "I ain' too old to work 'round dis place day and night. Ain' no ship, no ocean, gwina get da best of me, Miss Sallie. Please, Ma'am. Please let me go wid you and baby Hugh." Her cheeks were shining like ice on a brown stone.

I felt so badly, but I knew I had to stick by our decision. "We'll be back before you know it, then we're all going to move in with Mother and be one big family."

Sophy considered. "How come you all got to go? Da doctor, he oughta go and tend to his bizzness. You and da baby stay her wid me. And Miss Lamar? How come she gotta go?"

"Because Doctor Hagan and I want her to. That's the reason, Mammy."

"So you gwina take dat fool nigger gal, Belle, instead of yo ol' Mammy. Dat Belle, she ain' got da sense God gave a buckeye. All she is is frisky. No tellin' what trubble she get into wid all dose foreigners." She paused, then said, "Da Lawd hep dat po' doctor, dat's all I gotta say. Two women folks and a fool nigger gal traipsin' after him ever step he take!"

Through it all, the tears rolled down her face. I felt awful. I would so have loved to have taken her, but she wasn't nearly as strong as she thought. If anything happened to her I would never forgive myself. Then I thought if she should die while we were gone, that would be just as bad. The only happy solution would be to have her alive and well when we returned to Atlanta to live. Mammy couldn't see that far ahead. As I walked into the house, I wasn't sure I could, either.

The following week, we left for Charleston. It was early in April and the clean, cool smell of spring was in the air. Our trunks were packed and we had so many things to carry we had to take an extra wagon filled with Lamar's steamer barrels. Belle was making her first train trip, to say nothing of a crossing of the ocean. To hear her talk you would have thought she was a world traveler. The entire group of servants gathered around the carriages as we were about to leave. Belle was giving final instructions.

"Now when we gets back I'll be glad to teach y'all how we does things in Veeany. I might even speak foreign for you." That was more than Mammy Sophy could take.

"You git yo' fat behind on dat wagon and shut yo' mouf. If'n I heah you causin' Miss Sallie any trubble, I come ober dere an' wear you out."

"We'll all be fine, Mammy," I told her. "I want you to take care of Mother while we're gone. I'll feel so much better knowing you're here looking after her." I handed little Hugh up to Belle and put my arms around Mammy. I could feel her shaking but trying not to show how upset she was. "I love you so much, Mammy." That was all I could say because I was beginning to cry myself.

Mother was much more composed and I knew she would be fine. "When we get back, Hugh will be a regular little boy. He will grow up in this house just as I did," I said. She nodded and blinked hard, then took my hand and said how much she would miss all of us.

The trip to Charleston was uneventful, but the ship was a little worrisome. I had never been on shipboard and had heard frightful stories about seasickness, about the food and cramped quarters. This old steamship looked like it could give a ring of truth to whatever bad tale I had heard. The steam funnels were rusted and the peeling paint on the side of the hull looked as though it had survived many collisions. It was filled with cotton and tobacco as well as the few passengers. We would be going through the North Atlantic, and it was the time of year when icebergs were said to be in abundance. I had a hard time imagining a block of ice so large it could sink a ship, but I knew it had happened. Our boat appeared to be a likely candidate. And Belle was sick before we passed Fort Sumter. She was leaning over the rail retching furiously.

"Oh Miss Sallie," she wailed, when she had finished, "Make dis here boat turn 'round and lemme off. I didn' know we wuz gwina be outta sight of land." The waves were rolling high, and the ship was pitching mightily by the time we were off Cape Hatteras. I was beginning to wonder if we hadn't made a mistake. The cabin was no more than ten feet square with hammocks for beds. Little Hugh was the best of the group. We had some medicine that Hugh had given us for seasickness, but it didn't seem to help. Of course, Lamar had a cabin to herself and she treated the whole thing like it was a paddle down the Savannah river. If she was ever sick, I never saw it. Soon, she was a great favorite of the Captain and spent much of her time on the bridge where her official duty was to blow the horn whenever ordered which seemed to me quite frequently. By the time we got to New York, I was more than ready to call the whole thing off but, of course, that wasn't possible. As we sailed out of New York Harbor and up the coast of Long Island, I knew it would be a welcome sight when we saw it come into view on the return trip.

Fortunately, the worst part of the crossing was the trip up the Atlantic Coast. When we passed Newfoundland and headed out toward the Grand Banks, the weather improved and even Belle thought she might live through it. The problem of icebergs did not materialize, so my fears about that were allayed. Since Hugh was the only doctor on board, he set up a little practice for passengers who had problems. That kept him busy, and he had Belle help him as his nurse, which kept her mind off her miseries, although they were quickly being made worse by homesickness. When we reached the North Sea and Bremerhaven we were all feeling better, and the miseries of the first weeks were soon forgotten.

The harsh, guttural sound of spoken German was a shock. Although Hugh and I both spoke a little German, neither of us could understand much of what was being said, and spoken English was very rare. After much wild gesticulating and shouting, we managed to get all our belongings collected and transferred to the train station. Belle's eyes were as big as saucers, as were the looks of wonderment she received from many Germans who had apparently not seen a Negress before. The curiosity of the men was appalling. Belle was a beautiful girl, tall and full-bodied with skin dark as Dutch chocolate. Young men would stop and stare at her, then want to touch her face. She would react to their attention by stepping back and smiling at them, which only encouraged them. I finally would have to intervene, but since they had difficulty understanding me, the whole thing took on the air of a comic opera with Belle always circling to keep me between her and her would-be admirers. Soon, she learned to shout, "Nien, mein herr!" which had only a minimal effect. I must say, Hugh was not a great help in fending them off and irritated me by finding the whole thing amusing.

Once on the train, life settled down a bit. It was a long ride from Bremen to Vienna, but the train was much more commodious than the ship had been. We stopped for meals and had our first introduction to German food. In New York we had, of course, been to German restaurants, so we had some idea of what we would like. Getting fresh milk for little Hugh was a problem, and pasteurization was not something that was widely practiced. Frequently, we would have to buy raw milk that was scooped from big pails in which all sorts of debris was floating. Belle was highly upset that grits, collards and fatback were not part of the German diet, but she soon found that the sausages were quite a satisfactory substitute for sowbelly and chitterlings. She was a help and very good with the baby. To have done this without her would have been very difficult, and my decision not to bring Mammy had proven correct. The crossing would have been much too rigorous for her.

When we reached Vienna, our lucky star apparently had preceded us. We found a wonderful apartment on the Ringstrasse right opposite the emperor's gardens. Diagonally across the street was the Grand Opera House, scene of some of world's greatest musical presentations. In the center of the rooms, there was a wonderful salon, furnished with damask and silk settees and a variety of interesting high-backed chairs. In the corner was a harpsichord, which Lamar played as though she had been doing it all her life. The room was lit by a dozen sconces on the walls as well as a large candelabra. In the evenings, we had impromptu concerts that others in the apartment would come to enjoy. Lamar and her music were a wonderful introduction to our new neighbors. Our German improved rapidly and our house mates were certainly more patient than the roughnecks of Bremerhaven. Some even spoke English passably well, and within a week or so, I felt that we had settled into a new home. Vienna was so vastly different from anything I had ever experienced that each day was an adventure. Meals turned out to be just that. I had not anticipated that Belle would be useless as a cook; certainly, at first, she was. There was nothing in the markets that she knew how to prepare and although she gave it her best effort, I thought we might starve to death those first weeks, if she didn't kill us with some of the concoctions she had made from who knows what. Our downstairs neighbors were Colonel and Mrs. Frederick D. Grant, the United States Ambassador to the Court of Austria. They heard of our plight and sent one of their cooks to live with us. Elise was a Tyrolean master cook, and although she couldn't understand a word of English, she knew how to feed us and found in Belle an able assistant. I could hear them jabbering in the kitchen constantly. How they understood one another, I never knew, but they did. Much hilarity and giggles from Elise were more than matched by Belle and her knee-slapping laughter. It was wonderful to see them together.

The meals were prepared by both of them, but since Elise spoke no English, Belle was usually the one who served. One evening, as we were finishing dinner, Belle announced that Elise was going to leave. "How in the world could you know that, Belle?" Dr. Hagan asked. "You don't speak a word of German and Elise certainly can't speak English."

Belle regarded my husband with measured superiority. "I can speak German good as you, Dr. Hagan," she announced.

"Fine. Let's have a little conversation," he suggested.

"Oh, it ain' da kind of German you could understand, but I tell you what's a fact: Elise is gwina leave here."

"Why in the world would she do that?" I asked. "She seems perfectly happy, and the two of you are getting along so well."

"She say she ain' gwina work for no po' white trash. Dat's what she say."

"Poor white trash! Where in the world did she hear that expression? I never heard such foolishness," Lamar countered.

"Dat's perzactly what I tol' her, Miss Lamar. I say dey ain't no finer white folks no where dan you is."

"Well, what *is* she talking about, Belle?" Dr. Hagan asked.

Belle paused and looked back toward the kitchen as if she were afraid she would be over-heard. "Elise say she don' wanna cook for nobody dat wears the work clothes to dinner. She say you supposed to get dressed up wid yo' jewels and dem long coats in de evening. Da ladies supposed to have dere arms and necks showing. Dat's the way fine German folks does. Dat's what she said."

Lamar was speechless. So was I, but I really didn't think Belle knew what she was talking about until the next afternoon when Elise announced she *would* be leaving. We asked her to stay through that dinner, at least, to which she agreed. We dressed that evening as if we were going to meet the emperor. Lamar put on a long silk gown, purple and beaded with seed pearls around the bodice. I wore a royal blue gown with a lace choker collar. Between the two of us, we had on every piece of jewelry we owned. When Hugh arrived home from the hospital, he laughed. "I must have stumbled into his highness' palace by mistake. I was looking for some po' white trash."

"Well, you'll just have to walk down to South Fulton Street,

Dr. Hagan," Lamar cooed. "Only ladies of the highest fashion are allowed here." She took a sniff of his coat lapel. "And you'll have to do something about that awful ether smell, or I shall simply swoon." She put her wrist limply to her forehead and slouched to the fainting couch.

"I can match you quite handily when it comes to the finery, but the ether smell—I'm afraid that's become part of my body."

Hugh changed into his formal evening wear and came into the salon with a black silk ascot with a stick pin that glittered like a diamond. As we had our sherry, Lamar played Strauss waltzes and we did, if I say so myself, make an elegant threesome.

When Elise announced that dinner was served, her mouth fell open when she saw how elaborately we had dressed. She was obviously very pleased and even attended to the service herself. The next morning she asked if she could withdraw her resignation which, of course, we were delighted to do. She really had been offended by our causal dress and thought that we were definitely lower class. As long as we dressed properly for dinner she was quite pleased, but if either Lamar or I showed up for dinner with our arms covered, up went Elise's eyebrow, letting us know we were flirting with a problem. We never did find out how Belle knew what Elise was thinking when she nearly resigned. Somehow, through sign language, I suppose, Elise had gotten the message through to Belle that we weren't people with whom she should be associated. The customs of old Vienna were quite different from those of Atlanta, or even New York so we dressed for dinner every evening, arms showing despite the true chill in the air, a constant companion in Vienna that winter.

The Grants quickly became special friends. Their children were in early school and both spoke excellent German. Although Frank Grant was the ambassador, his German was not nearly as good as mine or Hugh's. He relied entirely on Captain Frank Hines, his military attache, to act as interpreter. Generally that worked out well, but one afternoon, about an hour before an important appointment with the emperor, Captain Hines fell deathly ill. He was unable to stand up, to say nothing of being able to perform his duties. Frank was beside himself when his son, Ulysses, walked in from school. The solution declared itself: Ulysses would act as his father's interpreter. Quickly, he was dressed in his finest and off to the palace he went, holding his father's hand. The meeting went well, and the business of state was conducted through the interpretation of a ten-year-old boy, the grandson of President U.S. Grant.

Hugh's work at the hospital was exhausting. Even as his skills in the language increased, there was another vocabulary to learn, that of neurology. He seemed frustrated by the enormity of it in the first months, but soon was back to his steady, if somewhat silent, self. The winter presented a special challenge: influenza. We had never seen anything like it at home. First, a sense of general malaise followed by muscular aching. Shortly, there would be chills and fever rocketing up to frightening levels, all of which was overlain with no appetite and a wracking cough. There was no treatment that seemed effective.

Children and the elderly were particularly hard hit, and by the middle of January the year that had started with such promise and pleasantry was assuming the proportions of a nightmare. Everyone we knew, except, of course, Lamar, had it. Hugh did not talk about it much, but I could tell from the look in his eyes that he was worried. Many died with pneumonia which settled in after a week or so. I was worried sick about little Hugh when he began to run a fever. The stories that mother had told of Uncle Howell's son dying when he was about little Hugh's age came back to haunt me. I hadn't thought of those tales for years, and now I seemed about to relive them in a foreign land. Homesickness settled in like a pall, and I'm sure that weakened me to the point I became ill, too. Lamar! Bless her heart. She took charge of everything. The cooking, the cleaning, the tending of all our needs—she was right there. And Belle was just as good. Mammy Sophy would have been proud of her, although she would rather have died than admit it. When I longed for Mammy's gentle touch, I was, at the same time grateful she wasn't there. At her age and weight, she would never have survived influenza.

The other great source of comfort during those difficult weeks was Mrs. Grant. Ida Honore Grant was a woman to be admired. She brought in wonderful broths and stews she said cook had prepared for Colonel Grant, but I really think she made them herself just for us. Although we were close, a formality common to diplomatic circles always remained. When the food arrived, it would be accompanied by a note written with Spenserian precision. Generally, it would read as follows:

> My Dear Mrs. Hagan:
>     I take the liberty of sending you a part of the dish we had for Luncheon. Colonel Grant pronounced it excellent. I thought perhaps Dr. Hagan might enjoy it too.
>     Please pardon my informality,
>                                 I am, very sincerely, your friend,
>                                                 Ida Honore Grant

The note, delivered on a silver tray by a servant, always preceded the presentation of the food. It was a Godsend, and Lamar enjoyed it more than the rest of us, since there was never anything wrong with *her* appetite and it gave her a respite from the cooking until Elise improved enough to resume her duties. By the end of January we were all improving, and the city began to emerge from what had been a long miasma of misery.

The Austrians took Lent very seriously, and in order to prepare for it, the social season picked up considerably before Ash Wednesday. The custom of extravagant parties with elaborate costumes, seen only in *Mardi Gras* in the United States, was apparent in *Fasching*. I was unclear about its origins, but happy to engage in the parties, nonetheless, once the influenza crisis had passed. Lamar was especially pleased with the upswing in the social scene. For more than a month she had been the mainstay of the household while we were ill, so she was more than ready for some new social interests. Even after Fat Tuesday the parties continued, although everyone dutifully made some sacrifice for Lent.

We were attending a party at the consul general's home one

evening. It was after Lent had started, so we had given up our costumes. Lamar was in excellent spirits and, I have to admit, she was a ravishing beauty. For all the years of our joking, I had steadfastly refused to admit that she was prettier than I, but in honesty I would have to say there were few women who could stand in her shadow, let alone cast one of their own when Lamar was present. She was seated in the corner of the side parlor on an ornate velvet throne-like affair. Someone said it had been in the home of Napoleon II, but that evening it belonged to Lamar. She was being closely attended by two handsome gentlemen, the sons of the Turkish and Serbian Ambassadors. She was chatting glibly along in French, the language most diplomats were using at the time, and both gentlemen answered her in impeccable English. I wondered how many of our Georgia friends could speak any language other than English, and most didn't do even that particularly well. Europeans were much more broadly educated than Americans, even those in New York.

I walked into the salon to join them. In addition to the ambassadors' sons, there was a coterie of other interesting young men. A number of them were in the same position as Hugh— taking a year at the University of Vienna in medicine, so I had something in common with them. As I seated myself to join in the conversation, Lamar shot me a look. No one else noticed, but I had seen the expression many a time sitting on the veranda of our Mt. Airy home. Why Lamar would ever have thought she would have competition from me, I could never understand. Now that I was happily married and a mother, surely she could lay that to rest.

"Well!" she announced. "I see the lovely Mrs. Hagan has joined our little group. She's the wife of Dr. Hugh Hagan," gesturing in his general direction, "a famous physician from New York who has come to Vienna to teach for a year." The assembled gentlemen all nodded appreciatively.

"Oh, really, Lamar! How you do go on. Everyone knows Hugh is a student. And you make me sound like a grand dowager. We're exactly the same age," I told her admirers. "And you're sitting there on Napoleon's throne like a re-incarnation of Josephine." Everyone laughed.

"Wrong Napoleon," corrected Jacques, an associate of Hugh's.

What a wonderful chance to play the dim-witted girl, the role to which Lucy Wellborn had thought I was so well suited. I decided not let them think I knew nothing of history. "Quite so, Jacques, but who knows, maybe the settee belonged to Bonaparte and it was passed down through the family."

There were a number of titled gentlemen in the group, and the conversation quickly turned to matters of custom in their homelands, to common history that European nations shared, to the rising tensions of nationalism in the unification of Germany when Bismarck had formed the North German Confederation. After the Franco-Prussia war, the southern German states had been taken into the Confederation which formed the German Empire with William I of Prussia as emperor. Austria had remained independent, and the conversation turned to how the failure to join the German empire would leave her in a vulnerable position. Having heard so much about and lived through the results of sectionalism and mistaken goals of nationalism, I was fascinated to be in the presence of men who really understood the history of their countries, all of which seemed infinitely more complicated than the issues of states' rights. Lamar listened patiently but was not interested in politics or politicians beyond securing their personal admiration. I thought the rest of the evening was glorious, but when we returned to our apartment, Lamar was furious.

"How can you expect me to gain any attention when you sit in the middle of them and quote political theories? When you got those books down from the library shelf and started reading about the life of Bismarck—whoever he was—I could have shot you. They were eating out of the palm of my hand until you started peering owlishly over that book at them."

"That's nonesense, Lamar. You sound like Lucy. These men are interested in intellect. If all you talk about is society matters, they'll become bored in an instant. If they find you have a mind of your own, then they'll become intrigued with the lovely Southern Belle and all sorts of things will happen."

"You think I don't know anything else to talk to about? You just wait. Tomorrow evening Baron Maporgo is calling. I will have an intellectual discussion with him, and you see if anything interesting in the way of romance occurs. I can promise you it will not. He'll talk about politics and *I'll* be the one who's bored to death."

"I'll bet it will be very different from what you think. Would you like to make a little wager?"

"Of course. I'll bet you a magnum of champagne that after I get him on the subject of languages, he'll not say a romantic thing the entire evening."

The following night we stationed ourselves in the main parlor downstairs where we did most of our entertaining. Normally, an unmarried woman would not be allowed alone with a gentleman caller, quite a different standard from what Lamar would have practiced at home. The Baron had no way of knowing I was there in any other role than a chaperone as I seated myself in the corner after Belle had taken his hat and cane. I peered, as owlishly as possible, over my book as Lamar launched into her intellectual conversation.

"Tell me, Baron, your views on the linguistic differences of the Germanic languages," she said, as if she were truly interested. "I know that you're well-informed in such matters."

"What an intriguing observation, my dear lady." He smiled expansively, as if he had been waiting for someone to ask this for years. "Each language, not just the Germanic ones, has a particular use. That's why it is so important to speak many tongues. For example, one should always argue in German. It has a harsh and guttural quality that make it ideally suited for disagreement. English, so free and fluid, so full of nuance and subtleties, is the perfect one for telling a joke. And, of course, as you know, Miss Lamar, French is the language of drawing room conversation and of diplomacy."

Lamar's look shot daggers at me. She was in for a terrible evening and it would take more than a magnum of champagne to elevate her spirits. There was a twinkle in the Baron's eye that made me think I had not lost my bet. He leaned in closer to Lamar and said in a soft voice, "Then there is Italian. That is the language of love." He leaned closer still and said something in Italian that I couldn't quite hear.

Lamar looked down coquettishly and said, "Unfortunately, I don't speak Italian."

"*Il ne pas de quois, mademoiselle.* I shall translate into your own tongue. I simply said, 'I love you.'"

I could practically hear the cork popping and tried to stifle my giggle. It had gone much faster than I had imagined. Leave it to an Italian to get right to the point. Lamar looked across the room, knowing the bet was lost, but I was deep into my book, fulfilling my position as disinterested chaperone and hiding my smile.

Lamar took another tack. "The customs in Europe seem so quaint, Baron Maporgo. It's difficult to get used to the concept of the chaperone, for example. At home, if we want to take a stroll with a beau, off we go. We go to the theater and to dinner and no one gives it a thought, but here, there always must be another lady present." She cut her eyes toward me.

"Ah, yes. I can imagine that does seem strange to you. I should be so fortunate as to find myself in America with such a lovely young lady as yourself. That would be truly grand! But in Vienna, if a Fraulein is seen alone with a gentleman, in the salon, in the opera, or on the Ringstrasse, then everyone knows the gentleman may do with her just as he pleases." He stopped and smiled at her then said a shocking thing. "It's a lovely night, although there is a bit of chill in the air. Perhaps you would like to exercise a bit of your American independence here and take a promenade with me down Prinzrengenstrasse. We can stop in at one of the music halls, have some champagne and listen to the band play Strauss. Afterwards, we can decide how to spend the rest of our evening."

I never knew if the Baron was teasing her. Was he flaunting his Italian charm, was he trying to embarrass me, or was he truly sincere? It made no difference. It was as bold a proposition as I had ever heard. I held my breath to see how she would respond. Lamar was totally undone by what she interpreted as an indecent proposal—and in front of me, as well.

"I think not, Baron. When in Rome, as they say. And I've developed a frightful headache, so I really think I must retire." She fanned herself briefly, gathered her skirts and fled from the room.

"Baron, thank you so much for coming. I'm sure that Miss Lamar will be feeling better after a bit of sleep, but rest assured I will be with her when she receives guests." I pulled the bell cord and Belle arrived instantly with his hat and cane. I suspect she had been lurking around the corner the entire time.

"*Vielen danke*, Frau Hagan" he intoned gravely, and was out the door.

"He look like a real prince, don' he, Miss Sallie? I bet he lives in one of dem castles down by der river. Is he gwina make Miss Lamar a princess"

"Oh, he's a prince all right, but not the kind you think, Belle. Good ol' Georgia boys are much more Miss Lamar's style. And she's a princess, already."

When spring came to Vienna, we began to enjoy ourselves again. The year would soon be drawing to a close. As we were sitting in the parlor one evening, Hugh was talking over his experiences of the year. Dr. Freud and his associates had been most kind, and the year had been fruitful from a professional point of view beyond anything either of us had imagined. Freud's reputation, although widespread in Europe, had not been felt in the United States. Hugh was fortunate to have been among his early students, but I don't think even he anticipated what a monumental influence Freud's work would have in the field of neurology and the beginnings of psychiatry. We had decided that we would return to Atlanta, as we had planned, after our European travels. Hugh would set up practice there and we would raise our family in the atmosphere I had experienced in my growing-up years. It all seemed so well-worked-out. Our plans were falling into place as effortlessly as can be imagined. One of the advantages of youth, I suppose, is the lack of recognition that plans can be changed in startling and unexpected ways. The idea of being invulnerable dies a slow death in youth. By old age, one feels quite vulnerable, indeed, but in the spring of 1890 we were living in a glorious time. The idea of tragedy seemed far removed.

During the last month of our stay, we attended many teas and parties given in our honor. Most of our friends were European and were planning to return to their homelands eventually, although some had settled in Vienna permanently. I hoped that we would be able to host them in a visit to Atlanta in the future. We tried to entice them with tales of the wonderful springtime, the dogwoods blooming in the gardens and flowers at every hand. The Viennese loved their gardens, but spring was late coming that year. In the cold, dank evenings, Georgia sounded positively idyllic. Our one close set of American friends was, of course,. Ambassador and Mrs. Grant. We had grown to love them, and I knew that I would miss Ida Honore greatly. She had been as helpful to me as Varina Davis had been to my mother when she, at my age, was learning the social ropes of Washington. Since my position in Vienna was that of only a wife, Ida Honore had no reason to take me under her wing and introduce me to the diplomatic circles of Austria. But she did. I can't think of how she could have been more gracious, particularly during the time we were all so ill.

On the evening before we were to depart for Paris, a letter arrived from the Grants. They were attending a party at the emperor's palace so they could not come to our final evening together. I opened the letter and read it aloud:

> My Dear Mrs. Hagan:
>
> How can I express the gratitude I feel over the flowers that Dr. Hagan sent yesterday and how we shall miss you when you have started your journey toward Paris and London Town. It would be selfish for us to wish that you were remaining longer, especially as your departure betokens the good health of the Commander of the Party, little Hugh,

who promises now to be in good health for the rest of the
summer.

We can only hope that the wonderful evenings we
have spent together and the friendship that we have formed
will last and can be renewed when we return to the United
States. Colonel Grant joins me in warmest regards for you
all. Do notice how I have learned to speak "Southern" with
my "you all?"

Your sincere friend,

Ida Honore Grant

What a gracious lady she was. What a gentleman was Colonel
Grant. Once again, I had learned that Union generals had wonderful
families. Little Ulysses was certainly a credit to his grandfather's
memory.

Then there was the matter of Elise, our Tyrolean cook. Belle
had decided that she would have to take Elise home with us. By
this time they had developed a third language—neither German
nor English—understood by no one but themselves. Elise, or so
Belle had told her, would come to Atlanta and the pair of them
would be head cooks for the household. I could scarcely imagine
the uproar bringing an Austrian into Mammy Sophy's kitchen
would precipitate.

"Oh, no, Miss Sallie. Elise, she gwina be jes' fine. She and me
be like sisters and Mammy Sophy gwina be glad to have her live
with us," Belle explained. I shook my head at the very idea which,
of course, we couldn't do.

"Belle, it just won't work. She will be miserable over there, no
one to whom she can talk; that would be awful. With her family
living all the way down in Graz, it's hard enough that she's so far
from them now, but if she went home with us she would never see
them again."

"Oh, she don' mind. She'll have me to look after her and I'm
gwina teach her to speak 'Merican."

When it finally dawned on Belle that Elise would have to stay
in Austria, she was crestfallen. The day of our departure, the two

young women held each other with much tearfulness and a sustained jabber that had bystanders wondering what in the world they were saying. I couldn't understand the words, but I knew their meaning: They had come to love each other and knew that they would never meet again.

The train trip across Austria, through the Bavarian Alps and on to Munich was wondrous. I was sorry that little Hugh was too young to enjoy it. The weather, although still quite cold was under the brilliant crystalline blue sky seen only a few days a year in southern Germany. As we left Munich headed for Nuremberg and Frankfurt, I realized what a gift this year had been. In Paris, we stayed on the *Champs Elysees* and enjoyed the sights of *Montmartre* and *La rive gauche*. When we saw *Notre Dame* from our river boat, Belle announced, "Dat's one whoppin' big church!" I doubt if, in its centuries-old tradition, it had ever been described quite that way. We took the boat train to La Havre and across the channel to England. In London, I noticed that Belle delighted in speaking her "German" to whomever she might meet. She did it such *elan* everyone assumed she was speaking an odd central European dialect that they should pretend to understand. Belle was enchanted by the looks of mystery on the faces of hapless bellmen and hotel clerks while she exposited in the lobby with great, sweeping gestures. I even aided and abetted by joining in with a more conventional German as if I understood everything she was saying. We would end up with a great fit of laughter, then I would ask the onlookers, "Don't you agree?" They invariably did. Hugh usually distanced himself from our antics, but Belle, Lamar and I enjoyed ourselves thoroughly. After a week, we traveled down to Southampton to sail home. I had given little thought to the actual journey. I didn't think it could be any worse than the crossing over. But I was wrong . . . dead wrong.

Although it was June, the weather had been unseasonably cold all spring. I had hoped for a warmer voyage, one in which we could enjoy being on the deck, but it was apparent immediately that wasn't to be the case. Before we had passed Plymouth and Land's End, the chill winds of the North Atlantic seemed to be seeking us out. While seasickness, which had been such a problem on the trip over, did not recur there was little incentive to be outside our cabin. We had better quarters than we had previously, as this was a passenger liner and not primarily a freighter. There were several hundred of us, a number who were finishing up studies, as Hugh had been, so we had much in common with them. I couldn't explain the sense of uneasiness that I felt about the trip. I had heard while at Southampton from disembarking passengers that icebergs were reported to be drifting toward the sea lanes. None had been seen on the trip over, and I felt confident that the ship's crew would keep us safe.

On the tenth day we were approaching the Grand Banks and Newfoundland. We began to see the ice. At first, they were little white dots on the horizon. In the morning sun they looked like little puffs of meringue that had settled on the sea, but as we came closer, I was astounded at their size. Some were much larger than the ship, and I felt as though we were sailing in a land of icy mountains with valleys of blue ocean between them.

The captain assured us that we would be safe, but he did mention that the fair weather was our best ally. Even at night, the ice would be clearly visible he said because the moon was near the full. I was feeling a little more comfortable after that chat, but Lamar was not pleased.

"When the sun goes down, and the air cools, there will be fog around all that ice. He won't be able to see a thing. What will we do then?" she wondered.

"Well, they've been through this many times and I'm sure they know what they're doing," Hugh countered. I certainly hoped he was right.

Late in the morning, the air was warmer and we were on the foredeck looking toward the west. On the far horizon something caught my eye. At the verge of the sea and the sky there was the thinnest of white lines. At first, I thought my eyes were playing a trick, but as the steady throb of the engines took us closer, I could see it was a fog bank. It looked like a giant white comforter pulled up over an indigo blanket.

"Fog," Hugh said with finality. Between us and the horizon there were no visible icebergs, but who knew what lay within that shroud? Most of the passengers were on the deck, watching tensely as the fog bank grew closer. Soon the intensity of the sun was dimmed by haze and we entered the fog as silently as a hand slipping into a glove, and with just as much visibility. From the foredeck, one could barely see the bridge and the funnels behind were obliterated.

A gentleman standing beside us said, "I've been on crossings like this before. There's ice all around us now. That's why there's the big fog bank. If we don't get out of this in a hurry, we're lost."

He said that in a such matter-of-fact manner I was shocked. Did he mean we were lost—as when you can't find your way out of a strange neighborhood? Or did he mean we were lost—as in dead?

Before I could sort that out, another man said, "Stop your whining. That's why they have fog horns. They can tell from the echo right where the icebergs are and maneuver right between them." I felt better after that. The foghorn had been bellowing its mournful sigh every ten seconds ever since we entered the bank.

First seating for lunch was called and I was glad to get below deck. Most of the passengers, even those for subsequent seatings, followed. Everyone was anxious to get away from the tension of the impending ice. We just had been seated and the steward was serving the first course when the collision occurred. It started as a feeling more than a sound. In the seat of the chair, there was a stubborn vibration, quite different from the customary pulse of the engines. In a few seconds the entire ship began to shudder, the cups dancing out of their saucers and shattering to the floor, followed immediately by the sound of rending metal and things crashing down from above. Some of the furniture was thrown into a pile against the front bulkhead.

"Come on, Sallie, we've got to get out of here," Hugh said softly, taking my hand and pulling the wide-eyed Lamar to her feet. Everyone raced to the deck and we were stunned at what we saw. The bow of the ship had disappeared under a mountain of ice. Tons of ice had fallen to the deck, reaching up to the superstructure, much of which had collapsed into a tangled disarray. The iceberg we had hit was floating alongside the ship, sliding by with a terrible scraping noise. Everyone was frantic. The crew members were trying to shovel ice away from blocked companionways and from the steps leading up to the bridge. The captain appeared on the bridge and announced through a megaphone that all was well. If that were true, I shuddered to think what it would take to make him think we were in trouble. The whole ship was listing to one side as we continued by the mountain of ice.

"Rest easy, ladies and gentlemen," he continued. "The ship is entirely seaworthy. I'm sorry for the little inconvenience and suggest you return to your lunch."

Well, lunch was scattered all over the dining salon floor, and no one was of a mind to eat. Hugh had collected Belle and little Hugh when the next complication presented itself. A young woman, about my age standing by the rail, suddenly shrieked and grabbed her abdomen. "Oh my God," she moaned. "I'm having my baby!"

The deck beneath her feet was awash with her waters, and she sank to her knees in the midst of it all. Where her husband was, no one knew, but she was right—her baby was going to be born on this ship that seemed, at least to me, intent on sinking.

Hugh bent beside her. "Don't worry, Ma'am. I will take care of you and your baby." He called for crew members to help her to the tiny sick bay with which the ship was equipped, then he turned to me. "Have Belle and Lamar stay here together. You come with me. I'm going to need your help."

"Come with you?" I shouted. "And leave Hugh up here on the deck of this sinking ship? Are you out of your mind?" I was yelling in a very unladylike fashion, but it seemed appropriate for the moment.

He took me by the shoulders, looked me right in the eye and spoke as calmly as if we were standing in Piccadilly Circus deciding where to have tea. "The ship is not sinking. Belle and Lamar will take care of Hugh. You and I will deliver this baby."

I stood there with my mouth open, but there was something in his manner that made me believe it was true. Lamar was standing, tight-lipped, holding onto Belle and little Hugh, who seemed to be enjoying the entire hullabaloo. Belle was wide-eyed and, for once, totally speechless. She stood there, an ebony statue, pointing at the mountain of ice that was now receding to the stern and mystically blending into the fog until it was quickly gone.

"Come on, Sallie," Hugh insisted. "They'll be fine and we need to get this woman to the sick bay." The crew members had loaded her onto a stretcher and were making their way down the deck, stepping around blocks of ice that were chest high. With Hugh close behind, pulling me along with him.

Her name was Gerta Polanski from Warsaw. Fortunately, she spoke some German and she was en route to New York where her family lived. This was her first baby and she was traveling alone, her husband having preceded her by several months. Obviously, she was terrified. Who wouldn't be? I had had my baby in the center of medical sophistication at Physicians and Surgeons and, even there, I had been quite nervous. Having a baby on a ship that might be sinking with a strange doctor and his wife in attendance was more than I could imagine. I decided my role would be one of comforter. I assured her that Dr. Hagan was more than competent to attend to the delivery and indeed it was so. As he was working away he found the baby was a breech, and I could tell he was anxious but showed no sign of it the mother could detect. I thought of my mother, helping my father in the hospitals during the battle of Atlanta. That situation was certainly more horrific than this. If she weathered that storm, I could certainly get through this one. After an interminable amount of pulling and straining, the little girl was born, feet first and screaming at the top of her lungs. It seemed a good omen. Surely, God would watch over this newest passenger in a special way. Gerta relaxed with the baby in her arms and I helped clean up the room a bit before telling Hugh that I was going back on deck to make sure everyone was all right.

The fog was as thick as ever and the wind, surprisingly, was whipping up. I had always associated fog with a calm sea, but that wasn't the case. The waves were frothed with foam and the ship was rolling significantly. The engines had shut down shortly after the collision, not because of damage, but because the captain thought drifting with the current was safer than plowing ahead in a sea that was filled with invisible ice. Rain, in driving sheets, followed shortly and we were all forced to go below, but not for long. The crew came through the decks distributing life jackets and instructing us to put them on and wait for further orders. I declined to wear one. If we were going into the water—there seemed to be very few life boats—death was an absolute certainty. We would freeze in a matter of minutes, and I didn't intend to prolong the agony by trying to stay afloat and watch little Hugh die in my arms. We would go down together—and quickly.

No dinner was served that night, obviously, and the ship seemed to be lolling away in the fog with no additional damage although icebergs as large as the one we had struck occasionally drifted by, silent sentinels from a world in which we were aliens. About nine in the evening, I decided to go to bed. Hugh had been attending passengers who were ill or had been injured. Belle and Lamar were in their cabins and seemed as resigned as I to the fate I felt sure the night would bring. Little Hugh went peacefully to sleep in my arms and I wondered if anyone would ever find out what happened to us. The ship would just disappear and no trace would ever be found. I slipped from the bed and wrote a short note to my mother detailing our ordeal. I put the time and the date on the bottom, emptied out a perfume bottle and stuffed the note inside. I set it by the porthole and would throw it into the sea if the ship was going down. Maybe someone might eventually find it and get word back to the family.

Shortly after midnight, I was awakened with a rumbling sensation in the bed. It did not feel like the collision had felt. Hugh roused up from his bed then said, "The engines! They've started the engines! I'm going up to the bridge and see what has happened."

I lay awake, tensely waiting for his return. Finally, he came back in the room, soaking wet and freezing. "That weather is still terrible. High seas, rain and still the fog, but the captain has decided that to remain adrift will insure our destruction. He's decided to get under steam and hope for the best."

That didn't sound like a very good plan to me, but who was I to say? Lying in bed, little Hugh nestled against me, breathing peacefully in his sleep as only a baby can do. So small! So trusting! The thought his life might never be lived was unbearably bitter. I tried to put the obvious out of my mind. The great engines of the ship had a comforting sound. Against all logic, I had the feeling that Hugh's prediction was going to be fulfilled: We would be safe and with that thought I drifted back off to sleep, but never losing the feel of those mighty pistons pulsing beneath us.

The next morning was a miracle. The sun was shining brightly and we had come out of the storm. On the deck, to the east, the fog bank could be seen disappearing from view. I have been grateful many times in my life, but probably never more so than that morning off the Grand Banks.

It was interesting to observe the reactions of the passengers once the danger had passed. Many, like me, had been certain we would never live through the night. Others had an equally unrealistic optimism about the whole thing. One thing we all shared was a sense of relief. Belle, of course, had her own view which she was more than happy to share with anyone who would listen.

She was such a strikingly pretty girl, and the mixture of her native dialect and the language she and Elise had devised made her announcements irresistible. She sat down in a deck chair in the midst of many passengers, little Hugh perched on her lap and explained the preceding twenty-four hours with such enthusiasm, one would have thought she was the only one who had been through it.

"Ich ben livin' un Dortchland mit der herr doctor. Ich haben been gavesen der wasser in da shippen lots." She waved her hands expansively. "Mein kinder und der missus be goin' ober dere to Georgia when allus ist ben Kersmash! mit der icebug." She pointed up to the broken railings in the bow. "Eben das cap'n spreken das boot da sinken in da wasser, but I knowed da gute Gott He be watchin'ober mein kinder und moi." She jostled little Hugh on her lap and everyone smiled approvingly. A refined-looking elderly lady seated next to Belle was drinking some water and little Hugh began to fret.

"Would you like a sip of my water, baby?" she asked.

Belle seated him firmly in her own lap. "Dis chile don' unnerstand no 'Merican talk. She turned to him and asked, "Hugo, wilt du wasser be haben?

Instantly, he broke into a smile. "Ja Ja! Wasser, bitte."

Belle took the glass from the woman's hand. "Dunker shern. Whad I tell you? Me and him bofe don' speak nuthin' but German."

"So you weren't afraid of the icebergs, Belle?" the American lady asked. "I was terrified."

"Nien, genedage frau. Ich not a'skeered. Ich knowed dat Gott und der life preserver would been be savin' us. Herr doctor, he kep' his clothes on all night, but Miss Sallie und Miss Lamar, dey get schlafen through der whole shebang. Miss Sallie, she sprecken dat she be ready to meet der Lawd, but be I willin' to keep meetin' Him in prayer."

Belle's commentary was a delight to behold. We were all so grateful to be alive that her story of how it all came to pass was just the comic relief we needed after such a close call. As my life progressed, with all the joys and sorrows that were to come my way, I have come to appreciate even more how close we came to losing it all.

When we arrived back in Atlanta, poor Belle, considered herself far above any of her contemporaries. After all, she had lived in Vienna for a year and she spoke German. Quick to tell everyone about her adventures, she was in for a rude awakening. As far as the servants were concerned, she was still plain ol' Belle, frisky but not too bright.

Mammy Sophy was particularly incensed by Belle. I had hoped she would have recovered from her hurt during the year we had been gone, but it had remained much on her mind. She never did understand why we hadn't taken her.

As soon as Belle started in with her airish ways, Mammy Sophy snatched Hugh from her. "Gimme dat chile! I wuz right all der time. You ain' got da sense God gave a mule, Belle. Talkin' like you know all 'bout eberthing. You can't boil water, girl, widout puttin' da fire out. Now you shet yo' sassy mouf an' git back der to da kitchen. Time I git little Hugh dressed you bes' have dem taters pelt for dinner. I ain' puttin' up wid no foolish from no low-down nigger. You git yo' tongue back after we gits through wid you, you jes' wait and see!"

I hugged Mammy Sophy. "I missed you so. I couldn't wait to get home and feel your arms around me."

"Shoulda' tuck me wid you, Miss Sallie, den you wouldna' had to wait."

I looked down in her eyes. There wasn't anything but love shining out. Thank God she was still with us.

# CHAPTER VIII

Just as I had not anticipated all the changes that would take place with my marriage, I had not understood how living in Vienna would affect my view of the world. The word *Zeitgeist* was as foreign to my thinking as it was to my tongue when we first arrived in Austria, but the association with men and women from all of central and eastern Europe broadened my horizons tremendously. When we returned to Atlanta, it seemed so provincial, almost agrarian, compared to Vienna. The sense of history, present on every side in Austria, France, and England was lacking in Georgia. Less than a quarter of a century earlier, the whole area had been an ash heap. Great strides were being made, but in terms of the span of history, the United States was a newborn nation.

Of the Europeans with whom we had been associated, I was impressed with all they knew of their native countries. Their knowledge made me realize how little I knew about our heritage. It was an important moment for me. Although America was young, it seemed vital to understand the roots from which she had begun to grow. That was my frame of mind when Hugh and I moved into our new home just a block from Mother's house. I didn't understand how important those feelings would become until Mrs. Mary S. Lockwood became interested in the women descendants of heroes of the Revolutionary War. It was a movement that quickly grew in popularity and spread across the country. Family Bibles were dusted off, stories were told that led to investigation of genealogies and soon chapters were being formed as heroic deeds of long-forgotten ancestors were brought to light. My cousin, Mary Rootes Jackson, started the Atlanta chapter, and when she asked me to join, I was pleased. It fit right in with my recent realization of how important it is to understand the history of our country. I was not planning on being anything more than an observer and a student of our family's history, but that soon was changed.

The first national meeting of the new organization was to be held in Washington the week of February 22, 1892. Appropriately, it would convene during George Washington's birthday and would be called The First Continental Congress of the Daughters of the American Revolution. Naturally, cousin Mary would attend as Regent, and she would be accompanied by Mrs. William Dickson, an equally prominent Atlantan, as a delegate. All was going well until cousin Mary was informed by Mrs. Lockwood that she would be expecting an address to be delivered by one of the Atlanta representatives. At our local chapter meeting, there was much consternation.

Cousin Mary announced that she certainly was too old to stand up in front of a group of strangers and give a speech, and at such an auspicious occasion. It was beyond possible, concurred Mrs. Dickson. I was seated in the middle of the group, slightly amused that they had gotten themselves into positions of leadership, yet seemed unwilling to take the role seriously. After a good bit of banter back and forth, cousin Mary looked at me and said, "Sallie, you can do it. You're very talkative and young—too young to be worried about your dignity—you can go with us and you can give the speech."

I was pleased. I enjoyed public speaking. And they were right: I wasn't burdened down with concerns about my dignity. A trip to Washington would be an adventure. They failed to consider my role as a wife and young mother, but assured me I could take little Hugh along with us. I was excited until someone asked what would be the topic of my speech.

Then it dawned on me. This would not be just a lark. I would have to actually come up with something worth saying. Ideas flashed through my head. A confusion of war heros about whom I had read in the family archives seemed promising, but most of those stories were of a single event, certainly not substance for a substantial speech to be delivered to women from across the country. I didn't mind being in front of an audience, but I did not intend to make a fool of myself. Every idea soon seemed shallow and flawed until the memory of my old friend, Henry Grady, popped into my mind. There had never been another orator like him. What would he do in this situation? I remembered his address to The New England Society, *The New South*. It had everything in a speech anyone could want, and made the strong case for nationalism which was why the Revolution had been fought. If the Daughters of the American Revolution understood *The New South,* they would form an organization that would wipe out sectionalism and reunite the country in friendship. It seemed like a perfect solution. My cousin was delighted. She wouldn't have to appear in public and she knew enough about me to think I would, at least, be entertaining. That was enough for her.

When I got home and explained it to Mammy Sophy, she put her hands on her hips and announced, "Well, I tell you one thing, Miss Sallie, you ain' gwina take Belle wid you on dis trip. She ain' been da same since she got on dat boat and you can't take her to no meetin' in Washin'ton. I'se goin' and dat's dat!"

"Of course you're going, Mammy. I took you to New York after we got back from Austria and we had a fine time. This will be just like that. You may even get to see the President."

"I ain' studying 'bout seeing no Prezzerdint. I don' want you up dere wid all dose Washington mens. You might start a wahr. No tellin' what might happen!"

I decided to see what Mammy was expecting from our trip.

"We goin' to der meetin' to heah da shoutin' and da prayin,'" she announced. I smiled to myself, wondering what she would think when she found this wasn't a camp meeting in a tent. I got a little inkling when we reached the train station. Mrs. Dickson, cousin Mary and I had assumed we would all be next to each other in the Pullman, but it turned out we were at opposite ends of the car. A friend of Mrs. Dickson's, a Mr. Burton, was in the same car with us and suggested that he give his lower berth to Mrs. Dickson and he would move to the unoccupied upper. That would get all three of us closer together. It seemed a workable plan and Mr. Burton insisted that he didn't mind. I hadn't noticed Mammy's eyes getting bigger, but after he was out of sight, she grabbed me by the sleeve.

"Come heah, Miss Sallie. Come heah to me!" I knew that look and I was in for a lecture.

"Wha'chu think you doin', lettin' dat man get in de bed above da wimmen? I neber heard such a thing. I gwina tell yo' ma. I gwina tell da doctor, too."

"Tell what, for heaven's sake?" I asked, exasperated.

"You knows whut I'm talkin' 'bout. I heerded ev'y bit wid my own ears!"

"Heard what? You must be crazy! I haven't heard anything."

"You mean to tell me you didn' hear 'bout de 'rrangement Miss Ma' Dickson made wid Mr. Burton?"

"Certainly, I heard that! What about it?"

"Whadda 'bout it? We goin' to a tent meetin', an' de mens and wimmens is foolin' around in da bedstead! Dat's whadda 'bout it." She put her hands on her hips, shook her head and said, "Well da Lawd bless my soul. I'm sho gwina tell yo' ma and da doctor."

"Listen, Mammy," I said, as patiently as I could, "You see this berth here the porter just made up? Little Hugh and you are going to sleep in that one.

"I knows dat."

"And I'm going to sleep in the one right above you."

"I knows dat, too."

"Now cousin Mary is going to sleep in the berth right there and Mr. Burton is going to sleep in the upper berth."

"Who say he gwina sleep? Who say he gwina stay put in dat berth?"

"Well, that's what one does in a sleeping car."

"Yes, well, I'se gwina stay awake and watch dat man. He come outta dat berth, I'se gwina crack his head open."

"Hush, Mammy. Don't let anyone hear you talking like that."

"Dat ain' all da talkin' I gwina do. When we gets back home, Miss Mary Willis and da doctor, dey gwina find out what kinda wimmen you been runnin' 'round with. Good thing ol' Mammy come on dis heah trip. You ain' got no mo' sense dan Belle!"

Fortunately, Mr. Burton stayed in his berth the entire night. I have no doubt that Mammy would have laid him out in the aisle had he tried to make a trip to the men's restroom in the dark.

One of the main reasons I wanted to make the trip to Washington was to visit Lamar. She had married Andrew Lipscomb, a childhood chum from Athens, and they were living in Georgetown. I had not seen her since her wedding the year before and was anxious to catch up on all the news. I remembered Andrew from my summer visits to Athens and had always thought he would be a good match for Lamar.

The carriage ride from Union Station to the Lipscombs gave Mammy a taste of how different Washington was from Atlanta. The tree-lined streets of Georgetown with the townhouses built one against another intrigued her. "Dey ain't got a sign of a yard. Where is da garden? Where do dey keep da chickens and da hogs?"

"They don't live quite like we do, Mammy."

"Dey sho' don'. No wonder dey all look so skinny and pasty-face. We ain' gwina move up heah, is we?"

"No, Mammy. We're going to stay right where we belong, but it's fun to see how other people live."

As the week progressed, she settled into a routine and found the Lipscomb's servants friendly and appreciative of her cooking skills. Mammy's head was hard as a hickory nut, but she could fit into any situation if she decided to make the effort. If I tried to put myself in her shoes, I wondered if I could adjust to her culture as readily as she did to ours?

The meeting of the Congress was held at the Church of Our Father. Cousin Mary and Mrs. Dickson took their seats in the front and I was advised, gently, to sit on the side. I was happy just to be in the building. The galleries were crowded and there wasn't an extra seat available. Women had come from all across the country.

The meeting was called to order by Mrs. Benjamin Harrison, wife of the President. The First Continental Congress of the Daughters of the American Revolution was in session. When Mrs. Harrison delivered her inaugural address she outlined the reasons for the organization, stressing that we should be something more than "a Ladies Aid Society." Her manner was gentle and her charm was obvious, but when it came to parliamentary skills she was at a total loss.

When someone had a point to make, she simply stood up and started talking. Mrs. Harrison, in an attempt to keep order, would tap on the podium with her fan, but she was roundly ignored. The result was several women would be talking at the same time and when they realized they weren't being heard, they would gradually work their way to the front of the hall and talk even more loudly. If a woman wasn't recognized when she stood to speak, she took it as a personal affront and started talking anyway. Mrs. Harrison, her head swiveling back and forth between the participants, soon had lost control of the meeting and sat down. General Shields was at her side, ostensibly to instruct her in Roberts' Rules of Order, but he never got a single point across to her. It was a free-for-all ranging from stories of heroism in the Revolutionary war to the proper way to prepare a Sally Lund. Eventually, Mrs. Lockwood stood and managed to get the attention of the assembly. She invited the DAR to hold its next meeting at the Exhibition Congress in Chicago the following year, 1893. Immediately, what had been intended as an effort to get the meeting back on track, degenerated into a violent argument. Many thought that would be a tacit endorsement by the DAR of the suffrage movement and there was strenuous opposition to such a stand. As I watched the melee, my sense of unease about my upcoming speech increased. The ladies from the north might storm the podium and ride me out of town on a rail. That Henry Grady had delivered the speech in "hostile country" with a superb result was no comfort; I was most assuredly *not* Henry Grady and felt there would be no shortage of women to remind me of that.

When the day of my speech arrived, I was prepared. I had read the text so many times that I had it committed to memory. As I sat on the stage next to Mrs. Harrison, I could see my cousin, Mary, and Mrs. Dickson. They were many years my senior, but I appreciated being considered a grown woman by them and being asked to participate in the meeting. My hands were damp and sweaty, and I hoped that my knees would hold me up as I stood to speak. The audience was large, a thousand or more, and there was a general undercurrent of conversation as I stood to speak. I suspect my age was an advantage. Most of the delegates were middle-aged or beyond. I was twenty-seven and a mere child in the eyes of many. They were, no doubt, curious to see what I might say. As I began, my voice seemed to carry better than I had imagined it would and the room became very still. I had worried that sectionalism might polarize the remarks, but I should have guessed that would not be the case. The words of Henry Grady about the returning soldiers of the Civil War stirred the emotions of us all. We were a group brought together to honor the heroism of our forebears and all seemed to recognize that Henry Grady's speech did the same thing, only in terms of more immediacy. He was talking about the fathers and the husbands of some of the women in the society. That alone prepared them to hear the words of reconciliation that were the heart and soul of the speech. I was concerned I would not remember all the points he had made and, in fact, I did refer to my notes from time to time, but the words came as naturally as if they had been my own. When I got to the final section, I felt as though Henry were there beside me and it was his voice speaking:

> "Every foot of soil about the city in which I live is sacred as a battleground of the Republic. Every hill that invests it is hallowed to you by the blood of your brothers, who died for your victory, and doubly hallowed to us by the blood of those who died hopeless, but undaunted, in defeat—sacred soil to all of us, rich with memories that make us purer and stronger and better—silent, but staunch witnesses in its red desolation of the matchless valor of

American hearts and the deathless glory of American arms—
speaking an eloquent witness in its peace and prosperity to
the indissoluble union of American states and the
imperishable brotherhood of the American people."

When I finished, I was exhausted. I hadn't realized the
emotional intensity of the speech would take so much from me. I
smiled faintly at the assembly, who silently stared at me for a
moment, then burst into applause that surrounded me like an
onrushing wave. I was stunned. The audience was on its feet, waving
flags and cheering. I turned to Mrs. Harrison who, for once, seemed
pleased to have the crowd out of control. She motioned me back to
the podium and I nodded to each side of the room in recognition,
then sat down. My knees were about to fail me. Mrs. Harrison
recognized a woman from the back of the auditorium who came
forward. It was Mrs. Edward Roby of Chicago. She had obviously
been crying. As she stood to speak she handed me a sheaf of papers,
then announced it was a copy of the National Anthem, autographed
by Francis Scott Key, which she wished to present to the society to
be given to the Daughters of the State of Massachusetts. Then she
turned to me and said, "I want Mrs. Hagan to make the
presentation in honor of the stirring words she has delivered to us
today."

In the midst of renewed applause, I knew I would have to
make a response. If only I could be offstage for a moment to compose
a fittingly patriotic reply, but there was no chance of that. Mrs.
Roby walked to my side, took my arm, and led me to the podium
and then stepped aside. The applause continued, but I held my
hand up and they became still, once again.

"In the memory of those who have died that we might live
together in freedom, I accept this document and present it to the
Massachusetts Chapter of the Daughters of the American
Revolution, knowing that as they first fought for our liberty, the
Daughters across the nation will stand together that all mankind
shall be free."

I stepped back from the podium and quickly left the stage,

trembling at the response I had received and wondering at the words I had spoken. I thought back to the drawing room conversations I had had with Henry Grady before I had married. I knew, somehow, that he was aware that his words lived on, and my part in delivering them had been a blessing to me. The following morning, cousin Mary came bursting into the sitting room waving a Washington paper in her hand. "Sallie, you won't believe this. Your speech made the front page. Just listen to this: 'Mrs. Hugh Hagan, a remarkably poised young woman from Atlanta, delivered a recitation of Henry Grady's famous speech to the New England Society. Although the message of *The New South* has been widely circulated since Mr. Grady's death in 1886, all who heard it agreed it was the high point of the convention of the First Continental Congress of the Daughters of the American Revolution. Mrs. Hagan possesses a stage presence that handsomely augmented the stirring words of the great editor of *The Atlanta Constitution.*' What do you think of that!" she inquired, laying the paper in my lap. I didn't know what to think. The whole episode had risen far beyond anything I had expected or, as far as I could tell, deserved.

"And here's some more news that I heard in the dining room this morning," Mary continued. "You're going to be nominated for one of the Vice Presidents General."

"That's not possible. I'm too young to be anything but a member of the DAR. You or Mrs. Dickson should be the ones who are the leaders. I just read that speech as a favor to you since you didn't want to stand up in front of all those people." I felt ashamed that I had moved ahead of my elders and by a trick of fate had stepped off with the honors that should have been theirs.

"Don't be ridiculous, Sallie. Neither Mrs. Dickson nor I has the ability to lead anything like you do. You *are* young, but so is this organization. If the leadership is filled with old biddies, then it will never amount to anything. You saw what happened to poor Mrs. Harrison the other day. She's a dear, but she certainly can't run a meeting. They need strong, young leaders like you. You'll make us all so proud of you, Sallie."

I thought about it and decided maybe I wouldn't be elected. I had seen the ugly head of politics raised before and I was sure that there would be some who agreed that I was an upstart whose only accomplishment was reading the speech a famous man had given years before. That certainly wouldn't qualify me for leadership. Mammy had been sitting on the floor playing with little Hugh taking in the whole conversation. The weather had been disagreeable ever since we arrived in Washington, so she and Hugh had been confined to the house. I had noticed she had been increasingly edgy.

When the election came, I was stunned at the unanimous support I received and very uneasy about my ability to live up to whatever expectations they had for me. My picture, along with those of the other officers, was on the front page of the newspaper. I sat down and read it to Mammy.

"Shucks, dat don't mean nuthin'. Nuthin' don' mean a thing 'less you serve de Lawd an' does right. We been here three days an' me an' dis chile ain' seed nuthin' of you 'cept when you come in an' change yo' clothes. Hit's da trufe." She was almost in tears.

Mammy had so looked forward to the trip to Washington. I knew she was counting on telling the other servants all the stories of "when me and Miss Sallie wuz in Washin'ton." She still had not gotten over the Pullman incident and was convinced that all sorts of things were going on that "no good woman, white or colored, would be doin'." Tender-hearted old Mammy had turned into a hard mentor and I felt badly that I had had so little time for them, but there was nothing I could do to change it. In just a few hours, the officers of the DAR were due at The White House to be received by President Benjamin Harrison.

"Mammy, as soon as all this is over, I promise I will make it up to you, but right now, I need you to help me get dressed. I walked to the closet and got out the Holtzward gown that Hugh had bought me in Vienna. There were dozens of hooks and Mammy was in no hurry to help me with them.

"Please hurry, Mammy," I implored, not wanting to be late for the reception.

"Don' matter if you be late to da 'ception. You better set yo' mind on bein' late to heb'n."

"Forget about heaven, Mammy. Mrs. Harrison will be furious if I'm late to meet the President."

"He don' matter, neither. Da Prezzerdint ain' no better'n nobody else when we stands befo' da jedgment seat of God. No, suh! Da 'postle Paul, he say . . . ."

"Mammy, for heaven's sake, hush up and get me out of here. I'm going to be disgraced if I'm late."

"Nuthin' ain' no disgrace if'n you behaves yo'self. I seen Miz Dickson in dat train car disgrace herself and now you fixin' to do da same thing."

As soon as I was buttoned I grabbed my wrap and was headed for the door, but not before Mammy got in her parting shot. "You sez you goin' to da Prezzerdint's house, but Jesus knows, I dunno whar you is going. Since Mrs. Dickson act dat way, no tellin' what you might be up to."

I was out the door without a reply. It was too ridiculous to dignify with discussion, but I was upset. Despite all my rushing around I was late getting to The East Room. The atmosphere was charged with *bon commaradie* but President and Mrs. Harrison had already received most of their guests. I was embarrassed to come to the receiving line by myself, but Mrs. Harrison saw me approaching and walked up to greet me. "Mr. President, may I present Mrs. Hugh Hagan," she announced. It had never occurred to me that I would be in a similar situation to which my mother had found herself forty-four years previously. I wished I had asked her for a bit of protocol before I left Atlanta, but the idea of a reception at The White House was the furthest thing from my mind. The President took my hand and bowed graciously.

"This is indeed a pleasure, Mrs. Hagan. My wife has spoken of your wonderful speech at the meeting the other day and I read the account in *The Washington Post*. A most impressive account, I should say. You should feel quite proud."

"Thank you, Mr. President. The credit, of course, goes entirely to Mr. Grady. I simply delivered his remarks."

"Ah, and well thought-out they were. Henry was a fine man. I often wonder what he might have accomplished had he lived. He might have been standing here instead of me!"

I moved on down the line, meeting the members of the cabinet and several senators. I found myself wondering if the counterpart of Mr. Lyons from Lyonsdale were in the room. Having heard the stories of Washington social life from Mother made the evening all the more enchanting. The following morning, *The Post* gave an account of the reception which I read to Mammy, hoping it would convince her I had not been "mis'havin' myself," as she had put it.

> Mrs. Harrison gave a brilliant reception from eight to ten last evening at The White House for the Regents of the Daughters of the American Revolution. The guests, after greeting the President and Mrs. Harrison, spent the evening in social fashion, strolling through The East Room, the Red Parlor, corridors, and conservatory which were all open, brightly lighted and decorated with plants and flowers. Mrs. Harrison's gown was of mauve satin and brocaded down either of the side panels in a broad, white-flowered border. The Marine Band in the outer corridor played throughout the reception. Shortly after nine o'clock a collation was served honoring the guests in the private dining room."

"There," I told Mammy, "That's where I was last night, not off into some mischief as you seemed to think."

"Don' make no difference where you wuz at. You warn't here with me and da baby. We shoulda' stayed on Peachtree," she said, shaking her head.

"Oh, Mammy, I'm so sorry. We'll stay an extra day and we will see Washington, just the three of us. I promise. Nobody will go but you, me and Hugh. That will make up for how busy I've been." Mammy's eyes brightened at the prospect.

The next morning when she was getting Hugh dressed, I overheard the conversation. "Put yo' foot in an' push. We gotta git yo' pants on 'cause we gwina go sight-see. We gwina go to da Corper's Art Gall'ry and da Smithers Instute an' all sorts of things.

Jes' me and you and yo mama. None of dem foolish folks she been runnin' round with is gwina bother us no mo',"she said with finality, giving Hugh a little pat on the rump as she buckled his shoes.

Just as we started down the steps the doorbell rang. Lamar called to Ellen, the downstairs maid, "I'm not at home!"

When Ellen opened the door, it was Mrs. Fitzhugh Pennington, a well-known lady of fashion in Washington.

"Mrs. Lipscomb's not at home," Ellen dutifully lied.

"Oh, of course she is, Ellen," Mrs. Pennington murmured, letting herself into the foyer. "Just tell her I'm here and I want to see her for a few minutes."

"I'll be right down," Lamar called over the bannister, as Ellen showed the guest into the front parlor.

Mammy took a look at me and I could see trouble brewing in her eyes. "Honey, did you heah Miss Lamar jes' tell dat lie? An' bless da Lawd, da woman kotched her 'fore Ellen had da words outta her mouf. Miss Lamar used to be a good woman 'fore she come up here wid all dese sinners."

Efforts to explain to Mammy how things worked in Washington were to no avail and Lamar was reduced to the ranks of the sinful along with cousin Mary and Mrs. Dickson. "Don' try to make it sound no better, Miss Sallie. She don tol' a lie and right here in front of dis chile. How we eber gon' teach him to tell da trufe if'n he hears lies all da time? We bes' be gettin' outta here 'fore we kotch dat lyin' disease. Eberbody in Washin'ton tells lies, I do believe."

We took our carriage to The Corcoran Art Gallery and were surprised to find they would not allow children in the museum. "Wha' chu' talkin' 'bout, mister man?" Mammy confronted the guard. "Dis here chile is a friend of da Prezzerdint's," she said, jerking her thumb in my direction. "I bet you don' want him to come down here and tell you what fo, does you?" She was persuasive, but to no avail. I took Hugh from her arms and convinced Mammy to go in with another lady, who volunteered to be her escort.

"Hugh and I will sit here and watch the carriages come and

go. You have a good time and we'll be here when you get back." Mammy seemed resigned, but she was intent on seeing the "Corper's Art Gall'ry," so in she went. In less than five minutes she was back, scurrying down the steps with her skirts flying behind. She snatched Hugh from my lap.

"Git outta here as quick as you can, Miss Sallie. I sho' gwina tell Miss Mary Willis what kinda place you tuck me to, das a fact!"

"Come on back, Mammy. You haven't seen a thing yet. I want you to see all the famous pictures they have here."

"Ain't seed nuthin', ain't I? I seed mo' nekkid wimmen dan' I eber seed before. Ain' a picture in dat whole place where da lady got her clothes on. Wha'chu mean goin' in dere? No wonder dey don' let da chillun go. What da doctor gwina think when I tells him 'bout dis? Ain' nuthin' but sin in dis whole city, I can tell you dat!"

It was pointless to explain, so we took our carriage down Constitution Avenue to The Smithsonian Institute. Mammy didn't say a word the entire way. Her mouth was clamped shut like a vise and looking neither to the left nor the right, she kept Hugh on her lap. He was enjoying himself immensely, listening to the rhythmic cadence of the hooves on the cobblestone. Once we got into the Smithsonian, things improved. She was delighted with the displays of the dinosaurs and the stuffed animals. She explained it all to Hugh in a loud voice which soon drew a following. The regular tour guides stepped aside and let her hold forth. Although the information she gave bore no relation to the actual facts, she was so enthusiastic it was charming.

"Lookit da size of dem teef," she exclaimed when peering up at a monstrous-looking lizard. "I bet he could eat a whole ham in one bite. But don'chu worry, Hugh. He ain' gwina get one sniff of you. Mammy see to dat!" Watching her explain everything to Hugh as though they were the only ones in the museum was a delight. Several patrons asked me who she was and I told them she was my special mother whom God had sent to help me. And she was, although she could be a trial when she didn't understand what was happening around her.

The trip to "The Smithers Instute" was the highlight for Mammy, but true to her word, as soon as we stepped out of the carriage at Mother's house, she reported in great detail with much gesticulating and rolling of her eyes all the sinful behavior of cousin Mary and Mrs. Dickson as well as the pictures of the naked ladies that I "made her look at."

Mother smiled and said, "Thank you for taking such good care of my family, Mammy. Things have changed a lot since you were a little girl. With all the new inventions, customs have changed and what seems odd to you is the way things are done now."

When Mother had finished her explanation, Mammy thought it over for a minute then said, "Miss Mary Willis, I jes' wants to ast you one mo' thing 'bout dat railroad car wid da bedsteads stacked up."

"Yes, of course. What is it, Mammy?"

"Is da men folks changed, too? I neber seed one yet what would stay in da bedstead by hisself."

"Of course, they've changed. A gentleman always conducts himself properly."

"But how you gwina tell a gent'mun from a jes' a plain ol' fashioned man?"

Mother smiled and looked at me. Neither of us had the answer to that, so we put our arms around Mammy and walked on either side of her into the house.

Our decision to move to Atlanta had been well-founded. With his Viennese training in neurology, Hugh brought a new dimension to medical practice in the South. His office was only a stone's throw from our house, which was large enough to accommodate his practice, had he wished to locate it there. I asked him about it, but he said that between Mammy Sophy looking over his shoulder and little Hugh running in and out of the office, he would never get anything done. As it turned out, it was a good thing that we had such a large house. Mother was becoming less able to get around by herself. Arthritis had set up in both hips, and even with the servants to help, she was somewhat limited. I decided that Mother needed to get out of her home and come live with us. We had plenty of room and I was expecting another baby. At first, Mother was reluctant, but when she decided that she should bring Mammy Phyllis with her, it would seem more like home. Hugh was most agreeable and took my mother in as if she had been his own.

The idea of another child was a happy thought. Hugh would soon be four and a half. He was such an active little boy and quite independent, but we felt that having a brother or sister would be a good thing for him. Had we known what lay ahead, perhaps we might have had second thoughts, but the undetermined nature of the future cannot keep one from making plans in the present.

When Willis was born Hugh was delighted with the addition of a brother. Mammy Sophy was in her element, and if Mother thought she would have an active role in looking after Willis, Mammy had a different idea. If I wasn't available, Mammy was right there to step into the action. I marveled at her stamina. No one knew how old she was, but she was certainly in her late seventies, if not beyond. Although she didn't seem to eat a lot, her weight continued to rise and it was hard for her to get around with the speed to which she was accustomed. I never heard her complain, and if she thought I was watching, she would not stop to rest when she reached the top of the stairs. Her sense of pride in herself was as strong as in any person I ever knew. I tried to get her to let Mother help.

"No, suh!" she announced when I suggested that she slow down a little. "I don' need to slow down. Dat's for ol' folks. I can do jes' as much work as I could when I was yo' age. I can do mo' work right now dan you can, Miss Sallie."

I had to believe she was right, but Hugh suggested that she might have something wrong with her heart because of the swelling of her ankles and her shortness of breath when she climbed the stairs. He tried to talk to her, too.

"If'n you stood on yo' feets all day long, yo' ankles be swoll up, too, Doctor. Ain' nuthin wrong wif my heart. Hit's jes' thumpin' right 'long." Hugh smiled and shook his head. He knew there was no point in pursuing it.

One of the real worries about babies was how many of them died in infancy. The cemeteries were full of tiny graves, children who had lived a month or less. Most died from intestinal problems which probably came from contaminated milk and drinking water. Very little was known of sanitation. The sewers ran open behind the houses and never far from the wells. Springs from which some of the water came flowed out from fields where livestock of all sorts grazed. Whooping cough, measles, chicken pox were diseases with which every child had to contend, but the real terrors were typhoid and smallpox. Although vaccination had been known for almost a hundred years, there were many who did not have their children take the shots. Hugh was insistent that ours would, and although I had heard stories of terrible things happening as a result of the vaccination, both our sons had no difficulty. Typhoid was another problem. There was no known treatment that seemed effective and, although it was thought to come from sewage and other filth, no one seemed too concerned about cleaning up the drainage ditches. Every time one of the children became cranky and developed a fever, I would fear the worst. Fortunately, in a few days they were usually back to their happy selves and I would breathe more easily until the next crisis. Hugh was less concerned than I was due, I suspect, to his medical training, but I found little comfort in that.

I realized how fortunate I was to have so much help around the house. Many of my friends had to do virtually everything for their children, leaving little time for outside interests. Had I been in that situation, I would have done the same, but with Mammy in charge, Mother became a willing assistant and I was able to devote considerable time to the DAR and other interests. In 1894 a project appeared which I found very exciting: The Cotton States and International Exposition which was scheduled to open in Atlanta in 1895.

When the requests went out to all the states to participate in the Exposition, the response was immediate and immense. The influence of Henry Grady was still at work, and enthusiasm for a national project was testimony that his words were being heeded.

The directors of the Exposition appointed Mrs. Joseph Thompson as President of the Woman's Board, and in that role she made the choices of those who would serve under her. The number of distinguished, albeit somewhat older, matrons was impressive, and many were anxious to be appointed. Mrs. Thompson astounded the community when she named Emma Mims as her first appointee. While Emma was well known in Atlanta society, she was not yet thirty years old and had been selected in advance of many more experienced women. I was amused at the uproar it caused, but my amusement was short-lived when a messenger from the Exposition Board arrived at the house informing me that I, too, had been appointed. I was slightly younger than Emma and not nearly as well known. Even worse, I had been appointed as chairman of Ways and Means, one of the key committees.

"What in the world are those people thinking about?" was the general reaction. "Emma Mims and Sallie Hagan are still children and they're put at the top of the committee. It's an outrage!"

Things quieted down a bit when the other appointees were of the more traditional nature. I certainly didn't want to cause a rift in the community, but it was an exciting opportunity. I suspected that Emma had been behind my appointment, but when I asked her she said that my work in the DAR as a Vice President General had caught the eye of many and that my personal friendship with Henry Grady had been a key factor. Whatever the reasons, I was grateful. There was one other reason they may have wanted me: I could act as a bridge between the society women and the rest of the organization; it was a position of political peacekeeping. There were women who needed to be appointed because we needed their husbands' support, but often they weren't really qualified to do any particular job. In some cases they could actually be a liability.

Sarah Lou Maupin was just such a case. Her husband, years her senior, was a major industrialist, but his community involvement was usually through Sarah Lou. Her problem was her beauty. She was strikingly handsome, taller by a head than most of us, had raven black hair, skin as fair as apple blossoms, and deep-set green eyes that could look right through you. She would be an ornament to any gathering, but she was wildly flirtatious. The older men would lose all sense of reason in response to her presence. The last thing we needed was some sort of blowup because of her. The older women were very suspicious of her, particularly when they saw more animation from their husbands than they had seen in twenty years. The younger women were jealous of her beauty and charm. I personally thought she was delightful and never knew her to do anything that seemed questionable. I had a little talk with her and she, although surprised, accepted my advice that she keep a low profile with any of the men. It would be bad for their hearts, I suggested. That was the first time I realized that Ways and Means was going to be used as a place of refuge for women who might cause a problem. In the end, it all worked to my advantage because the committee became quite large and was filled with women of special talent. Some were old, some were young, some were socially very prominent and others not, but they all worked together as good friends and learned to respect each other. I was fortunate to be able to blend such a diverse group into a cohesive unit, but much of the credit goes to some of the older women with whom I served. They had influence that I could not have wielded, but they had the maturity to use it in a way that I might not have understood even if I had had the power. Mrs. Black, whose sons were Judge William Black of New York and Eugene Black of the Board of Governors of the Federal Reserve Board, was my chief ally. Mrs. Grant Wilkins, the mother of Dr. Charles Wilkins, one of the most prominent physicians in Atlanta, was the committee treasurer. The success of Ways and Means was due, in no small part, to them.

The strongest committee was the Colonial Committee, headed by Mrs. William Lawson Peel. It was her job to collect treasures from the Colonial period, not just from the original thirteen states, but from all over the country, and she did just that. Her *piece de resistance* was convincing the City of Philadelphia that the Liberty Bell would have to be moved to Atlanta for the Exposition. I have no idea how she brought that about, but for the year of 1895 the bell was the centerpiece of the Colonial Exhibition. I don't think it had ever left the city before and certainly not since. At the opening ceremony, Mrs. Adlai Stevenson, wife of the Vice President said it was appropriate that the bell should be in the "Mecca of the New South." It was a grand moment. If only Henry Grady could have seen it.

As part of the symbolism of unity, the committee planned a Grant-Davis day. The widows of General Grant and Jefferson Davis were invited to attend. When I told Mother that Varina Davis might be coming to Atlanta, she was delighted. She wrote Varina and extended a personal invitation to stay with us. Since I had met her several years before, I was just as excited. We waited long days for her reply.

Guene's Inn
Narragansett Pier
September 5, 1895

My dear Mary Willis:

I should have long since answered your kind letter but for the hope I vainly cherished that I could come to the Exposition and my sincere desire to make it a certainty before writing you. To the proposition of the ladies to make a day for Mrs. Grant and myself, I can only answer that any respect and consideration given to Mrs. Grant by our own people would give me pleasure and I feel sure we should mutually have enjoyed meeting under such auspicious circumstances, but I am too much an invalid to encounter the fatigue of visiting the Exposition.

I shall look from a distance with much pride and expectation of your complete success.

Mrs. Grant has just left here with Mr. Jackson and you could not have had a more enthusiastic and judicious advocate than she has proved. I, for one, was most sorry to give her up.

Neither you nor your family has passed out of my tired heart. I cling to the memory of our dear old times when brother Howell and sister Mayon were in the strong current of their successful lives, when you and I were girlish friends. I was twenty-two and you were only nineteen. How time does fly.

Since I have found out the same blood flows in our veins I am doubly anxious to see you again. Kiss your daughter for me and thank her for the invitation.

I hope we might be able to meet next spring if I am able to get home in March. With dear love, I am,

Affectionately yours,
Mrs. Jefferson Davis (Varina)

Mother was saddened, as was I, that we would not see her again. She was such an important figure in Mother's early life, and my exposure to her, although brief, several years earlier was a pleasant memory.

I worried that my involvement in civic affairs were taking time from Hugh. His hours were long, and increasingly he was called to give lectures at the Atlanta College of Medicine or in other universities around the South. He seemed tired most of the time, although he never complained about it. Quiet by nature, he seemed more so now than when we had first married. His involvement with the children was infrequent since they were usually in bed by the time he arrived home, but he was an attentive father. My efforts to include him in my activities only added to his busy schedule, and I felt guilty about asking him to attend gatherings when he seemed so tired. Gradually, we drifted into a level of accommodation where we each understood the demands time made on the other.

Fatigue was a problem for me, too. One afternoon when I was returning from the Exposition in a state of collapse, Mammy sidled up to me with a smile on her face.

"I seed da Prezzerdint and his lady today."

I was too exhausted to care, but I smiled and said, "I'm so glad you did, Mammy."

"I talked to Miz Prezzerdint, too." She beamed at me.

"I'm sure you did," I replied, wondering if Mammy was making up the story. She could see the skepticism in my eyes.

"You think I done forgot how to talk?"

"Lord, no, Mammy. That's something you'd never forget. I was just wondering how you stopped the procession and had a conversation the President and his wife."

"Sposin' da carriages stalled right in front of our yard where me and da chillun was playin'?"

"Even that wouldn't give you a chance to talk to the President or his wife."

"How come it wouldn't? I 'spect if'n a lady bow an' smile an' wave her hand at me, hit look like she want to pass a word or two, don't it? Well, I tuck it dat way and I walk out to da carriage wif da chillun. Hugh, he act like a reg'lar gent'mun. He tuck off his hat and bowed to da lady and Willis he wave his hand. Den I says, 'Howdy,' an ax how she gettin' along? She say de chillun is pow'ful sweet. I tells her dey da chillun of Dr. Hagan. She say she know you an' axt where you is at and I sez you off in da crowd runnin' da whole shebang. We neber had no mo' chance to talk 'cause da carriages tuck off down da street, but she wave an' me and we smiled at each 'nother right considerable."

I was convinced. Having met Mrs. Harrison, I could imagine how gracious she was. The picture of her having a chat with Mammy under the spreading magnolia with my children standing at her side is one I still treasure.

The next afternoon, I was leaving the house to finish up some Exposition business when Mammy called me.

"Hold on, Miss Sallie. Miz Lowe want to speak to you on da telerfome."

"Tell her I'm not home," I called over my shoulder.

"Who me? No, suh! I ain' gwina tell no lie."

"It's not a lie. I'm out here on the sidewalk," I told her, continuing to walk.

"Come heah, chile. Dis minute. I'se gwina tell yo' ma. You ain't been right eber since yo'cousin Mary went wrong in dat sleepin' car. Come on back heah!"

On the phone Mrs. Lowe started into an excited conversation

of which I understood little because of Mammy's ongoing tirade about the truth.

"And don't fail me, Sallie. Be at my house at three o'clock sharp," she instructed.

"I'll come as soon as I can, Mrs. Lowe, but I have to meet Mrs. Black at the lawyer's office at three."

"Break it! Break it! I'll never forgive you if you fail me," she shrieked.

Mrs. Lowe was always one for drama verging on hysteria, but I promised and was able to get to her house only moderately late. I still didn't know what all the excitement was about. Instead of the usual elegance and order of Mrs. Lowe's house, I was surprised to see all the furniture on the first floor had been cleared away and replaced by row-on-row of chairs. I found a vacant seat off to the side and began to wonder at the assemblage of women who filled the house.

"Where were you, Sallie? You've just missed hearing Jenny June speak." An attractive woman in her late fifties was just taking her seat in the midst of lady-like applause.

"I told you. Mrs. Black and I had to meet with the lawyers about some Exposition finances. It went well and I'm sorry I'm late." That was the truth, but I had had little understanding of the legal matters of finance. That was Mrs. Black's job and I was there for moral support. Mrs. Lowe wrinkled her nose.

"Finance! I didn't know you were good with numbers."

Before I could reply, she had scurried to the front of the room at the announcement that the floor was open for nominations. Nominations for what, I wondered?

The whole thing had an air of being pre-planned but I still didn't know what the organization was about or why they were electing officers. Mrs. Lowe was elected president and Mrs. William A. Hemphill, vice president. As soon as that office was filled, Mrs. Hemphill asked for the floor.

"Madam President, my thanks to the society for honoring me with the office of vice president which I accept with the provision that I shall no longer be addressed as Mrs. William A. Hemphill, but rather as Emma Belle Hemphill." Without further explanation she took her seat.

I caught my breath, as did many others, at such a display of feminine independence from such a gentle and conservative woman as Emma Belle. I leaned over to Mrs. Lowe and asked, "What in the world is all of this about?"

For an answer, I got a pinch and "Hush and listen!"

Sarah Grant Jackson was elected secretary, then to my amazement, I was nominated for treasurer. I rose to object, but Mrs. Lowe pulled me back to my seat. "Just sit there and be quiet," she hissed. "Don't ruin this wonderful meeting."

"Wonderful meeting of what? And treasurer? I can't even keep account of my own money! I can't be an officer in this thing— whatever it is—and certainly *not* treasurer."

"Just be quiet, Sallie. I'll take care of the money, but I need you in this office," Mrs. Lowe whispered.

While our discussion was going on, I was elected by acclamation. "Please, Mrs. Lowe," I begged, "Let me resign now. You know I can't attend the meetings. I have too much to do already."

"You're the duly elected treasurer and that's that," she announced. "I'll look after the money for you if you can't be here."

After the meeting, I finally found out what the organization was: The National Organization of Women's Club. I had no idea what their purpose was or why I should be involved in it, even at a local level, but it turned out to be Providential in what life would hold for me in the future. I would never have dreamed that what I learned from Mrs. Lowe, her associates and The National Women's Club would change the direction of my life in a city of which I had never heard.

I had apprehensions about my inability to function as treasurer and they were more than justified. I attended the meetings when I could, but in my absence, Mrs. Lowe would collect the dues, and dump them in a paper sack along with a list of who had paid. Unfortunately, the amount in the sack never came close to matching the amount on the tally sheets. I tried to enlist Hugh and Mother's help, but they were thoroughly amused at my predicament and laughed immoderately at my distress.

"They're going to put me in jail for embezzlement," I wailed, when I found I was fifty dollars short.

"Don't worry, Sallie. Mammy will bring you extra food and we'll come visit on weekends," Hugh laughed.

They may have thought it was amusing, but I was anything but happy. I went to Rob Maddox, a friend whose father was president of The Bank of Atlanta. I told him my sorry predicament. and I was fearful that I might be short even more money. He was cheerful about the whole thing and assured me he would find the missing funds for me. The next day he called and said that I was fifty dollars to the good. Where in the world that money came from I have no idea. I even wondered if Hugh had slipped some extra into my sack, but it really didn't matter. I was a nervous wreck about the whole thing and was off to the board meeting to hand in my resignation, no matter what. When I told them that I had more money than I was supposed to, they were delighted and said I was the *perfect* treasurer. After an inordinate amount of jesting at my poor expense, they accepted my resignation, but insisted that I remain as an active member. I was happy to do that, but resolved that I would never handle anyone else's money again. Leading an organization—that I might be able to do, but leave the finances to someone else.

At dinner that evening, Hugh and Mother were relieved, too, I think, that I was out from under a job that I couldn't do. I asked Hugh and Mother if they knew anything about the extra funds and they looked at each other and smiled. "Of course not. You just counted wrong some where," Hugh suggested.

"And that made the money grow? I don't think so, Hugh." But there was no budging them. It was a good thing Mammy didn't understand what was happening or they would have gotten one of her lectures about honesty.

Hugh's schedule and his duties in the medical society continued to increase during the year. I was so pleased he was doing well. I took time to reflect on how blessed our lives had been. It was a time of wonder and of joy. Except for the death of my father, not a ripple of sadness had entered my life. My girlhood had blended so perfectly into the life of a comrade husband who lived his ideals and inspired all those around him. I heard from many sources how his brilliance brought comfort and cure, regardless of their economic status. Hugh and Willis, now nine and four, were a joy for us all. Mammy, although she was tired and aging rapidly, never lost her sense of how important she was to all of us. Mother, despite her infirmities, continued to be an active part of the family. It was, in many ways, an idyllic time. At age thirty-three, I suppose most of us thought life would always go on in such a wonderful way. There's a sense of invulnerability that youth carries, but it can be stripped away with no warning.

Looking back, there were warnings, but both Hugh and I ignored them. His sense of fatigue was getting the best of him and there was no denying that. In the spring of 1898, it was apparent that he needed a rest. I suggested that Hugh and I should take several weeks of rest at Stone Mountain. There were a number of homes there available for such a purpose and Howell Clark arranged for one where he and his wife had vacationed. We set out early on the morning of March 20, the first day of spring. Mammy and mother would look after the boys while we were gone. I remember so well them standing on the porch waving good-bye.

We talked little on the ride through town, but as we were entering the countryside east of Atlanta, I noticed that Hugh had been looking to the left for quite some time and didn't seem to be paying much attention to the horse or the road.

"Hugh, what are you thinking about so hard?" I asked.

He didn't reply, or turn to look at me so I leaned over to see his face. His eyes were fixed in a stare but he didn't appear to be seeing. His mouth was drawn to the left and his left hand had dropped the rein. As I watched his left arm slid away from his lap and he began to toppled from the carriage seat.

"Hugh! What's the matter?" I screamed, but of course he didn't answer. I had startled the horse who began to skitter off the road. Somehow, I was able to keep Hugh in the seat and stop the horse.

I jumped down and ran to the other side of the carriage so I could see him better. It was obvious he was having a stroke. A farmer in a nearby field saw I was in trouble and came to help. We laid him in the back of the carriage and then some men helped me get the carriage back home.

The doctors came but there was little they could do. After all his study and brilliance in the field of neurology, it was a one of the diseases that he had sought to understand that was taking his life. Family and friends gathered, but on March 22, 1898, my dear Hugh died.

Little Hugh was stunned, but he understood what had happened. Willis, only four and-a-half, had more trouble. For months, he would sit on the front porch in the afternoon, looking down Peachtree, waiting to see his daddy quickly stepping toward home. By dinner time, he would silently come in and climb up in Mammy's lap.

Mammy cried as if it had been her own son who had died. She held me in her arms most of that afternoon, saying over and over, "Don'chu' fret none, Miss Sallie. He be waitin' for you on da other side." She meant well, but I was on this side and what would I ever do without my dear, sweet Hugh?

On the afternoon of the funeral I couldn't find Hugh. Willis was in his room with Mammy, but Hugh was no where to be found. Finally, I looked in his father's study and there he was, sitting at Hugh's desk, a large medical book open in front of him.

"Oh, Hugh! What are you doing? It's time for us to be going to the church."

He looked at the clock on the all and said, "Yes, it is. I'm studying to be a doctor so I can take care of you and Willis. I'll just leave these books here until we get back."

And that's just what he did. In the days ahead while Willis was waiting from his father, Hugh would be looking at the medical books and trying to read them. It was a sight the recollection of which still brings tears.

The children became the central focus of my life. Many of my activities with the DAR and the Woman's Club, I left to others. Being with the Hugh and Willis seemed to be the most important thing, but in the months that followed, I felt a sense of increasing restlessness. By the spring of 1899, I was beginning to get out more and think of what I would do with the rest of my life. The boys would be grown before I knew it, and I didn't want to be passed by without plans of my own. Before I had time to act on those feelings, Mother died. She had been suffering from arthritis for years, and in the months after Hugh's death, the zest for living which had been such a part of her life seemed to wane. Her death came peacefully, but no less painfully for me. With my husband and both parents gone, I would have felt quite alone in the world had it not been for Lucy and Wellborn along with the multitude of friends that I had from across the country. They were a support without which I couldn't have survived. By the sympathy of friends, God expresses himself, and it was largely for their sakes that I kept my aching heart largely to myself.

The house on Peachtree, once so full of life and joy, was as barren as a dogwood in December. No matter what I did, I couldn't seem to shake the gloom that was all around. Lucy and Wellborn came to my rescue. They suggested that we move in with them. Their children were grown and they had more than enough space. Mammy could come with us, but for the rest of the servants, I had to find other positions. The day we walked out of the house I felt as though my life had become a book with no writing on the pages. I knew that Hugh would want us to move on, to find a new life, but it was going to be a long, hard struggle.

As I began to re-enter normal life, it was just around the edges— a dinner gathering here, a meeting of the Woman's Club there. I felt as though I was drifting, but I had a longing and spiritual hunger for adjustment that was eating into my soul.

It was my old friend, Clark Howell, who first brought a new outside interest to my life. His mother never quite got over our not getting married but he now had a wonderful family of his own. I still remembered vividly the near-duel at Mt. Airy that I had precipitated, but we still remained close friends, just as we had been growing up in the same neighborhood. One afternoon, we were sitting on the veranda discussing nothing in particular, but just enjoying the warm, fall weather when he said, "Sallie, why don't you write?"

"Write? What would I write about? Are you making fun of me, Clark?"

"Of course not," he answered. "Now listen to me," he really looked quite fatherly, "You've imprisoned yourself here for months. That's no way to live. Hugh wouldn't want it and certainly your mother wouldn't, either. Don't lose touch with the world and rear those boys without teaching them the wonders waiting out there for them . . . for you, too."

"Oh, Clark, don't be stupid. I read and keep up. I'm seeing that the boys are exposed to lots of different things."

"That's true, but you're reading with your mind in the past. You're thirty-six and you've got half your life to live. I don't know anyone who can tell a story better than you, and you've certainly had wonderful experiences all over the world. You should write about them. Write about the dinner party scene—that would be a laugh or two. I'll publish whatever you do. Try it—just for fun."

After he left, I thought about it. He was right about one thing: I had seen a lot and I did enjoy talking about it. The real question was what could I say that would be of interest to anyone else? As I sat there, pondering, Mammy Sophy walked across the front yard, She was bent over and always had her head down, watching every step she took. Her hickory stick left a dent in the grass at every placement, so much weight she was putting on it. I thought about what a remarkable woman she was, about all the outrageous things she said, fully believing them to be true. And a kinder, better woman never lived, I was certain of that. Maybe I could write a story about her. Growing up as a slave girl and becoming like a mother to me and my children. The idea had possibilities. As I was mulling this over, Mammy Phyllis, almost as old as Mammy Sophy, came walking down the street. They were related in some way, although we could never figure out exactly how. Before the war, it was difficult to straighten those things out.

Mammy Phyllis had just gotten back from a trip to Michigan with our neighbor, Mrs. George C. Smith. She had needed a servant to make the long trip with her and I had asked Mammy Phyllis to go. She plopped down in the chair next to me on the porch and launched off into a recounting of her northern adventures, particularly the northern servants.

"Lawd, honey, I'm so glad to git home agin," she panted, as she moved her carpet bag to the side so she could rock.

"Didn't you enjoy Michigan?"

"Michigan's all right, an' so is da white folks, but dem Yankee coloreds—I'm tellin you—whoopeee! Honey, dey thinks jes' 'cause dey got edgercation dey's fust class. Dat's da trufe. Dey's jes' like po' white trash dat gits rich an' thinks dey know eberthing. Edgercation done ruint da whole passel of'em!"

"But Mammy Phyllis," I interrupted, "You know how important school and education are. Your son is over in Tuskegee at Booker T. Washington's school and we're all so proud of him."

"I knows dat, but Booker T is differ'nt. Booker T, he learns'em to be gent'muns even if dey got a edgercation. Dem colored Yankees think as soon as dey can spell C-A-T dey's full quality folks and dey can't even fry an egg wit'out busting it up. Neber seed da likes of'em."

Maybe there was a story there—the difference in the life of the southern and northern Negroes. "Didn't they ask you to go to parties or anything? Did you feel left out?" I probed.

"Oh, dey ast me, all right, but I nev'r went."

"Ah, Mammy, I'm afraid riding in Mr. Smith's private rail car has turned your head."

"Tain't so. My head's settin' jes' like it always sets. But honey, dem private cars sho' is grand," she giggled. "Yes, my Lawd, and dat colored cook, he be fust class. Fust class, you hears me? He like to bust me wide open wid all dose vittles."

"Tell me about some of the things you did that you enjoyed—beside the food on the train, I mean."

"Well, da onliest 'joyment I had was goin' to a funeral. Some big somebody next do' to da house died, an' I went out on da sidewalk to see how folks up yonder laid out da dead. But Lawdy,

Miss Sallie, it wuz da most unfair funeral I ever seed! Yes suh! Instid of da widder comin' out to da gate where ev'body could see her, she made'em drive up to da side do'. She got in da carriage an ain' nobody got a look at her. Couldn' tell nuthin 'bout her veil, her bonnet, her frock, not nuthin'. How anybody gwina know if she be grievin' les' we gits a look at how she dress? Oh, it 'twuz a shame. Dat's what 'twuz," she said, shaking her head.

"Mammy, I believe you like to go to funerals."

"'Course I does. Eberbody likes to go to da funerals of dere friends, don' cha think? Oh, yes, I fergit to tell you day got da Daugthers of da Revelation up dere, too. I tol' Miz Smith dat Kitty and I try to get you to change da name to da Daughters of Zion. She say she thought dat were a purtier name than de Revelation and den she bust out laughin'.'"

"Didn't you go to church?"

"I never had to go to no church 'cause da white gent-muns come to see Miz Smith's ma and 'fore he went he pray da purtiest prayer I ever did hear. Lawd, honey, dat white man prayed like he was black as da ace of spades. I ain' never heerd a colored preacher pray no better'n dat. I tol' da cook on da private car he was da fust white man I ever seed who had a 'ligion good as a colored preacher. Yes, ma'am, dat man's heart was black, I don' care how white his face wuz. He could flat out talk to da Lawd."

For the next weeks, I listened carefully to Mammy Phyllis and her stories and soon had enough to write a short piece about her trip to Michigan. Clark, true to his word, but me in touch with *The Century Magazine*. It was accepted and placed in the Christmas issue. I was pleased that it had gone so well, but I really didn't think much would come of it. Shortly after its publication, a friend from New York sent me a clipping from *The New York Times*.

> From the land of Uncle Remus and Mars' Chan comes
> a new writer, a woman whose work will doubtless take its
> place among the writers of the Old South. The December
> issue of *The Century Magazine* carried a story, "Phyllis Visits
> Michigan," which chronicles the escapades of an elderly

servant from the deep South on her first trip to the "land of
the Yankees." Mrs. Hugh Hagan shows a skill in telling a
story which, while humorous, makes an important point
about the coming together of ethnic differences Her voice
will, no doubt, be heard again. We certainly hope so!

Well, that was a surprise. I had never expected that anyone
would think there was more where the Phyllis story came from,
but perhaps there was. I started writing down incidents from the
past that were important to me, but doing it in a light-hearted
style that I hoped would be of interest to others. I had no plan
about what to do with the work I was producing, and the benefits
of having something I enjoyed doing seemed reward enough in
itself. My writing was giving my life a focus that had been lost
since Hugh's death. I had devoted myself almost entirely to the
children, and my social contacts, by my own, choice had been
limited. I found a new sense of freedom in sitting down with a
blank piece of paper and watching the ink flow into a story that I
was recounting. Most of my friends knew of my writing and
encouraged me to keep it up, but I was surprised when a delegation
arrived one morning with the request that I do a public reading.

"Who in the world would come?" I asked, startled at the idea.

"Everyone we invite," replied Marsha Lane, who seemed to be
in charge. "We're going to rent the Grand Opera House and sell
tickets. The whole thing will be managed by The First Baptist
Church and we're going to use the proceeds for our orphanage. It's
wonderful cause and you're the perfect one to do it, Sallie. Your
family is well known, and since Hugh died, you can just imagine
what it must be like for children to have no father or mother. Your
little boys are so lucky, but many children aren't and you can help
them." She shook her head like a little exclamation point as if that
would settle the whole issue.

"Well, I don't know, Marsha. I've written a lot of things and
I've enjoyed doing them, but I'm far from sure I'm ready for a life
upon the wicked stage."

She looked offended. "This is anything but the wicked stage;

this is The First Baptist Church of Atlanta and we know a good thing when we see it."

"Oh, I was just teasing. Of course, it's a wonderful project, but I don't think I'm the one to do it."

"Well, you are and we've already had the pamphlets printed." She handed me one from her purse. There was a daguerreotype of me on the front over the title, "Stories of the Old South." Beneath there was a picture of a fine old mansion, carriage in front, with servants attending an elegant couple while children played under the live oaks.

"It looks as though I don't have a choice," I said, pleased, but a little distressed at their presumptuousness. "I'll do the best I can, but I wouldn't be surprised if there's no one there but you and me."

"Don't you worry about that, Sallie," Marsha assured me. "We'll fill the place. Everyone will have a wonderful time and we'll make a pile of money for the orphanage."

After they left, I hoped I had not made a big mistake. The idea of entertaining a whole theater full of people for an hour or more was a daunting prospect. It wasn't like writing an article which people could read—or not—at their leisure. There would be no place to hide if it fell flat.

Mammy Sophy was in her usual doubtful frame of mind. "I neber thought I'd see da day," she shook her head. "Dr. Johnson, he roll over in his grave if'n he knowed his daughter wuz tellin' stories in da thee ater."

"Oh, Mammy, he wouldn't either. He'd be glad we were trying to do something to help the orphans. And all the things I have to say will be interesting, don't you think?"

"Dey oughta let me give dat speech. I'd tell'em a few things about railroad cars, and wimmen folks that have pitchers made of'em wid no clothes on. Dat's whut I'd tell'em."

"And you would probably draw a big audience, too, Mammy." I had to bite my lip to keep from laughing.

As the day for the performance drew near, I wondered if I were about to make a fool of myself. Suppose there were only a handful of people who showed up? That wouldn't be my problem, I decided.

I wasn't the one who thought this up. The evening of the show, I was sitting in the dressing room at the Grand Opera House wondering what in the world I had gotten myself into. There had been a time, during my "Shakespeare period" at Waverly, that I would have given anything for a stage. Now that I had one, I wished I were anywhere but there.

As I stood in the wings, Marsha made an overly generous introduction after thanking everyone for their support. When I walked on to the stage, I couldn't see anyone for the footlights, but from the applause, I could tell the theater was full, from the pit to the second gallery. It wasn't me they had come to hear, but to support a worthy cause. When the Baptists decide to do something, they don't go half-way.

Lent had just started and I knew a number of people had just returned from *Mardi Gras,* so I started off with a story about what happens to prominent and dignified people from Atlanta with a little too much bourbon on board when they fall into the hands of Cajuns with an interest in voodoo. Of course, I made the whole thing up, but it had enough of the ring of truth to set the audience on its heels. The people I mentioned may have wondered if I had been in New Orleans spying on them, since I hit the nail on the head more than once. After the laughter quieted down, I told a story of moonshiners in North Georgia with whom some of my audience had more than a casual acquaintance. While the tale was largely true, it was a tragic story ending in a death. I think the contrast of the stories I told kept the audience wondering what would come next: laughter or tears. Of course, Mammy Sophy made her appearance more than once. Many of those present knew her and had a special appreciation for her wry insights, misguided though they might be. I closed with a story of a Peachtree dowager who encountered a beggar on Whitehall, and after imperiously dismissing him found, as the tale unfolded, that he was her nephew. It was a serious note on which to close that we should never make assumptions about people who were down on their luck. It could be any of us and that was the whole point of the evening—to help children who, through no fault of their own, had no place to go.

When I made my curtsy that I had perfected as a little girl, the warmth of response was more than I could have wished. I felt as though it had been a wonderful time for all of us and especially for the children. I was called back several times, and the mayor even brought be a bouquet of roses.

As I was sitting in the dressing room, well-wishers came by to thank me for an entertaining time. Standing at the back of the crowd was a stately looking gentleman who waited until most had left, then he stepped forward.

He introduced himself with appreciation of my "performance," then handed me his card. J. Adams Smith, Theatrical Agent it, read. "Mrs. Hagan, I am here to offer you a lecture spot at the New York Chautauqua."

I was astounded. "The New York Chautauqua! They don't take unknown's like me. They have William Jennings Bryan, Elwood Hubbard—famous people. Why in the world would you think I could compete with them?"

"It's not a matter of competing, Mrs. Hagan. Mr. Bryan and Mr. Hubbard will certainly be there, but their reputations are established. Our patrons know what to expect from them, but a fresh voice such as yours is what gives the Chautauqua its magic. The anticipation of the unknown is always an attraction to the audience. You will accept, will you not?"

"Well, of course I will!" How could I turn down an opportunity to meet and be on the same platform with Elwood Hubbard, certainly the most famous of the Chautauqua speakers. And William Jennings Bryan—everyone expected him to be President one day, despite having been defeated in 1896 and 1900. I couldn't wait to meet him.

In June, I took Hugh and Lucy's son, Lamar Hill, a little older than Hugh, for the summer at Chautauqua. It was a wonderful experience and Adams Smith had been right: the audience was ready for something a little different than the wonderful lectures of Mr. Hubbard and others. The invitations to lecture at northern universities and colleges came quickly as did speaking engagements from many parts of the country. It exceeded anything I could have possibly imagined, but it all came to an end late in August.

Hugh came to me one afternoon and, looking older than his twelve years, made an announcement. "Mama, I'm proud of your success, but I don't like all these men and women chasing after you. I don't like it. It doesn't seem like my mother." He was frowning.

In an instant, things became clearer. I had certainly been caught up in the swirl of prominent people I had met. The invitations were alluring. The celebrity I was gaining seemed to have much momentum, but that wasn't what was important. Perhaps that would come later, but Hugh and Willis were my primary responsibility. All the invitations were canceled and I finished out the Chautauqua in August and we headed back to Atlanta. I sometimes wonder where it might have all ended, had I kept at it, but I never once questioned the wisdom of my choice and was forever grateful that my growing son stood up and said exactly what he thought.

# CHAPTER IX

Although I was determined to be at home for Hugh and Willis, that was not the end of my travels. Mrs. Rebecca Lowe had become president of the General Federation of The Woman's Club and she frequently invited me to go along with her as a "charter member of the Atlanta Chapter." I noticed when she used that in an introduction, she failed to mention my role as treasurer. Usually I declined such invitations, but when she needed a companion to accompany her to Los Angeles, I was tempted. Willis had been running a fever for several days and I was very concerned about typhoid, which frequently started indolently, only to blossom into a life-threatening illness. Because he was sick, I refused, but when Dr. Hull saw him, he thought that he had malaria and a change in climate would be good for him. Aggie agreed to look after Hugh, so with some reluctance I accepted.

It turned out to be a most interesting excursion. Willis did seem to improve, although I was never sure he wouldn't have gotten well just as fast in Atlanta. Mrs. Lowe's suite was the gathering place for numbers of interesting people, all of whom I found most educational for me. Among other things, I was pressed into service to read a speech when one of the participants fell ill. Having no speech to give, one was hastily written by George Gunton, an editor from one of the New York papers who was covering the meeting. It was an excellent speech, and I decided my calling must be the reading of other people's work, but I added a number of personal notes that made it partly mine. The most important part of the trip was getting to know Rebecca better. Although she had always been gracious to me, since the death of Hugh and my mother, she had taken a special interest in me. After the meeting, she suggested we return home via San Francisco, where we had a wonderful visit with friends of the Lowe family. We sailed across the bay to the quaint town of Sausalito, an interesting mixture of artists' shops and bawdy-looking saloons. Northern California was quite different from Los Angeles and, although enjoyable, I was ready to get back to the South. The train trip home through the Rocky Mountains was spectacular and much more interesting than the outward-bound trip across the deserts of the Southwest. Willis was recovered and spent most of his time, unsuccessfully, looking out the train window for cowboys and Indians. After we reached Chattanooga and the red hills of George began to roll into view, I was glad I had gone, but happy to be home.

As we were about to leave the train, Rebecca said a surprising thing. "Sallie, the trip for Willis has done him so much good, and you look more rested, too. I want you to bring, Hugh, Willis and Mammy Sophy and spend the season with me at "The Hot.""

"The Hot? Where is it?"

"Hot Springs, Virginia. The Homestead has been there for more than a hundred years. Mr. Lowe and I have a cottage there and we spend the summer season in it. The weather is so much better than Atlanta. You will love it. It will keep Willis from having a relapse of his malaria and Hugh will have a grand time. I insist on it."

It didn't take much convincing that it would be a good way to spend the summer. In a week my little family and I were on the train again, headed north to the mountains of Virginia. The train wound its way from Charlottesville through the mountains and tunnels until finally, we backed up the mountain to The Homestead. There was no place for the train to turn around, so they backed up all the way from Covington, Virginia. It was the most interesting train trip Hugh had been on, but Willis was quite jaded by his cross-country jaunt and, for once, had the upper hand with his older brother.

The Lowe Cottage was anything but that. I had expected

something on the order of the Mt. Airy cottage of my courting days, but this was a full-fledged house with a third story for servants. It had been built before the war and was still in good repair. Elegant was the only word to describe it.

The season at The Hot was busy. There were concerts and lectures, as well as activities for the children. Hugh had a pony that he rode and Willis, a little too small for that, developed a stable of "ponies" that he kept under the front porch. They were constructed from sticks and fitted with bridles made from cloth strips. He amused himself endlessly galloping across the green lawns. Willis always made friends easily and one morning, as we were coming out to go to the baths, I saw that he had lent one of his ponies to J.P. Worthington, one of the owners of the Union Pacific Railroad. Mr. Worthington, who must have been in his late seventies, was galloping along with Willis with as much dignity as if he had been riding a Tennessee Walker.

The horseback riding for Hugh resulted in a nasty cut from a fall, requiring stitches. He insisted that he did not need either, and I watched the doctor sew his leg up while he gritted his teeth. He was braver than I would have been. When it was done, he asked, "Would it be all right if I cried a little now?" So grown up so soon, but still a child!

Our lives were leisurely paced and we paid little attention to the meetings that were constantly being held at The Homestead. The American Bar Association met there in the latter part of the season. Lawyers from across the country had gathered for their annual meeting as well as some golf. I was aware that there was an unusually large contingent of handsome and elegant-looking men in the dining room, but thought little of it. My hands were full with the boys. One morning in mid-week, I received a note asking me to call on Mrs. Charles Evelyn Smith of Richmond. I wasn't sure who she was, but suspected that she might be an acquaintance of Hugh's family. I had an engagement for riding at noon, so I decided to send her a note that I would contact her when I returned. As I was going to the hotel desk to ask them to deliver the note, up walked Colonel Scruggs from Atlanta, who had arranged for our ride. I told him I would catch up with him, but he insisted the horses were waiting and he would see to it the note was delivered.

The ride was lovely, down a wonderful mountain stream that connected the Upper and Lower Cascades. By the time we returned it was too late to get in touch with Mrs. Smith who would, undoubtedly, be dressing for dinner. The following morning, Rebecca and I were scheduled to play golf, but before going, I needed to get in touch with the elusive Mrs. Smith. I hoped she wouldn't be offended by my lack of attentiveness to her invitation. Rebecca called after me as I left the house, "Offer her the use of my carriage for the day. She'll be so delighted to get something free around this place, she'll forget she ever invited you."

I was standing at the desk, writing a note to Mrs. Smith when a gentleman stepped to the front and asked the clerk if he knew where he might find a Mrs. Sarah Johnson Hagan.

The clerk replied, "This is Mrs. Hagan standing here, sir."

The very distinguished looking gentleman turned to me, and held up a card. "I received your gracious note, madam, and was so curious to meet you that I canceled a meeting with the Governor of Virginia." He smiled good-naturedly.

"I beg your pardon? I have sent you no note. There must be some mistake." My tone was, I'm afraid, bordering on indignant.

With no less dignity, he confronted me sternly. "This is your card, is it not? I am Lucian Cocke, of Roanoke, and it was delivered to my suite. Actually, it was delivered to my mother-in-law, Mrs. Francis H. Smith. Since she is not acquainted with . . ." he consulted the card again . . . "a Mrs. Sarah Johnson Hagan, she asked if I would be so good as to inquire as to the nature of your call."

It all became painfully clear. Colonel Scruggs had addressed the card to the wrong Mrs. Smith. No wonder she was mystified. I was beginning to blush with embarrassment over my rude treatment of the gentleman who was acting in a most courtly manner when Rebecca walked up to us. She had seen the whole thing and was making my discomfiture even worse with her laughter. "Mr. Cocke, you must forgive poor Sallie. She doesn't get out of the cotton patch too often and she's fearful of being abducted by a handsome gentleman such as yourself." Mr. Cocke laughed loudly, as did the hotel clerk and everyone else within ear shot. Then Rebecca added, "She makes herself perfectly ridiculous with her prudery!"

"Actually, my sister is President of Hollins College and I thought this had something to do with an application." He was still laughing, seeing that I was far beyond college age.

I shot an angry glance at Rebecca who was enjoying the whole affair entirely too much, but she, in her usual gracious way, saved the day. "Mr. Cocke, you must bring your mother-in-law, the *real* Mrs. Smith, to tea in my cottage at four. We look forward to getting to know you and your family better. In the meantime, I will try to teach Sallie some manners."

That afternoon, Mr. Cocke, along with his mother-in-law, Mrs. Francis H. Smith, and his sister-in-law, Mrs. Charles W. Kent, were scheduled for a four o'clock arrival. The concept of "tea" was something Rebecca had refined to a science and The Homestead staff were more than equal to the task. Special Darjeeling tea, *petit fours* which resembled museum porcelains, an assortment of tiny sandwiches of cucumber and Smithfield ham and closing out with a selection of sherbets—that was the offering of the day. From the hotel entertainment staff, she had secured the pianist and the violinist for background music.

As the servants were laying out the impressive spread, I asked Rebecca why all the fuss. We had tea each afternoon, but not on this grand scale. She stopped powdering her nose and looked at me incredulously.

"We're having Lucian Cocke and his family for tea, my dear. Surely, you understand the importance of this."

"What importance? He's a pleasant-looking sort of fellow who we would never have met had it not been for the bumbling of Colonel Scruggs. Why go to all this trouble over an accidental meeting?"

"Accidental? Accidental, did you say, Sallie? I don't believe in accidents. Good Presbyterian that I am, I feel certain there is a purpose behind every encounter; it's our job to be clever enough to figure out what it is. Look at your own life. How many times have you profited from some 'accident,' as you call it. Your address to the DAR Congress in Washington; Your Atlanta performance leading to your appearances at Chautauqua—more than an accident, I would say. And Mr. Lucian Cocke—even if meeting him was happenstance, you would be a fool not to look into the matter." She smiled knowingly.

"I still don't understand what you're doing. I have no interest in this man and I'm sure he has none in me. Is that what you're up to—trying to introduce me to a man who is probably happily married?"

"Oh, Sallie! How can you be so smart and at the same time, so obtuse. Lucian Cocke is a widower and beyond that, he is one of the most admired and successful lawyers in the state of Virginia. His father was the founder of Hollins College and his sister is the president of the school. He's a man of great charm but it does not exceed his ability. He will revel in meeting a woman with your intellect."

I reflected on what she had said. How totally opposite from what I had been told by my well-meaning sister, Lucy Hill, when I was a young girl. "Show your brains and you'll spend your life alone," was her assessment. I had never believed that and certainly my life with Hugh had been a vindication that I was right, but I had never thought a man would be attracted to me just because I was more-or-less intelligent.

"How long has he been a widower?"

"His wife died three years ago. She was Lelia Marie Smith and they had four children, two boys and two girls. They range from about fifteen down to about nine years old, I would guess."

"How do you know all this, Rebecca? I didn't know you're in matchmaking business."

"I make it my business to know. I've done my homework on Lucian Cocke but I'm certainly not trying to make a match. On the other hand, you know how much I care for you. You have much to offer as a wife and a mother; now, you're missing half of that. I can tell you that motherhood, as wonderful as it is, will pass—or it should. The children will grow up and start families of their own and then where will you be? I'm sure you will find much to do with the rest of your life. Your writing, your speaking, your civic involvement—all of those things will pick up when Hugh and Willis are grown, but you may end up missing the best thing of all: sitting by the fireside on a cold winter's night and being close to the one who chose you and with whom you choose to share."

There was a wistfulness in her voice and I felt as though she was talking more about herself than about me. I didn't particularly like the idea of being paraded in front of someone but, on the other hand, I certainly understood what she was saying. When the entourage arrived, I had decided to approach the afternoon with a little more care than had been my intention when Rebecca, presumptuously, I thought, proffered the invitation.

Mammy Sophy took one look at all the preparation and announced, "Sumthin' 'bout to happen heah, I can tell dat," and she shooed Willis and Hugh back upstairs for dressing. They protested having to change their clothes just because guests were coming and I heard Mammy tell them as they turned from the landing, "Yo' mama got two of da fines' lookin' boys in da world and I aims to make sho' dat whoever is comin' for tea knows dat. Now git in da bathtub an' don' you come out till you's shinin' like a new penny."

Lucian was indeed the picture of elegance and charm. He was dressed in a tightly fitting dark blue waistcoat and a white Ascot. He wore his clothes as though it were a totally natural thing to be dressed so finely for an afternoon tea. I had selected my clothes with more haste than I normally did and wished that I had been more thoughtful. Mrs. Smith, his wife's mother and her daughter were equally grand in their tailoring. If people are dressed neatly, I rarely paid attention to what they had on, but in this case, the trio were eye catching. As they were introduced to us, the music started and the tea was served, I wondered if the whole afternoon wasn't going to be rather stiff. The conversation flowed easily, but everyone except Rebecca seemed to be somewhat guarded. The boys were taking the cucumbers from their sandwiches and trying to get them in their pockets without being seen, but Lucian was too quick for them.

"Trying to hide the evidence rarely works, Hugh," he laughed. "I can remember my mother trying to get me to eat an asparagus sandwich at a tea and trying to hide it in my pants just like you're doing. I thought I had gotten away with it until I stood up and remembered that I had a hole in my pocket. If you've ever had a handful of cold asparagus run down your leg, you can imagine there's no way to explain the unexpected whoop and their appearance on my shoe tops. I decided after that I would just try to swallow them without chewing them. That didn't work much better."

The idea of this dignified man with cold asparagus in his pants was just what was needed to lighten things up. Lucian turned to the violinist and suggested, "Let's have a little jig instead of Bach. I want these boys to dance and see if they've got holes in their pockets." After a few rounds of "Turkey in the Straw," and "She'll Be Comin' 'Round the Mountain," things lightened up considerably. The boys immediately liked Lucian and Mrs. Smith was remarkable in her poise. I wondered how she felt seeing her deceased daughter's husband so clearly enjoying himself with another woman and her family. She answered that quickly by calling Hugh and Willis to her side to tell them about her grandchildren and how like Francis and Lucian they both were. She had pictures of them and told a little story to illustrate what they each were like. I wondered if the roles were reversed if I could have been as gracious as she. As the afternoon ended, I was amazed at the sense of camaraderie that had developed. And beneath that was a sense of excitement, of anticipation.

As Mammy was clearing away the remains of the refreshments, she looked at me and said, "Sho' nuff a nice man, Miss Sallie. Too bad he live way up heah in hilly-billy land." "I'm sure that he lives in a very nice place, Mammy. Not everyone who lives in the mountains is a hillbilly. You've seen that for yourself in Mt. Airy."

"I ain' seen nobody whut lives dere dat ain' wild as a billy goat. All da nice folks come up from da city and dat's da trufe."

Rebecca came back into the salon in the middle of the conversation, but she immediately joined in. "Unless I miss my guess, you'll be finding out a lot more about Mr. Lucian Cocke, Sallie. He was quite taken by you—just as I knew he would be the minute I laid eyes on him. And you weren't too shy yourself, I might add."

"Don't be ridiculous, Rebecca. I was a perfect lady just as you have trained me to be."

Rebecca laughed and sat down beside me. "Be that as it may, you must plan your next move carefully. He will be calling back soon, I'm sure of it."

"I'm not planning anything. You really are quite a busybody, Rebecca Lowe. I'm certainly not prowling around looking for a man, if that's what you have in mind."

"Wait and see," she said, "You wait and see."

I didn't have to wait long. The following morning, the footman from the main hotel was at the door with a large arrangement of freshly cut flowers. The note that was attached was written in an elegant style and thanked Rebecca for her hospitality. At the end was a second note to me, asking me to join him for dinner that evening. I had really planned on eating with the boys, but when I asked them about it, they were enthusiastic that I keep the appointment. Hugh, particularly, seemed delighted at the idea and, as was usually the case, Willis followed his brother's lead.

When the carriage called for me, the footman said that Mr. Cocke planned to meet me in the main hall. I was surprised that he had not come to fetch me himself, but when I saw him in the hall, I understood why. He had arranged with the bell captain a private seating area off to the side of the main lobby. The violinist was there and the whole area had been arranged much as a parlor in a fine home would have been.

"Good evening, Sallie," he said, bowing slightly. "Since I cannot entertain you in my own home, I thought I would set up a little area that reminds me of my parlor. James, the bell captain, has been most helpful. I'm so pleased that you have agreed to join me."

A waiter appeared with juleps and hors d'oeuvres as we sat on a damask couch facing the west grounds. The sun was just setting and the first hint of fall was in the air. I had worried if conversation might lag without the children present, but my fears were groundless. It seemed as if we had known each other before and there were, in fact, a number of Richmond and Washington connections that we shared. When time for dinner to be served arrived, we were escorted to a private dining room set for two. I had been in some wonderful dining halls, particularly in New York and Vienna, but I had never seen one with the charm and warmth this showed. The meal was rack of lamb with wonderfully tender asparagus, all complimented with a Burgundy Lucian had personally selected. As the evening progressed, I realized that things were moving at a rapid pace. Scarcely twenty-four hours before I had not even known the man, but now I was having a wonderfully intimate dinner with him.

He told me of his wife and what a wonderful mother she had been. Her illness and death, at such an early age, had been a terrible trial for the children as well as himself, but he felt strongly that Lelia would have wanted the family to move on in their lives. Although neither one of us was talking about it, I'm sure we were both thinking that when our holiday at The Homestead ended, we would certainly be seeing one another. As we were riding back to the Lowe Cottage, he made it plain that he intended for that to happen.

"Since Lelia's death, I have not had an active social life. It certainly has been available, but I have met no one in whom I had an interest. My legal work has kept me quite occupied and I'm sure that I have used that to fill some of the lonely spots. Thank goodness the Bar Association was meeting here. Thank goodness old Colonel Scruggs got the message delivered to the wrong Mrs. Smith. I really don't believe any of this was an accident, but since it has happened, whatever the cause, I can tell you that I fully intend to capitalize on my good fortune. I will be coming to Atlanta in the middle of next month on a banking matter and certainly hope that it will be convenient to spend some . . . let me amend that . . . most of my time with you."

I thought of Lucy and her coyness so I put on a little show that I'm sure would have pleased her. Looking over my fan, I murmured, "Oh, Mr. Cocke, I will certainly do what I can to work you into my social calendar." He looked taken aback, but as I winked he realized I was teasing him. "Next month can't arrive soon enough for me," I assured him.

As he helped me from the carriage and up the steps, he took my hand in his and looked at me as I had not been looked at in a long, long time.

After Lucian's first visit to Peachtree Street, word spread through Atlanta as if something remarkable was happening. Sallie Hagan had a boy friend! Nothing could have sounded more ridiculous than to describe Lucian Cocke as a "boy friend," but whatever he was called, interest abounded. As usual, there were on every hand women who knew "exactly what I should do," as they put it. I ignored all of their advice, but enjoyed the consternation it caused when they realized that a marriage might be in the offing.

"You've got two boys and he's got four children, Sallie! Have you thought about that?"

"Yes, of course I have thought about it," was my standard reply.

"Well? What have you decided?"

"After considerable thought and meditation, I have come to the conclusion that makes four boys and two girls—a total of six children." I suppose I should have treated their inquiries with more respect, but the look on their faces when I gave them my answer was too good to miss. Lucian and I had talked long about the blending of the families. My roots were right down to the granite in the Georgia clay and his were equally deep in the limestone of his beloved Virginia. His work was well established, and despite my love for Georgia, I knew that I could live happily anywhere so long as the boys and I were together in a situation where there was love. "And besides," I told my friends who were aghast that I would leave Atlanta, "They outnumber us." By then, everyone had given up on advice and was just filled with good wishes. Since Hugh and Mother had died, much of my past seemed disconnected from the present. Many of the servants, including the famous Belle, had moved on, but Mammy Sophy was still with us. The idea of leaving her behind was more than I could imagine, but taking her to Virginia seemed an unkind thing to do. She had never known a home other than ours. Her first memories were of plantation life as a slave. To think of her in those terms was more than I could manage. She had been such an integral part of my life and the life of the boys, I was in a real quandary about what to tell her. Sadly, the problem began to solve itself.

Not many months after Lucian and I met, Mammy's health began to fail. She tried hard to ignore it, but getting up out of a chair became almost impossible. "Gittin' lazy. Dat's why I don' git outta da chair," she would explain. The other servants tried to help her with her work, but she refused. Most of her time was spent with Hugh and Willis which required little more than sitting in the rocking chair on the veranda and watching them play, but even that was tiring. Soon, I realized they were actually looking after her. I moved her from the cabin to a downstairs bedroom in the main house so she would not have to make the walk through the back yard. When she didn't object to the idea, I knew she recognized that her life was drawing to a close. In the late summer of 1903, I took her breakfast into her room and found her sitting at the front window in her rocking chair. I laid her tray down and walked over to her, wondering why the shade was drawn and she was looking toward the window. The instant I touched her shoulder, I knew she had died during the night. That shoulder on which I had cried as a child . . . and sometimes as a grown woman . . . was cold as any winter's stone. If ever there was someone who deserved heaven, it was Mammy Sophy. I just hope she will be merciful when she tells the Lord about "Miss Sallie and her misbehaving." The last reason for my staying in Atlanta had moved to a better place, but the light in our lives seemed a little dimmer.

On October, 26, 1903, I became Mrs. Lucian H. Cocke of

Roanoke. As the train rolled out of Union Station and started toward Virginia, our lives would begin. I had been through the mountains of Virginia, but never to Roanoke before I met Lucian. It was a charming little city, much like a sister of Atlanta, I thought, but with somewhat of a western, frontier-town look. There had been a settlement there for years with the unlikely name of Big Lick. A beautiful river ran nearby and there were numerous deposits of salt in the valley. The deer would come down from the mountainsides and mingle with the farmers' livestock for the salt. Originally, the village had been called "The Lick," but as it grew they added the "Big." When the Norfolk and Western Railroad chose the area for its headquarters, someone rightly thought they needed a name with a little more dignity and "Roanoke" was chosen. It is an Indian word meaning "money," and from the boomtown atmosphere, it seemed that there would be plenty of that. The city was growing by leaps and bounds. There was an air of excitement about it that was infectious.

The city lay at the southern end of the Shenandoah Valley, surrounded on three sides by the mountains. Lucian's home, Cockspur, sat on the crest of Orchard Hill. It was a wonderful house with gables and a large porch perfect for the cool summer evenings. The grounds were immaculately kept and the gardener had flowers blooming most of the year. To the northwest we could look over downtown toward the railroad and all the activity up and down the tracks. Such places existed in Atlanta, but they were far removed from Peachtree Street. Here, it was close at hand. The sound of raucous evening activities drifted up the hill and if the wind was right, it was uncomfortably common to hear gunfire from the saloons and houses of the evening ladies along Lick Run, the creek that bubbled out of a spring in the middle of town. I had not anticipated being quite so close to the seamy side of local life. To the southwest, the view was quite different. Mill Mountain rose like Stone Mountain of Georgia but was velveted with the brilliant hardwood colors of autumn. From the base of the mountain flowed a wondrous spring, coursing down to the river which ran through rich bottom land. It was easy to see why this had been a wonderful place for settlers: unlimited timber, crystal clear icy water in great supply and a climate that, although substantially colder than Atlanta, was temperate when compared with upstate New York or Vienna.

I had some trepidation about moving into a house with the history of another mistress. Lelia Cocke must have been a remarkable woman. She was a gifted artist and had done a portrait of Lucian's father, Charles L. Cocke, when he was president of Hollins College. Lucian understood how I felt and was quick to solve that problem. The pictures that Lelia had painted were still in the house and I certainly didn't mind that, but we were cramped. We needed more space since we now had six children. A wing was quickly designed and added to accommodate guests without displacing the children from their quarters. I had thought that I understood what an active social life entailed, but Cockspur was a gathering place for young and old alike. The neighboring children used our home as headquarters for whatever adventure they might conceive, and the business associates of Lucian and his friends seemed to find their way to Cockspur on the way home most evenings. It reminded me of a continual house party but one where there was never any of the intrigue that sometimes accompanies such events.

I so wished my friends in Atlanta could see how well the children joined into one family. The boys, Francis and Lucian, became instant best friends with my boys while Mary Stuart and Janie never seemed to feel excluded. I could not have imagined a group of children with whom so much happiness developed so quickly. I had wondered if the novelty for Hugh and Willis suddenly having four new siblings would wear off, but it never did. They remained as close as any blood kin I have ever known. Even as they became grown men and women, their love and affection for each other never dimmed. My marriage was, all in all, a happy blending into a charming community.

During the first winter and into the following summer, I began to see a different side of Roanoke. There was not a paved street in the city. After a rainstorm, the streets became a sea of mud. In Atlanta, there were many streets that were dirt, but it was packed so hard that the water ran off just as if it had been cobblestone. Not so here. During the spring rains, people would slog through the mud as if it were the most natural thing in the world. What I had initially interpreted as "charm," now appeared to be primitive . . . far more so than I had first realized. The industrial area along the railroad was the location of countless saloons and brothels. Additionally, the second industry of the city seemed to be the distilling of whiskey. In the surrounding mountains there was a booming business in bootlegging, but right in town there were a dozen or more distilleries. I wondered how a population of thirty-thousand or so could keep them all operating, but they did. The combination of whiskey and women was not a healthy one, and complicating the whole affair was Lick Run. It coursed through the center of all this activity and was nothing more than an open sewer. The Hotel Roanoke, owned by the railroad, was as fine a structure as you would find anywhere. They announced with pride that the entire hotel was connected to a sewer system. While that sounded fine, all it amounted to was the raw sewage coursing down the hillside into Lick Run. The rest of the establishments along the banks weren't so sophisticated: They just carted their sewage to the creek and dropped it in.

The most alarming thing was that no one seemed to be particularly concerned about it. I suppose my years with Hugh had heightened my sense of sanitation, although you certainly didn't need an education to understand the place was an epidemic waiting to happen. Just to the east of the center of town in the farmer's market was the city fountain from which the livestock drank, as well as many patrons in the market area. I was astounded to see water taken from the fountain in large pails and carted off to schools for the children to drink.

The epidemic came in 1905. It was called "Big Lick Fever," or by the more enlightened, "Roanoke Fever." Of course it was typhoid. I had seen it before and every mother lived in dread of it. I instructed the children to be very careful about where they got their drinking water, but the pail and dipper in school was all they had available. I knew that they would frequently drink from Crystal Spring over by the mountain, but that didn't concern me. Our water came from a similar spring at the foot of Orchard Hill and I had no worry about it's purity. I stood it as long as I could then mentioned it to Lucian.

I had, in fact, been mentioning it to him ever since I moved to Roanoke but, he, like everyone else, seemed uninterested. Lucian had been the mayor before we were married and I chided him for not taking a more active role in getting these problems corrected. He listened patiently, but nothing happened.

That summer there were thirty-five deaths from typhoid, cholera and dysentery, fifteen of them children. Some seemed to think that was not an inordinate number for a city our size, but I reminded them it was far more than one would find in Atlanta which was ten times the size of Roanoke. If something were to be done, it appeared that someone other than the city fathers would have to initiate the action. I decided to take a little tour downtown one evening.

I knew what the conditions were; I had seen some of it, but much was by word of mouth. If we were going to get anything done, we would need to have the facts. It was just getting dark when I stepped from the carriage next to Lick Run. The saloons were already in high gear and the ladies of the evening were plying their trade with a vengeance. I stood on the south side of Lick Run and would have walked over to Norfolk and Salem Avenues for a closer look, but there was no way to get across the creek except a log foot bridge that had no railing. It was worn smooth as a glass by thousands of feet that crossed it every day. I wouldn't have tried to cross it in my bare feet, let alone with high-top boots with heels. I watched a man come out of a saloon. Although it was only nine o'clock he was so drunk he must have gotten an early start. As he approached Lick Run, I wondered if he would attempt to navigate the crossing in his state. He stepped onto the log and staggered to the center where, to my horror, he unbuttoned his pants, relieved himself in the stream and then, apparently thinking he was in a bathroom, stepped back to admire his contribution. The fall was impressive and was greeted with great whoops from the onlookers. The creek was only waist deep and he managed to wade to the shore. He started back into the saloon, but the keeper barred the door and wouldn't let him enter.

"John, you smell like an outhouse. I ain't lettin' you come back in here." John shook his head, sat down on an empty whiskey barrel next to the door and was soon either asleep or passed out.

I had no doubt the scene I had witnessed was repeated countless times each day. There wasn't anything charming about downtown Roanoke at night. It was beyond primitive. We would get something done about it, of that I was determined. If the men didn't think it was important, I knew I wasn't the only woman who was concerned.

There was a major advantage to being part of a larger social scene. The circles in which we moved were populated with women who, like me, had moved here because of their husbands. The railroad, centered in Philadelphia, had relocated many of their officers in Roanoke as the Norfolk and Western expanded. Their wives had come here from Philadelphia, from Hagerstown, from Baltimore which, just like Atlanta were substantially more civilized than I was finding Roanoke.

One evening in the late fall of 1906 we were entertaining friends at Cockspur. The men were off talking politics and I suppose they thought the ladies would be swapping recipes, but the conversation was quite different. Molly Coxe, Willie Walker Caldwell, Mary Alice Markley, Ann Bryan, and Minnie Stone were gathered on the back veranda when I served tea. Someone asked what I was having prepared for dinner and I mentioned it was turkey.

"Did it still have feathers on it when you bought it?" Molly asked.

"I don't know. I didn't notice. Why do you ask?"

"I assume you bought it from Gilley Bush on the market?"

"Yes, I did, as a matter of fact."

"Well, our good merchant, Mr. Bush, has been selling buzzards as turkeys. That's why you shouldn't buy anything unless it's got enough feathers to tell what it was before Gilley killed it," Molly advised.

"Not just turkeys, either," interjected Willie Walker. "I'm pretty sure he sold me a groundhog the last time I thought I had bought a rabbit."

The conversation went on about the conditions on the market and I took the bird—whatever it was—out of the oven and convinced myself it *was* a turkey, then I returned to the porch. The sense of outrage had increased during my absence and more stories were coming out about the terrible conditions in the city, about the lack of our husbands' interest and the total apathy of the city fathers.

"I suppose we can talk about this forever, but nothing seems to be happening. That's the really discouraging part about this," Molly sighed.

"We all came here because of our husbands. We never had to live like this in Philadelphia," said Minnie. "If you saw a cow or a bunch of chickens walking down Walnut Street you would have thought you were having hallucinations. Last week, I stepped on a live chicken right in the middle of Mothner's Mercantile. I know Edwin likes his job here, but that was about the last straw. Now I find we may be having breast of buzzard for dinner, Sallie."

"Don't worry. It's a real turkey, I can promise you that, but the issue is still there." No one spoke for a few minutes, but then Ann said, "You know, if the men are going to sit around and do nothing, maybe we should get together and talk this over."

"Who do you mean? With our husbands? They won't do anything," I suggested.

"Of course they won't. But we don't need them. We can get all the ladies together and make a plan about what to do. If a bunch of us put our heads together, I think we can make some changes around here."

Everyone was thoughtful for a minute or two. These were wives of prominent men. We saw our roles as supportive of the work our husbands did, as raising responsible children and keeping the household well-organized. But we weren't uninformed. Similar problems—and worse—existed in the major cities of the country. Much was being written in the national press about it.

"Muckrakers," they were called by their opponents, but Upton St. Clair, Ida Tarbell, and Jane Addams certainly were making their views known. They were famous people, but there was no reason we couldn't accomplish the same thing on a smaller scale.

"Ann, that's an interesting thought. We could all meet and I'm sure we could come up with some ideas," I answered.

The response was immediate. Molly said, "Each one of us should make a list of fifteen or so women who we think might be interested and write them a note telling them we want to see some changes made in the market."

"No more buzzards from Gilley Bush, for example," Willie Walker laughed.

"Let's do it," I said, more loudly than I had intended. "We can get our butlers to deliver the notes telling them the time and place we'll meet. I'll bet we can get fifty or more women to come."

"Do you think it will make our husbands mad?" asked Ann.

"They don't even have to know. After we get ourselves organized, then we will recruit them to be on our side. I suspect we all know how to do that," I said. Everyone laughed.

"No more country ham for breakfast until you change your attitude, Edward," said Minnie.

"When will we do it?" Mary Alice asked. "And where will we have it? None of us has a house that can handle a big crowd like that."

I thought about it a minute. We could get everyone in Cockspur, but it would be better if it were on neutral ground rather than in a home. "Let's plan on two weeks from this Friday. That will give us plenty of time to invite the women who will be interested. As for the place, I think we should have it at the YMCA. There's a bit of irony about using a men's club to plan what they should have done a long time ago."

Everyone laughed again and there was a sense of excitement about the whole idea. Before we had time to make any further plans, Lucian and the others came up from the side garden. He looked us over and we must have had a curious demeanor about us. He turned to the men and said, "I think something's afoot here. Maybe we shouldn't have left them alone."

"Quite the contrary, Lucian. The ladies and I have been discussing our shopping habits. We're tired of ordering our food from Philadelphia and Baltimore just because the railroad likes to carry it for you. Local shopping needs to be improved."

He thought about this for a minute and said, "And that brings up the question: What are we serving for dinner?"

"Buzzard," was all I said. The ladies smiled knowingly; the men looked nervous.

Over the next two weeks the word got around that we were concerned about the level of sanitation in the market area and were planning to do something about it. We had hoped that we would have fifty or so women who would show up, but were amazed when more than one hundred appeared at three o'clock on the appointed afternoon. By then, even the newspaper had heard of our plans and wanted to attend, but we decided they had already had their chance and we would have our first meeting behind closed doors. We weren't at all sure how we would be organized, and until we had a plan it seemed best to keep the newspaper at bay.

When all was said and done, we had reached a consensus: Action would be taken. The reporter, who sat out on the sidewalk, filed a somewhat cryptic report about our get together but said no one was able to find out exactly what we talked about. It was actually very straightforward. We would call ourselves The Civic Betterment League. I suppose, because the idea had its origins at my house, I was elected chairmen. Anyone of the group present could have done the job just as well, if not better than I, but since I had a reputation of speaking out, the gavel ended up in my hand and Willie Walker Caldwell was vice chairman.

At dinner several evenings later, Lucian asked me what all the commotion was about. The notes flying back and forth among all of us was definitely unusual.

"You, Mr. Cocke," I informed him, "are about to witness The Petticoat Rebellion."

"The Petticoat Rebellion? You mean you're going to stop wearing them?"

"Oh, no! We'll be wearing them, but we're going to put on our hats and have a little meeting with City Council about all the problems on the market."

"Oh, that. Well, I wish you luck but I wouldn't expect too much to happen."

I thought about that a minute then said, "I don't think you quite understand. If one hundred women walked into your office all at the same time and demanded that you listen to what they had to say, I suspect that you would pay attention . . . and if you're half as smart as I think you are, you might well learn something. That's exactly what we're going to do with the City Council."

He smiled, patronizingly, I thought, then said, "And what do you expect them to do?"

"Well, to begin with we want them to appoint a city health officer. We need a doctor who will enforce the regulations about quarantining of contagious diseases. We want him to be in charge of sanitation on the market. Gilley Bush and his ilk should be closed down. They're a public health menace. Lick Run is a six-block-long outhouse and most of the city buys its food right from the banks of that sewer."

Lucian looked thoughtful. "And how do you and your petticoat parade expect to have City Council help you? Suppose they refuse, which they probably will?"

"We intend to boycott every merchant and green grocer on the market until something is done. We'll get at them through their pocketbooks. I haven't seen a business yet that doesn't pay attention when sales drop off to nothing."

"Where will we get our food if we don't use the market?" he asked.

"The same place some of us have been getting most of it all the time: from Philadelphia, Baltimore, and Norfolk. Of course, we'll be eating a little more simply, but it certainly will be safer."

I'm not sure how convinced he was, but he certainly knew we weren't talking through our hats. When the day of City Council meeting came up, six of us piled into Minnie Stone's car and off we went, leading a parade of carriages with more than one hundred fifty women. Minnie's was one of the first cars in Roanoke, and she was certainly the first woman to drive. As we were driving into town, I was in charge of the klaxon, honking loudly that we were on the way and those who valued their lives should be up on the boardwalks. The brakes were anything but reliable and there was much swerving through ruts and puddles. Mayor Cutchin and the honorable gentlemen were flustered at all the hullabaloo and let us know that the place for women was in the home, attending the children, and that our public appearances should be limited to church. I gave them to understand that we would appear where and when we liked when we had something to say and suggested that we would be in frequent attendance at their meetings until our demands were treated with respect. Although I never heard the word used, I am quite sure that in private conversations we were described as "uppity."

Uppity, or not, we carried the day . . . actually it took some time and not until our market boycott was in place did things begin to happen. One of the things we had counted on was the support of our husbands. Once they understood the magnitude of the problem and that when the war cry of, "Ladies, put on your hats!" was sounded we were on the march, they rallied behind us. These were men of great power. They would have done this themselves had they been paying attention, but in their professional lives, they were looking beyond the local scene. They became our allies. They were instrumental in helping us implement some of our plans. Once the mayor and council realized that we were all banded together, things began to change. The men of the market knew that we meant business and conditions improved. Meat was no longer left uncovered where flies visited it freely. Sewage restrictions were passed. A city health officer was employed, and the hideous single pail of water with the dirty common dipper disappeared from school as fountains were introduced. The City Council even voted money for two new schools. We were more than pleased with the reception we had received.

Much of the success was due to the obvious merit of our suggestions, but the ladies were such diplomats that they persuaded the city fathers to take action and did it without making them mad. Once we had made progress with our initial plans, The Civic Betterment Club—that was the official name on which we settled—began to look to the future.

Roanoke had grown in such a rapid fashion in such a short time, it was sometimes called The Magic City. The Woman's Club even had a song about its wonders:

> In the Blue Ridge Valley of Virginia
> Mid mountains crowded with oak
> You'll find a gem of the Southland
> The Magic City of Roanoke.

There was nothing magic about what needed to be done to make it a better place for all of us. And if it was a gem, it certainly needed a little polishing. It was obvious we were just getting started, and equally obvious that money would be required. There had been no planning or organization to the growth. The city had grown wherever and however people chose to let it happen. We needed a city planner to give us direction for the future. And that was going to cost money.

At a meeting the discussion centered on that problem. Mrs. Frank Brown came up with an idea that really took hold. "We need to have a festival in the market. Look how much improvement has taken place in the last year. The market doesn't even smell badly anymore. It would be a wonderful place to have a bazaar."

We decided that we would sell homemade foods, jellies and jams, as well as needlework and things that would appeal to the general public. There would be games and contests and lots of food. We ended up with fifteen different food locations, each featuring an ethnic group and the foods they liked best. It was a great success.

In November of 1907 we started with a big parade and opening music by a brass band. The place was thronged with people. We had no idea how popular it would be, but we were thrilled. We published a daily newsletter called Festival Facts and Fancies. It was filled with a list of the activities for that day as well as stories and poems that people had submitted. Each day, the paper was distributed throughout the city and was a reminder that people should come to the market. The weather cooperated, although if we had waited until spring, it might have been a little more seasonable. One thing I learned about the Civic Betterment Club: When they decided to do something, they weren't planning on waiting around to start. Even in the late fall, the crowds and sales were so brisk that we made over five thousand dollars! That was certainly enough to launch us to the next phase, which was to hire a city planner.

We talked to city officials in Baltimore and Philadelphia, asking for recommendations of who might help us. One name kept coming up: John Nolen of Boston. He was willing to come for a fee of $2100. He spent several weeks with us and came up with a wonderful plan utilizing the natural beauty of the area with the rivers and streams flowing through and blending it with the unalterable presence of a major railroad running right through the middle of the city. He proposed parks and green space that would offset the grime of fifty steam trains passing through each day.

His plan was dramatic and we certainly got our money's worth from John Nolen, but then we ran into a roadblock with the city fathers. I suppose it was the cost that bothered them the most, although I think the immensity of the plan escaped some of them. I found myself, as well as did the others, becoming irritated that once we had gotten the sanitation problems more or less under control, the leaders of the city didn't see the vision of the future with the same enthusiasm we did. Then, of course, they were quick to remind us that they all had jobs to do and all the Civic Betterment Club had on it's mind was our projects. If the plans of John Nolen had been adopted, I truly believe that some of the problems that later came to roost would have been avoided. Of course, in retrospect it is easy to think that is true. Maybe the money that was not used to implement the Nolen plan was spent in ways that were more urgent, but I believe that present needs cannot be emphasized to the point that future plans are ignored. As far as we were concerned, that was what happened.

One of the benefits of the Civic Betterment Club had to do with Cockspur: It had become a frequent gathering place for our meetings and a rallying point before we fired up Mimi's Oldsmobile and headed down Orchard Hill. It was an unusual day that found us without house guests, both local and from out of town. It certainly kept the place lively and the children were right in the thick of it. Frozen salads had just come into style and they were a favorite with the children. Although the kitchen help was quite good, frozen salads and desserts were a little beyond their usual fare, so when the State Democratic Convention met in Roanoke, we knew there would be many dinner parties in the house and the children were anxious to have frozen salads as often as possible.

We had just finished luncheon and while the guests were chatting, I slipped back to the kitchen to make sure cook was getting along with the salad for the reception we were having that evening. Obviously, she needed help.

"Lawse, Miss Sally, I don' know nuthin' 'bout feedin' folks ice for food," she said.

"Don't worry about it, Emma, I'll help you." I set about the task, but Mrs. St. George Tucker soon showed up in the pantry.

"Get me an apron, Sarah. I want to see how you make a frozen salad."

In short order, the Honorable St. George Tucker himself showed up and settled in to watch the proceedings. Since he had been the guest of honor at the luncheon, soon the entire guest list was in the kitchen, chopping fruit and shaving ice. Emma took a seat to the side and let us do all the work for her. Senator Daniels seated himself at the head of the table and the discussion of what was to take place at the convention continued in the pantry just as if we had been in the main salon. That was one of the endearing things about Cockspur. It seemed to bring lightness to everyone and a sense of being at ease. Having six children racing through the house certainly was an ice breaker. As we finished up our work, I realized that Emma probably hadn't learned a thing, but there would be other times. Senator Daniels, as he was leaving, said, "Let me know when you have another 'pantry party.' I will certainly be here. We got more work done while making that salad than I usually accomplish in an entire afternoon in a committee room at the Capitol. And it was, I must say, I'm sure it will be the best frozen salad I have ever made!" He tipped his hat as he stepped into his waiting car.

I enjoyed entertaining and Cockspur was such a gracious house in which to do it. When someone suggested that we should host the Confederate Reunion that was to be held in Roanoke, I was delighted with the idea. I was not involved in much of the planning, but knew that we would have many guests in our home during the week. It did concern me that all of the activities seemed to be planned for officers and their families with little or no thought being given to the foot soldiers, many of whom living in Roanoke were old and poor. I thought we should have had a special party just for them, but much more attention was paid to the prominent generals and their staffs.

On the first day of the reunion, we were attending a reception at Hotel Roanoke and I had been leaving our cards in the quarters of the officers, many of whom seemed to be away for the afternoon. I was sitting on the veranda, a grand porch looking down the hillside, the railroad being just beyond the hedgerow. Friends and I were visiting when suddenly the air was split with a cannon blast, bugles blowing, drums beating and the most blood-curdling of screams coming up from the railroad. Shortly, there appeared a rank of veterans marching, more or less, up the street from the station to the hotel. They were old and scruffy-looking, but dressed in their gray uniforms. Many were crippled and had to be helped up the walkway, but the intensity of the Rebel yell had not lessened with all their infirmities. When they reached the veranda, they were all panting and trying to sing "Dixie." Looking at them was a heart-wrenching sight. These old men, many of them amputees, all of them beaten down by years and scarred by the war, were standing in front of the grand hotel, not quite sure what to do next.

A young lady of obvious wealth was standing near the center of the porch. She stepped in front of the group. "What do you want?" she asked, and none too pleasantly, I thought. "What's the meaning of all this fuss and noise? Why, it's enough to wake the dead!"

The noise stopped as suddenly as it had begun. An old man stepped forward, using his rifle as a cane. His face was lopsided with a scar, a saber slash, I suppose, that ran from his forehead to his chin. He pulled himself to attention, then saluted the young woman.

"We came to pay our respects to the General, ma'am."

The young woman, whoever she was, responded with a snap. "The General is asleep. Now you get out of here. And be quick about it."

The old soldier looked at her. It was hard to see what was in his eyes, those eyes that had seen horrors that young woman could not possibly imagine. He just shook his head, tipped his hat, and limped back to the men standing behind them. They were gathering up their things and starting down the hill, but I couldn't stand it. My parents had told me enough of the war that I understood some of what those old men were feeling. I turned to a gentleman standing next to me. I didn't know who he was but I said, "Don't let them go without some word of thanks." My resentment at the way they had been treated got the best of me. "And when you've done that, tell them they are all invited to Cockspur for a lawn party tomorrow afternoon at four. Tell them they will be the guests of honor; it's a party just for them."

The lady who had spoken to them with such rudeness stared at me as if I were crazy. "You'd better lock up your silver if you let that bunch of hoodlums on your property," she snapped.

I looked at her sharply, then said, "Miss, if it weren't for those men and all those like them, you'd be lucky to *have* any silver. I don't know who you are or where you're from and, frankly, I don't particularly care, but I *do* care about those men. My father and many of my family were part of that army and I will not have them dishonored."

After the gentleman issued the invitation to the old men not a word was spoken, but the entire assembly moved away and left the young lady standing alone as the gray uniforms slowly disappeared around the hedgerow.

Dr. St. George Tucker, of New York, was a house guest during the week and he put himself in charge of assembling the veterans. He even hired a special band and the following afternoon, the soldiers marched through the main streets of Roanoke and up Orchard Hill to Cockspur. We could hear the Rebel yell long before we could see them. A number of officers arrived, too but they stepped aside to let the rank and file walk onto the lawn. It was to be a party for Johnny Reb. Under the magnolia tree we had set up a table for refreshments. Several new wash tubs served as punch bowls and each was filled to the brim with ice and mint julep,. The old soldiers spread across the lawn, hundreds of them, a few in wheelbarrows because they couldn't walk. They were careful of the flower beds and courteous to the extreme. I watched one old man as he tottered over to another and held the cup for him to drink—his friend had one arm and no hand on that one. After he had finished his draft, he smiled at me and touched his stump to his cap in salute. The thoughts of my father and mother, working in the hospitals of Atlanta were never more vivid than that moment.

As the juleps flowed, the spirits became more free. There were campfire songs and stories and more than a few tears shed. Many toasts to the women were soon offered and the ladies mingled among the soldiers as if they had been friends for years. I looked around for the young lady from the hotel veranda but did not see her.

When the time came to leave, I believe every one of them came by to give his thanks. We shook hands with hundreds and all looked at us with gratitude. "Good bye, Lady." That's what most of them said. And a lot of "God bless you all." When I think back to that afternoon, I believe it was one of the best parties we ever gave. It warmed my heart for years to come whenever I thought about it.

Although Lucian never was active in politics after his term as mayor, his counsel was frequently sought by those who were. He invariably supported the Democratic ticket and through those associations, many a political conclave was held at Cockspur. When the business had been concluded, enjoyable evenings generally followed, and none were more memorable than the many times William Jennings Bryan was a house guest. He had run for President in 1896 and 1900 and was expected to be a candidate in 1908. His command of current events, domestic as well as international, was extensive. His daughter, Grace, was a student at Hollins College, where my sister-in-law, Mattie Cocke, was president. Whenever Mr. Bryan would come to visit, he would always stay with us. While the conversation had a serious side, equally memorable were the wonderful stories that were told. Lucian was a great raconteur, as was Mr. Bryan, and they would swap stories until late in the night. Former Governor Tyler was a frequent attendee and was so impressed with the tales passing around the room that he usually took notes. It was not unusual to find one of our stories coming back to us in a public address that one of our guests would deliver. Mr. Bryan was such a courtly gentleman but full of surprises. One of his trips to visit Grace came without much warning and I had already made plans to leave for Washington on some DAR business on the midnight train. With William Jennings Bryan as a house guest, I could not imagine abandoning him.

"Don't give it a thought, Sallie," he said. "My banquet address at Hollins will conclude no later than ten o'clock. That will allow plenty of time for both of us to catch the train. I'm on the way to Washington, myself."

It seemed a workable solution and Lucian was delighted to drive us from the college to the station. The Pullman porter, Charles, was an old friend. He seemed to know everyone who was boarding the train except Mr. Bryan, the most famous person to make the journey that night, or any other, for that matter. Mr. Bryan did not take offense at not being recognized and we soon settled into our accommodations for the overnight trip to Washington. The journey went along uneventfully when I was awakened from a deep sleep by Charles.

""Scuse me, Miz Cocke, but the gentleman in number nine say he want to have breakfast wid you."

"Breakfast? We should be in Washington any minute, Charles. Why would we be stopping for breakfast?"

"Dere was a wreck at Rockfish and we done spent mos' of da night settin' on a sidin'. We gwina stop in Charlottesville for some food since we ain' got no diner on da train."

"Well, you tell Mr. Bryan I will be delighted to have breakfast with him. And Charles, he's a special man. He may be President next year."

"I don' know nuthin' 'bout dat, Miz Cocke, but I hopes Mr. Lucian don' git mad 'bout this."

I laughed and thought to myself what a ludicrous idea, but it turned out not to be so ridiculous after all. As soon as we stepped from the Pullman and started toward the station, everyone recognized Mr. Bryan and all wanted to speak to him. It was immediately apparent everyone thought I was Mrs. Bryan. As we walked along the train shed to the restaurant, all the passengers formed lines making an honorary passage for us. When we entered the restaurant, the proprietor had been forewarned and with a great flourish and much ostentation, showed us to the best table where we dined alone. Neither of us referred to the obvious mistake and we were glad to re-board the train and be off to Washington.

As we entered the car, Mr. Bryan removed his coat and asked, "Do you have a needle and thread? My wife is not at home and I have a hole in my coat pocket. Do you think you could mend it for me?"

"Certainly," I said, taking the jacket. "You men are all the same. No matter how important you are, you men can't get along without your wives. I'll tack it back together in a jiffy."

He sat in the seat opposite, reading the Charlottesville paper he had bought at breakfast. There was a Supreme Court decision pending in which he was interested. As I sat mending his coat, he reading the paper, we made a nice little domestic scene. A young man approached Mr. Bryan and said, "May I speak privately to you, sir?"

He folded his paper and said, "Certainly. Shall we move to the end of the car?" Even with all of his fame, he always had time to talk to anyone who took the time to ask. I continued sewing away when another gentleman approached my seat.

"Mrs. Bryan, may I sit with you and chat while your distinguished husband is away?"

I looked up at him. His was a handsome and earnest face but another person who had made the wrong assumption and I would have to deal with it. The little triumphal entry into the station after alighting together from the train; my mending his coat while he was reading his paper—it was a natural mistake for anyone to make, but I could not let it pass. I thought quickly, and demurely replied. "Why I am not Mr. Bryan's wife. I am his mother."

The gentleman blinked and said, "Well, madam, I wouldn't have believed it except that it came from your own lips. I will say you hold your age better than anyone I ever saw. You look much younger than your distinguished son." It was not jest. He was in dead earnest. Before I could get myself in deeper trouble, Mr. Bryan returned and took his seat. He shook out his paper and began reading about the impending court decision.

"And what, Mrs. Cocke, do you think the court will decide?"

"Lucian and I have discussed it and I believe he is quite right when he says the court will side with the corporations rather than with labor."

He wrinkled his impressive brow. "Great heavens!" He threw up both of his hands. "You have absorbed your husband's corporation ideas."

"Quite the contrary. Lucian is a corporation lawyer, but he is careful to see both sides of an issue. He rarely makes a mistake in his judgments, so I listen carefully to what he says. You would do well to follow his advice."

I don't think Mr. Bryan was accustomed to hearing such a remark from a woman. He shook his head with resignation, took up his paper and, although the remainder of the trip passed pleasantly, he did not ask my opinion on any further topics of importance.

Leaving Mr. Bryan to his paper and his dismissive attitudes, I went back to my own seat, but was surprised to find a woman sitting in it. On closer look she appeared ill and explained that she had moved to my reservation because riding backwards had made her dizzy.

"You're Mrs. Bryan, aren't you?"

"Heavens no! And I'm not his mother either, which is what I told some poor misguided soul." I explained to her the mixup and then sat in the backwards-facing seat that had caused her trouble. She and her husband, a writer, had been to Lexington on their honeymoon. Her husband had been collecting historical data on Washington and Lee as well as the Virginia Military Institute for a book he was writing. Being a writer myself, I was interested in what he had discovered which she readily shared with me. Some of the stories she told about both schools I had never heard, but I was amazed to find she did not know how Washington and Lee University became known by that name.

In the spring of 1865 the South was in a state of devastation. Jobs were non-existent and everyone was trying to avoid starvation. This included everyone right up to General Robert E. Lee. Everything he owned, including his beloved home, Arlington, had been confiscated by the federal government. He had no property and no income but then was offered the presidency of a large New York insurance company. He refused, believing that he should not live in luxury while others suffered so terribly.

Little Washington College in Lexington was preparing to reopen its doors but had no president. Colonel Bolivar Christian, a board member, hesitantly suggested the name of General Lee, but the board felt it could not expect the greatest man in the South to accept such a humble position. Despite his fame and offers of help to his family, no one had offered him a job in the South that he felt he could accept. It was decided: They would approach him with the offer and Judge Brokenbrough was chosen as the emissary. The Judge was a man of brilliant career, an imposing figure and elegant appearance, but he had only threadbare clothes to wear. The board scrounged up a suit of clothes sent by a board member's northern son, borrowed money from a woman in Buckingham County who had sold a tobacco crop and equipped the judge for the trip. After the visit with the General, he consented to serve and on September 18, 1865 General Lee, the most famous military figure in the United States, rode into Lexington on his horse, Traveler, to assume the presidency of Washington College. After his death in Lexington in 1870 the school name was changed to Washington and Lee.

The rest of the trip passed uneventfully and I was happy to be removed from my undeserved position of honor as "Mrs. William Jennings Bryan."

Several weeks later, Mr. Bryan announced his opposition to the views that Lucian had expressed, and when the Supreme Court handed down its decision, it was in favor of the corporations. Mr. Bryan's strong stand for labor in this case caused much public reaction, and many said it was the decisive factor in his defeat by William Howard Taft. That was the last of three attempts to become President, but it wasn't the end of his political career.

After Woodrow Wilson's election in 1912, Lucian and I were in Richmond to hear a speech Mr. Bryan was to deliver at The Mosque. After the address, we went back stage to greet him.

"Lucian! How good to see you. I was about to get in touch with you. I've been offered a Cabinet position by President-elect Wilson. Do you think I should take it?"

"What is the position?"

"Secretary of State."

Lucian thought for a minute. He recalled his comments about the Supreme Court case in 1908. "Mr. Bryan, I hesitate to tell you my thoughts, but since you have asked, I will give you an honest answer. You will be a much more effective leader as Ambassador to Great Britain than as Secretary of State. Your background in foreign affairs is weak, but from the Court of St. James, your oratory powers can be put to great use. Your influence will quickly spread through England and then to Europe. You will not be able to garner such power as Secretary of State."

Mr. Bryan looked dismayed. An ambassadorship had much less prestige than a major cabinet post. "Not accept Secretary of State?"

"I would certainly not advise it. I was at Princeton and The University of Virginia Law School with Wilson. I know you both too well. It will not be a good match."

The eyebrows went up. "Oh, pshaw!" he responded. Since he had been instrumental in securing the Presidential nomination for Woodrow Wilson in 1912, the Secretaryship was offered and Mr. Bryan accepted, the second time he had ignored Lucian's counsel, and this time the results were equally devastating. As Secretary of State, he proposed a system of arbitration between nations involved in international disputes. Thirty-one countries agreed in principle to new treaties that would allow for a year of "cooling off" while an international forum debated the issue. Unfortunately, before implementation, the First World War erupted, and when the Germans sank the Lusitania in the Irish Sea, Mr. Bryan was furious. President Wilson's weak response to the sinking was the end of the road for his secretariat. An avowed pacifist, he resigned from the Cabinet. If he had listened to Lucian and others who gave him the same advice, who knows what the outcome might have been; certainly, not the dismal end to which his political career came.

# CHAPTER X

In 1909, Lucian and I attended the Poe Centennial at The University of Virginia. The principal speaker was Dr. Barrett Wendell of Harvard. The conversation around the dinner table was excellent, but much time was spent discussing where Edgar Allen Poe actually had been born. I had always thought it was Baltimore, but others insisted it had been Richmond or Philadelphia. Dr. Wendell settled the matter—at least in his own mind—by stating with conviction that Poe was born in Boston. Dr. Alderman, President of the University, tried to make the case that no one knew for sure . . . no one except Dr. Wendell, of course. I suppose it was the conversation about Poe and his literature that set the stage for the dream I had that night.

Before Lucian and I married I had published an article in *The New Century* around the stories of Mammy Phyllis. It had been well-received and I had done other writing in Atlanta but had not tried anything on a larger scale. After our marriage, life was so busy that I hadn't given much thought to it, but the discussions about Poe and his works from Dr. Wendell must have set my mind in motion. Certainly, I had no inclination to write tales of horror that seemed to flow from the pen of Poe like black clouds, but that night I dreamed of Mammy Phyllis. She was seated in the back yard of our house on Peachtree Street, and gathered around her were all of the children from the neighborhood while she told them of what happened to Sister Cat and Brother Dog when they got into the cookhouse then ran into Mr. Pig. It was a story that I had never heard and I didn't remember the details of it in the dream, but I did remember when I awoke laughing how entranced the children had been in the dream.

"What are you laughing about?" Lucian asked.

"Just a funny dream about Mammy Phyliss and her stories." I rolled over and planned to go back to sleep, but the idea of writing again, or putting all those stories down on paper, kept running around in my head. The next morning, I told the assembled group at breakfast of my dream and even told them a story or two that I remembered. The discussion of the birthplace of Poe was set aside and Dr. Wendell said, "Mrs. Cocke, you should write those stories down. It's part of a tradition of southern literature that has received too little attention. If it's not preserved, then it will be lost forever."

My life was too busy to think about writing, I told myself. The boys were getting to the age of thinking about college, and the girls were approaching debutante age; I had too much to think about to scratch the itch of writing. No matter how much I tried to put it out of my mind, it wouldn't go away and I found myself awakening long before daylight with Mammy Phyllis talking to me just as she had for so many years. Eventually, I gave up. I went into my dressing room each morning and started putting the stories on paper. I had no real plan about what to do with them, but in the back of my mind, I thought it would be a book. Lucian was supportive, but he had never met Mammy Phyllis; he had known Mammy Sophy, however briefly, so he acted as consultant. The servants in his family, although excellent and devoted, did not have the exciting history that my family had enjoyed.

In the spring of 1910, I went to New York to visit my cousin, Helen Glenn. She came into my room one morning and found me hard at work, still in my nightgown.

"Writing your sweet husband again? That man must get more mail from you than any other man you know," she said.

"Well, actually, I do write him often, but this is a book I'm writing. I do it in the morning before I get all wound up in the day."

"A book! A book about what? Your comfortable life as a

hillbilly?" Helen was certain that in the Blue Ridge we had a still in every backyard.

"No, these are stories about a mammy who was with our family from the time she was born until she died. She had more tales to tell than a dog has fleas."

Helen took the papers from my hand. "Sallie, for a sophisticated woman, you certainly have a homey way of putting things. I'm going to read this."

Lucian was the only person with whom I had shared the stories, and I had read them to him. They were all written in dialect and that would be as foreign to my New York cousin as Swahili. "No, please don't. I'm not sure they're worth reading."

"Don't be ridiculous, Sallie. How could you do anything that's not perfect. Remember what your daddy always said, "Sallie can do *anything!*"

"But I was a little girl then. This is different." She paid no attention and sat down on the edge of my bed to read. Soon she was putting her hand to her mouth and starting to giggle. Cousin Helen was not one to giggle, but she was doing it. Then she was laughing out loud.

"Sarah Johnson, this is the funniest thing I ever read. What are you going to do with it?"

"Well, I really don't know. After I finish writing it, then I suppose I will send it off to a publisher. Probably nothing will happen."

She looked thoughtful. "You don't need to wait until you're finished. You're in New York. This is the publishing capitol of the world. You should take this to one of those houses while you're here. You get dressed and march yourself down to E. P. Dutton; that's a big publisher. I don't know anyone there, but that won't slow you down. You just walk in and tell them you have a book for them to publish!"

"I wish I thought it would be that easy, but . . . . :

"But nothing! No one's going to come walking up Park Avenue, knock on the door and ask if anyone inside is writing a book for them to print. You have to go see them!"

So that's what I did. The horns of the bull and I were old acquaintances, and Helen was right: Unless you took some action nothing was going to happen.

E.P Dutton and Company was on West Twenty-Third Street. It wasn't hard to find but getting anything done was. The clerk looked at me with ill-disguised disinterest. People like me were sitting all around the waiting room and they had appointments. I explained that I was from out of town and needed to be seen that day. He nodded imperceptibly and motioned toward a chair. After thirty minutes, I was beginning to despair and was thinking about just walking out. This had been a hare-brained idea and I had wasted an entire morning when I could have been in the Metropolitan Museum. After another hour, I stood up to leave and the clerk, as if he had been waiting to see if I was still alive, said, "Mr. McCrae will see you now."

I was ushered through several offices and a door with gold letters, edged in black that said, "The President." He was a normal-sized man, but Mr. McCrae looked about ten feet tall when he rose to greet me. "Busy" was written all over his face and I was a nervous wreck. I tried, pitifully, I thought, to explain what was on my mind. He continuously moved papers from one stack to another while I was talking to him. I wondered if he was listening to anything I said. Finally, he asked me to read a sketch, which I did—miserably. There was one redeeming fact: I was in a strange city, embarrassing myself in front of a man whom I would never see again. No one need ever know of this little debacle and I certainly would never tell anyone. After I finished the reading, President McCrae said, "Leave the manuscript. I will look it over this weekend. Come back on Monday." His face was expressionless. I couldn't tell if he liked it, hated it, or thought that was the only way he could get this hillbilly who spoke in dialect out of his office. I was in a black gloom.

Monday morning found me back on the El and down to the Lower West Side. At ten o'clock I was sitting humbly in the outer office, the same diffident clerk meticulously stacking papers. After he collected them up, he banged a clip through them and then moved to another batch. I wondered if my little manuscript was among them. Instead of the hour I had waited before, in only fifteen minutes the clerk looked up and, as if seeing me for the first time, ushered me into Mr. McCrae's office. He rose from his chair and gave in greeting what almost appeared to be a smile. I was so disconcerted I had trouble following what he was saying, but the gist of it was I needed to write twelve more Mammy stories before they could go to press. I don't remember any of the details, but in short order I found myself back on the street and walked all the way uptown to Cousin Helen's house. I was exhausted and fell into the nearest chair, weeping.

Crying was not something I did, so Cousin Helen was alarmed. "What did he say?" she asked. "It must have been awful to make you cry so."

Between sobs, I recounted the meeting as best I could. Helen thought a minute, then said, "Well, as best I can understand, he plans to print it. He just wants more stories. Is that right?"

"Well, I suppose so. He told me to get back to him when I had completed my writing. He even said it was as good as Uncle Remus, but then he seemed to take it back."

Helen was overjoyed. "Dutton is going to publish your book! Isn't that wonderful? You must start writing immediately."

When I was finally convinced that things had gone well, I knew she was right. She brought me a pencil and pad, showed me to a desk, and expected me to turn out a story before dark.

"It doesn't work quite like that, Helen. I have to get back home where I can think.

"You can't think here? You're making up all this stuff and you can do it in New York as well as you can down there in the sticks."

I tried to explain, but to no avail. All the parties, the trips to the opera and the museum would have to wait until another time. I had a Pullman reservation by that night and, much to Helen's chagrin, I was off to the "sticks."

When I arrived back at Cockspur, everything else was put aside and Mammy Phyliss began to live again. The work went amazingly fast and in 1911 I was back at Dutton, seeing Mr. McCrae. He held the manuscript in his hands and said he was delighted. He thought it would be a real success. When he handed it to the same clerk I had met the year before, I could tell he was impressed only that he had another sheath of papers to get set in type. *Bypaths in Dixie* was published later that year. It had a handsome blue cover with a rooster silhouetted against a gold background. The reviews were favorable, and to my surprise invitations began to come from colleges throughout the north to appear as a lecturer. The most prestigious came from Columbia University wanting a lecture of southern folklore. I was delighted and started to prepare a talk entitled Moonshiners and Darkies, but my now grown son, Hugh, objected. I was never sure why. He was looking after himself by then, but Lucian agreed that it wouldn't be proper for a "southern lady" to appear in a northern college with such a topic. I declined the invitation because both of them seemed dead set against it, but I thought it a splendid opportunity and I let it slip away from me.

Other chances appeared. *The Saturday Evening Post* published "The Rooster and the Washpot," followed by "Men Fokes' Doins'." Soon I was a regular contributor to *The Post* and was grateful to the dour Mr. McCrae and his sullen sidekick for giving me the opportunity. Cousin Helen should get some of the credit, too. She never did explain why she came up with the Dutton company, but it was a wonderful bit of serendipity. It was almost enough to make a Presbyterian out of me . . . but not quite.

My writing life continued, and the family was able to look after themselves much of the time. While most of the time I found living in Roanoke a delightful climate, the summer was an exception. Although many of the streets had been paved by 1912, the problem with dust was frightful. The winds blowing up from the market carried not only the aroma of food that may have been left too long in the sun, but the air was yellow with dust. As if that wasn't enough, the cinders and smoke from the ceaseless train traffic added to the discomfort. If April and May were dry months, a patina of dirt and ash covered everything like an alien frost.

Fortunately, we had a respite from that. Near Botetourt Springs, just to the northeast of the city, Lucian and his family owned a large farm. It was on this land that Hollins College had been founded, and there were still hundreds of acres in use for the dairy farm, growing crops from which came most of our food, as well as some manufacturing. A brick fabricating plant was there where Hugh and Willis worked in the summer. I often thought it was that hard work that further inspired the boys to more education; they certainly didn't want to do that kind of work for the rest of their lives. As soon as school was out we would move to the farm, but there wasn't adequate housing except at the college, so we stayed in the vacant dormitories. As long as the whole family was there, everything went along fine. We ate in the main dining hall and had the run of the campus as well as the farm. It was much cooler than the city and, thankfully, the nearest train tracks were two miles to the east. It wasn't quite as entertaining when Lucian was away on business and I was left to entertain myself.

In the summer of 1913, we had been settled into Hollins for about a month when Lucian announced one evening that he would be going to Philadelphia for ten days. He was general counsel for the Norfolk and Western, but their alliance with the Pennsylvania Railroad, headquartered in Philadelphia, was close. His trips were frequent, but rarely that lengthy.

As the train pulled out of the Hollins station bound for Hagerstown and on to Philadelphia, I felt a little twinge as I watched the red lanterns disappearing into the distance. I thought I knew myself pretty well, but I was in for a big surprise. The boys were off at their summer job and the girls had interests of their own so I was left to visit with the other ladies who were summering on campus. It wasn't even noon of the first day and I was getting restless. My rocking chair companions on the porch of Main Hall were quite content to sit and rock until time to eat, then rock some more. Not one of them had a single comment of interest to make, nor did they seem to be interested in anything I had to say. I tried everything: life in Vienna, opera in New York, Mother's adventures in Washington as a young lady, growing up in

Atlanta after the Civil War, college affairs—none of it evoked the slightest response beyond, "Oh, really?" or "You don't say." Well, of *course* I say. I had just said it! The short, sad truth was I was bored. Even my writing didn't appeal to me. I could imagine Lucian's return and finding I had turned into a silent matron, rocking aimlessly all day long. If my companions couldn't join in some entertainment, I would just have to do it myself.

Mattie Cocke, Lucian's sister, was president of the college. Her older brother, Charles, had been slated to succeed their father as president, but when he died, the job fell to Mattie. She approached her job with a vigor that was admirable. One of the things in which she most prided herself was attracting young women from the northeast to come to Hollins and absorb some of the gentility of southern culture.

I took a carriage down to the train station and sent a telegram to cousin Helen in New York, asking her to forward the enclosed second telegram to Hollins College, attention Miss Mattie Cocke, President of Hollins. Then I sat back to see what would happen; it didn't take long. That evening at dinner, Mattie came in to the dining hall waving a telegram in her hand.

"Well, ladies, we're going to have a visitor, even though it's summertime. I just got this from New York," she referred to the note in her hand, "from a Mrs. Helmut Simon. She is a recent widow and is considering sending her daughter to Hollins in the fall, but she's coming next Monday to inspect the facilities, as she put it. We must be on our best behavior. I suspect, given the Park Avenue address, she must be of the famous German shipping family. It could be quite a prize for the college."

The table seemed faintly interested, but I told Mattie I was sorry I wouldn't be able to meet her guest as I planned to spend next week at Cockspur doing some gardening. If she was disappointed, she didn't show it.

On Monday, I packed up, went to Cockspur, dressed in my best widow's weeds with a veil so heavy that I could barely see through it, then had the butler drive me to Vinton, just two miles east of Roanoke. When the New York train came through, I got on and rode to the Roanoke station where Mattie had arranged for a carriage to meet Mrs. Simon.

As the train rolled to a stop, steam hissing and cinders settling, I got off and was immediately identified by Samuel, one of the college coach drivers, as his quarry.

"Miz Simon? I'se to take you out to da college. If you step this way I'll have you out there in a jiffy. Did you have a good trip?"

"Zee-mon. Mrs. ZEEmon, dat's de vay ve pronounce my name. Oh, ja! Der trip vas gute. Long und tiresome, but gute." Samuel smiled obligingly and we were off to the college. Mattie was waiting in front of Main Hall when the carriage pulled up to the entrance.

"Oh, Mrs. Simon, we're delighted to have you visit Hollins. I know it will be a place your daughter will be very happy," she said.

"Zee-mon," I corrected and looked sharply—as sharply as I could through my veil—to see if there was any sign of recognition, but she was busy extolling the virtues of the college and then paused to ask if my family was from Germany.

"Nein. From Vienna. My husband died this winter from influenza and I'm left all alone with der Gudrun. I vant to see how she vould live if she comes to these places . . . Hollins, you call it?"

Mattie looked puzzled. "Da Gudrun? That's your daughter's name?"

"Ja, ja. I vanted to call her Brunhilde, but Herr Simon wouldn't hear of it."

That information didn't slow her down, so Mattie was off and running with how the college got started, the money from the Hollins family in Lynchburg, her father's founding the school, and all the famous Virginians who had sent their daughters there. She was having such a wonderful time showing the school off, I almost felt badly that I was putting her through this, but it was really just a theater for me.

"Vo ist der firehaus?" I asked.

Mattie looked puzzled. "The firehouse? Why, it's over in the village. Why do you ask?"

"All der buildings ist of vood made. If you haff a fire . . . Poof . . .

allus ist kaput! My poor little girl, da Gudrun. It makes me very . . .
how do you say . . . nervous?"

Mattie was genuinely distressed. "Oh, that would *never*
happen. We haven't had a fire here since year before last."

"You haf already had a fire? Und der firehouse is vay off in der
village?" I shook my head.

The tour concluded with dinner served in the dining room,
with candles blazing everywhere. I commented on how close
they were to the draperies and Mattie was quick to have them
moved, but I told her I would have to have my meals served in
my room. I hadn't figured on having to eat with my veil in
place.

As I was leaving, I said,"Of course, if der vas a fire, den you
could collect lots of insurance money. My late husband, der Helmut,
vas insurance person. He said many times, colleges burn down to
get der insurance. Do you haff insurance, Miss Mattie?"

"Of course, we do, but I really don't understand your
preoccupation with fire, Mrs. Simon—Frau Simon," she corrected
herself.

After dinner, I went back to the main salon to fetch my shawl.
As I was rounding the corner to retrieve it, I could hear Mattie
talking to the other ladies in the dining room.

"That woman is crazy as a bed bug," Mattie was saying. "All
she thinks about is fire. I wonder if someone didn't send her here
to burn the place down. I can tell you one thing: When she gets in
her room, I'm going to have Samuel lock her in and sit on the
porch all night. If she comes out of there, I'm going to call the fire
department."

I was so amazed and amused at my success that I didn't dare
go back in the dining room. I knew I would break out in laughter.
I probably should have whipped off my veil and exposed the whole
ruse, but I held my tongue. Sure enough, I heard the key turn in
the outside lock and I could see Samuel sitting on the porch in a
rocking chair. It occurred to me, if there were a fire, maybe I couldn't
get out. It would serve me right!

The next morning, Mattie asked me if I had rested well.

"Der bugs in der bed. They haff made me crazy! Haff your horse man take me to der bahnhoff, bitte."

By that time Mattie was more than happy to have Samuel deliver me back to the station. I caught the next train headed east, got off in Vinton, rode home, changed clothes and went back to Hollins.

Mattie met me at the gate. "Sallie! You won't believe what happened while you were gone." She recounted the whole visit in great detail, to which I listened patiently, then said, "It takes all kinds, I suppose."

"Well, that kind should stay in Austria with all the other crazy Huns."

Several weeks later, I told Mattie that I was the "crazy Hun." She held her hand to her mouth in surprise, then said, "I should have expected as much! You should have been an actress, Sallie. There's no telling what might have happened to you with a life upon the wicked stage," then she hugged me.

Not far from the campus was Kerncliff, the summer home of Senator John W. Kern of Indiana. All through the Allegheny mountains were many summer homes of senators and congressman, so there was a summer parade of distinguished folks visiting the area. Frequently we were guests at Kerncliff and spent many pleasant evenings in distinguished company, but the best time we ever had was in May of 1914 when Vice President Thomas Marshall and his wife came to visit. A reception was to be held at Kerncliff and there was much stir about the vice president being the guest of honor. I'm not sure what brought it to mind, but I suspect it was all the pomp and circumstance that was being built into the occasion. I had met Vice President and Mrs. Marshall on visits to Washington, and I had been struck by the sense of humor he had. He always enjoyed a joke, even when it was on himself. I remembered a similar high-toned reception about which my mother had told me when she was hostess for my uncle, Governor Cobb: The lawn party had been crashed by a bunch of Georgia crackers. A similar event could easily happen at Kerncliff, I decided, given its location at the foot of Tinker Mountain, the home of numerous real, live hillbillies. I decided I couldn't leave their appearance at the reception to chance, so I enlisted the help of my good friend, Joe Turner, the college treasurer. On the afternoon of the tea, we rode down the mountainside on a borrowed mule. We had blacked out several teeth and were dressed in overalls and straw hats.

As we rode into the yard, the tea and wafers were just being served. Vice President and Mrs. Marshall looked at us with interest. Most of the guests had a look of alarm. After I got down from the mule and walked over to the vice president. I could see the guests getting edgy.

"Ma' man and me jes' come down from the mountain to get a look at ye. We heer'd there wuz vittles and wanted to git some for the chillun."

The Vice President smiled. "I'm delighted to meet you, but I didn't catch your name."

"My name's Lizzie and this here is Lem, my present husband."

"Well, we're glad that you came down. I'm certain that Senator Kern will be happy to have a basket of food packed for you."

As we were waiting, I said, "I've been a'wonderin'—what does a vice president do?"

Several guests looked shocked, but Vice President Marshall threw back his head and laughed. "You know, madam, if I knew the answer to that I would surely be glad to tell you!"

I took off my straw hat, wiped the charcoal from my teeth and immediately everyone recognized who we were. Laughter filled the yard as the "basket of vittles" appeared.

"Well, one thing we can all say," Senator Kern said, "When Sallie Cocke is on the loose, even a vice president may get a surprise or two."

The following afternoon we had a reception for the vice president and his wife at Cockspur. Men from the Vice President's entourage decorated the house with red, white and blue bunting, hanging from every gable. The police patrolled the neighborhood in an open-air Maxwell in an effort to keep the children from running through the yard and disrupting what was supposed to be a formal occasion. The newspaper carried a long article the next day, giving much more importance to the social standing of the people in attendance than to the truly democratic nature of the crowd.

As Vice President and Mrs. Marshall left, being escorted by the police car with four officers in attendance, he said he would look forward to his next visit from his favorite hillbillies.

If it were hillbillies he was interested in I could have shown him a few real ones right in the neighborhood. Moonshiners, particularly over Bent Mountain and into Franklin county, would have given him more than he would ever have wanted to see. Despite all the distilleries in town, moonshining was a vigorous business. Much of the mountainous rocky terrain wasn't suitable for farming, but there was an abundance of cold, fast-flowing streams, a necessity for a good moonshining operation. From time to time there would be shootings and assorted violence around the stills, usually involving the revenue service, but sometimes between the families who operated the stills. I had been curious about the way they lived, in such stark contrast to the life our family enjoyed, but there was no way to really get to know any of them. It seemed an ideal subject for a novel, but getting the facts was something I had not been able to do.

Then a letter from my cousin, Lamar Rutherford Lipscomb, arrived. They were still living in Washington where Mammy Sophy and I had visited them, but their Georgia roots had called them home—at least for the summertime. Lamar and her husband had built a mountain home in North Georgia, not too far from Mt. Airy where we had shared so much as young women. "Come for a visit, Sallie," she had written. "The setting is perfect for a book about moonshining." How she had known that I was thinking about just such a project was a mystery, but we had always had a sixth sense about each other. "We are entirely surrounded by moonshiners and their families. You'll be amazed at what nice people they are!"

Well, I *was* amazed—amazed that Lamar, the most prim and proper of Washington matrons, was consorting with criminals, but as when we were children, Lamar suggestions for an adventure were hard to resist, so shortly after Easter in 1915, I was off to Georgia and the whiskey-makers.

In my years in Georgia, I had picked up the lore of the land. As the train was leaving Chattanooga and crossing Moccasin Bend into the mountains, I could see the flowers of spring beginning to bud. I remembered the old Indian story of the naming of the state flower. These woods had been the home of the Cherokee before the settlers came, and to the south, the Seminoles ruled. The two tribes were bitter enemies, although occasionally they would come together peacefully. As the legend goes, a Seminole warrior was gravely wounded while fighting in Georgia. He was captured by the Cherokee who routinely burned their enemies at the stake. In a rare gesture of humanity they would not burn an injured or ill prisoner—not until he was well. I doubt that it was really concern for the prisoner's welfare, but more that they wanted to make sure the death was fully protracted. In this particular case, the chief's daughter looked after the injured Seminole and as happens, they fell in love. They ran away together, to the land of the Seminole, but the girl took a sprig of the plant growing by her father's tepee. She wanted to plant it in her new homeland. In the sunny land of the south Georgia Seminole, it grew and spread wildly among the jasmine and magnolia. It became known as the Cherokee rose. I hadn't seen that flower in many years, and looking at its blossoms along the track side, I knew I was coming back into a land where my roots still lived.

Lamar met me at the station, and it seemed as though we had never been apart. I was surprised there was no carriage to take us to their home, and as we trudged up the mountainside, dragging my luggage along with us, I was impressed with the wildness of the surroundings. The Lipscomb house in Georgetown was the picture of hospitality, and I had assumed the mountain lodge would be similar. As we rounded the last bend, I stopped in my tracks when I saw the rustic structure she had referred to as "The Lodge." It was little more than a shack.

"You stay out here in the sticks in *that* place?" I asked.

"Of course. The nights are cool, but never too cold to be comfortable with fire and blankets. Couldn't stay here in the winter, though," she said, starting up the final hill.

"I couldn't stay here in the summer, Lamar! What about the moonshiners? They must be all over the place." In the valleys I could see wisps of smoke trailing up above the poplar and oak. I knew they were fires from the stills. Whenever I stood still I could hear the sound of rushing water in the distance. "They might come up here and slit our throats."

"Don't be ridiculous, Sallie. These people wouldn't hurt a fly."

"Well, I know that's not true, at least not in Franklin County back home. They would just as soon put a bullet between your eyes as spit. I'm not staying up here without protection. I thought your husband was here."

"Oh, he was, but he went over to Athens to attend to some business. He'll be back in a few days."

In a few days we might both be dead, I thought, but there was no choice. In the little town at the foot of the mountain there hadn't been a sign of a hotel.

"The moonshiners are gentle as lambs, Sallie, particularly when it comes to women. Most of them are a lot less suspicious of you than you are of them, once they get to know you. They're a lot safer than many of the 'gentlemen' we might encounter in Georgetown."

She picked up a handful of the soil. "Look at this dirt. It's mostly clay and sitting right on top of granite. You can't grow a thing up here except the scraggly corn we've been passing on the trail. That's what they use for the whiskey, and from the money they get they can buy food and clothes for their families. When you see how they live and what nice people they are, t you'll want to help them like I do."

"As you do? What do you do to help them, Lamar? Buy their whiskey? Aren't you afraid it will make you sick? I've heard of people at home going blind after they drink the stuff."

"No, I don't buy their whiskey, but I try to help the children learn to read and write. Most of them have never seen a book, and the women don't know much about cooking. They can weave, but they don't have the things they need to really make clothes. You'd be amazed how excited they get over the needles and thread I bring them, to say nothing of the cloth. It's wonderful fun. You're going to love it, and I'll bet you write a wonderful book about them."

She stopped for a minute and looked back down the trail. An old man and a boy were bringing the rest of my luggage. "There's Mr. Phillips and his grandson. Let's wait for them. I want you to meet them."

Shortly they came across the field toward us. There was a ghostly, unreal quality about them. Although they were walking on stubble, they made no sound. Mr. Phillips was tall and angular, his skin as tanned and tough looking as whit leather, but he had a full head of wavy, white hair. His eyes were deep set and looked as though they had seen things I couldn't imagine. The clothes they both wore were tattered and dirty. Mr. Phillips, if you cleaned up and put good clothes on him, would have looked like a tent evangelist . . . or a senator. I thought about Vice President Marshall and wished he were there to see what a real hillbilly looked like. The boy, who appeared to be about sixteen, was a young copy of his grandfather. There was a grim determination about the pair of them that was unsettling.

"This is Miss Sallie, Mr. Phillips, and this is Bob, Sallie. Bob is my right-hand friend."

Mr. Phillips looked steadily at me, then said, "I'm glad to know ye, Miss Sallie. Miss Laymar's been tellin' we'uns about ye."

Bob picked up the rest of the luggage and took it into the house. Lamar invited them to "sit a spell" on the porch, but Mr. Phillips sat down on a stump.

"I'm from Virginia but I used to spend summers at Mt. Airy. I never had a chance to meet any of the local folks, except those who worked in town, so I've been looking forward to getting to know some of you."

He wasn't one to respond quickly, but after thinking it over, he replied, "I'll tell ye, Miss Sallie, most don't take no count of us

folks up here. Perticklerly, the guv'mint. They don' take no notice
of how poor the land is and how much trubble we have tryin' to
farm it. The corn is so scrubby we can't sell it, and we're 'bliged to
make likker out of it to feed our folks. Our folks is 'bliged to eat
and we're gwina feed'um if we haf to kill ever revenoor in Georgia."
His voice was quiet, but filled with emotion.

He was quiet for a minute, but he could tell I was interested,
so he continued. "I'm gwina tell you sumthin' that'll show you
how low down them revenoors is." His voice got softer still, but it
was so full of hate it was chilling. "Right up yonder at the top of
the hill they kilt my son at his still. He warn't doin' nuthin' but
drawin' off the juice. When he didn' come home that night, his
wife took their baby and went up thar to git him and they shot
her, too. Like a pair of dogs, they shot'em dead. When I didn' see
no lamps in their house, I went alookin' for'em and I found'em
both stone dead, lettle Bob here a'cryin' and a'crawlin' acrost his
ma's breast lookin' for sumthin' to eat. Do ye blame me for killin'
ever one of'em I can find?"

I was speechless. That explained the look in their eyes. They
*had* seen things that I couldn't imagine. I thought of my children
when they were small, the six of them, romping through the hillsides
and down to the river. There was always motherly concern for
them, but never the thought of danger like that Mr. Phillips and
his grandson Bob had lived with for generations.

The plot of a book began to form in my mind during that
visit, and when I returned to Virginia, I began to write but soon
realized that I had nowhere near the amount of detail I needed to
make the story believable. One evening in the summer Lucian and
I were sitting on the veranda and I told him I was having trouble
weaving it together. I needed more information than I had. Lucian
had always been supportive of my writing, and this time he was
particularly so.

"It sounds as though you may be on to a good story and it
would be a shame to let it drop. Why don't we all go back there
and you can spend as much time as you like. We can take my
railroad car and Hugh can go with us. It will be good vacation for

him before he starts his internship. We can live in the car and you can do all the research you like."

It was a wonderful idea. The private car the Norfolk and Western had assigned to Lucian was like a home on wheels. It was finished in mahogany paneling with blue velvet seats. It was equipped with its galley and staff with enough food on board to last a week or more. We had traveled many places on the car, particularly when the children were small, but never to the wilds of north Georgia.

Mr. Phillips, Miles was his first name, lived within sight of the tracks, and when the old locomotive that had brought us up from the mainline pushed the car on to the siding, Miles and Bob were standing in the brush watching.

"Mr. Phillips, I want you to meet my family," I called to him. They moved out of the woods and were surprisingly friendly. In my previous visit Miles and I had become friends, although Bob had little to say to anyone. Given what he had been through, that was easy to understand.

We invited them for dinner, and I am sure it was the first time they had ever been in a railroad car, to say nothing of the private car of a company official. We talked about the mountains and about the way the stills were operated. I told Miles that I really wanted to see one. I could tell he was turning over in his mind whether this was a safe proposition, and after a few quiet words with Bob, he said that he would take me up the mountain, but that he wanted one of the family members to go with us. He looked the group over. Lucian, in his starched collar, probably didn't look like the type for an adventure like this. He pointed to Hugh Hagan. "You look like a strong young'un. You come with us." Hugh was not a "young'un" but a grown man. He may have been the youngest doctor Miles had ever seen, I suspected.

We left early the next morning. I could tell Lucian was having second thoughts about the whole thing. He'd been many places in the world. He was first-name friends with a number of Presidents, but he had never seen anyone like Miles Phillips. We left in a small canoe and were soon deep in the forest as we paddled upstream. Eventually we pulled into shore and Miles hid the canoe under branches and leaves a hundred feet or more from the river's edge. We then began walking up the mountainside. He constantly broke off twigs and left them behind.

"Why are you doing that? Won't we be able to find our way back?" Hugh ask him.

"I could walk outta here with my eyes shut. I leave those twigs so if'n somethin' happens to us, Bob'll be able to find us."

As we rounded a little knoll there was a waterfall tumbling off a precipice. Miles held out his hand to stop me.

"What is it?" I asked, a little more edgy than I was willing to admit.

"Jes' stand real still," he s said, bending with his knees only to pick up a rock, his eyes fixed on something I couldn't see. Before I had time to worry about it he had hurled a rock so fast I didn't see it hit the rattlesnake coiled just beside the path. Miles took my hand and led me by the dead snake and across big rocks to the other side of the branch. After that, I imagined there were snakes under every rock

The climb was almost vertical. I had a difficult time holding on to Hugh's hand and trying to pull myself up the face of the mountain. Miles was walking ahead with the ease of a fly climbing a wall. He turned and looked at my struggling.

"Cain't ye make it?" he whispered. I noticed that he hadn't spoken a word out loud since we left the river. "Ye'll jes' have to set in ye boy's hands and let him poosh ye up."

I've never stood too much on my dignity, but I thought if my Roanoke lady friends could see the fix I had gotten myself into, I would never hear the end of it. "Hugh, if you ever tell a soul about this, I'll never forgive you," I hissed. He laughed because he wasn't doing a whole lot better than I was.

After about an hour of this, Miles stopped and I thought to myself, "Well, finally he's gotten tired," but that wasn't it at all. He was listening. You could see him straining to hear every noise in the woods, and when he heard something that he didn't recognize, he turned his full attention to it until he was satisfied he knew what had caused the sound. I was grateful for the rest and so was Hugh, exhausted from having pushed his mother halfway up the side of this seemingly interminable mountain. Eventually he turned to face a series of branches and vines falling down the mountainside and carefully held them aside. It concealed a cove which contained the still. The copper coils were barely visible in the dim light, an orange snake serpentining under a little waterfall.

"Tain't been long since we started usin' this here still agin. The revenoors don' forgot about it and they think don nobody use it." He paused. "The smoke goes up through them trees and hit's so high up, it spreads out in the wind 'fore anybody can see hit. Right where you is standin' is where they kilt my son. Down the path yonder is where they shot Bob's ma and I found the pair of em, his dead ma and the young'un 'bout to fall off the side of the mountain. If'n the revenoors hada still been here, wouldn' none of em have left here with his head on his body." He touched the knife stuck through his belt.

As I stood there looking at him, thinking about what he had been through to even get to the place, what he had lived through, I was overcome with the resolute strength of Miles Phillips. He had killed because people he loved had been killed. He was looking after his family the best way he knew how. That people in the world down below couldn't understand it, that they ridiculed the mountain folk hurt me in a way I couldn't explain, but I knew it would give me the inspiration to write about it. The Master of the Hills . . . that was who was standing in that dim light where his family had been killed. That was what I would call the book.

When we returned to Roanoke, I began to re-write the book and the words fairly flew from my fingers. Dutton was quick to publish what I was sure would be a best seller. When it was released in 1917, it received excellent reviews, but no one was interested in reading anything. The United States had entered the war. My two sons were enlisted; Hugh became a captain in the Medical Corps and Willis as a Regular Army Lieutenant. Lucian, Jr., and Francis were officers in Army Aviation. I wondered if Miles Phillips and his friends even knew there was a war They had been fighting a war all their lives and now we all lived with fear we might suffer as great a loss as had the mountain people.

# CHAPTER XI

## Epilogue

With the children grown and with families of their own, it gave me a time to look back over my life. How varied it has been. How exciting. I would never have dreamed that I would live through such times; times of great happiness and some of great sadness, too. Looking back, I realize that my life as a woman was different from that of many. I had opportunities that I took for granted, particularly when I was young, but I came to realize their presence in my life had been a gift by accident of birth. My parents, particularly my father, always encouraged me to do what ever I felt I could do. I grew up encouraged not to believe in limits, but in my ability to accomplish.

I was sitting on the veranda of Cockespur many years after the excitement of my life had given way to the comfortableness of old age. The wisteria was in full bloom, and in the early summer air the perfume of the flowers was heavy. To the west, I could hear the rumble of thunder coming from clouds rolling in from the mountains. To the east, the sun was still shining brightly, but the wind was picking up, blowing the oak leaves and showing their silver undersides. I thought how much the scene capsulized my life with all of it's changes.

One of my most difficult times came in 1928. It had been a turbulent decade after the war. Prohibition had certainly been a boon to the Miles Phillips of the world. Prosperity was at every hand and there seemed no end to the good times. Lucian had retired from the railroad and we were looking forward to old age together.

One afternoon, Lucian came in from working in his roses, holding his thumb. He had broken a thorn off in the tip of it. He had tried pulling it out with tweezers, but a small shard remained embedded. We thought no more of it but in several days, it was apparent that infection had set in. The thumb was swollen and quite painful. Hugh, who had a large medical practice just down the street, looked at it and I could see the alarm in his eyes. He prescribed soaks with Epsom salts, some cod liver paste called Icthyol, and drained some of the pus from it. For a day it looked better, but then the swelling returned and there was no further drainage. We continued the warm salt baths constantly, but nothing seemed to help. I will never forget changing the dressing on the tenth day and seeing the red streaks—a pair of them—coursing up his the base of his hand and toward the arm like faint, red snakes. Blood poisoning! I called Hugh immediately and he confirmed my suspicions. By late afternoon the chills had started which Hugh told me was a sign the germs had spread all through his bloodstream. We spent the next several days alternately trying to cool Lucian from the burning fever and warming him during the bone-rattling chills. His mind began to drift, and by the next morning he was unable to take fluids. The children had assembled, along with the grandchildren, and a pall lay over the house as the end came swiftly.

The day after his death, I could barely take in how fast it had happened. One day, a vigorous man of 70, a minor injury promptly attended to, then an inexorable slide to death. It taught me a lesson I already knew, but needed reinforcing: Life is precious, and it is tenuous. Each day should never be taken for granted and should be celebrated. Our lives together had been wonderful. Hugh and Willis had accepted Lucian as their father and he, them as his sons. The children of the two families remained close all through their growing-up years and into adulthood—they still remain the best of friends. Having them about me after Lucian's death was a

wonderful comfort. I don't know what I would have done without
them.

And this afternoon, a storm on the way, with grandchildren
scampering through Cockespur so much of my life seemed close at
hand. I never intended to be an elderly grandmother, the matriarch
of a large clan. The picture of a bespectacled old lady sitting in her
rocking chair, with a cap on her head, did not fit the image I had
of myself. "Grandma" was not the person that I was becoming. I'm
not sure where the name originated—probably from one of the
older grandchildren, but it suited me just fine: Ma-MA, with the
emphasis on the last syllable. Soon, that had replaced "Sallie" with
every one of my friends, except the servants who still called me
"Miz Sarah," when addressing me, but when talking to the
grandchildren, I was "yo gran'ma."

The children, on the other hand, came up with some
appellations of their own which I was forced to correct. One
afternoon, I was reading a story to little Bobby and his cousin,
Sarah, in which an old hag was prominently mentioned.

"What's a 'hag,' Ma-ma?" Bobby asked.

"Oh, hush, Bobby," Sarah interrupted. "A hag is an old woman
like Ma-ma. Please go on with the story."

I did but not until we had a little discussion about the difference
between their grandmother and an "old hag"!

Despite the fullness of my past life and the joy of my family,
after Lucian's death I found myself fighting the loneliness of old
age. Cockespur seemed cheerless and dark. Years before, it had
been the scene of so much gaiety, bunting draped from every corner
with nationally important guests visiting and wonderful parties in
the gardens for the children, for our friends. I could imagine myself
slipping back into the dark shadows of this place, living on memories
that fewer and fewer people could share. It was an unhappy thought,
one which my pride would not let me entertain for long. I was 67
and I had a legacy I wanted to pass on to the children of my
children's children. I wasn't seeking anything for myself, but to be
sure they were instilled with the same sense of civic pride and
duty, the zest for life that my forebears had bequeathed to me.

Through the years I had kept a diary, a memoir of sorts. Maybe I should re-write that. There was so much that I hadn't included; so many stories that really served to illustrate a point. I could spend the rest of my life putting all of that down, but who would read it? Despite the things I had published, I wasn't sure who, beyond the family, would find the story as compelling as the living of it had been. As I was thinking over the possibility, little Billy Hagan, the youngest son of my son, Hugh, came scampering onto the veranda. Mammy Singleton was huffing along behind him.

"Make a bow, Billy, and tell yo' gran'ma 'Good mawnin'.'"

"Hello, Ma-ma," he called out, but not slowing in his pursuit of the cat that had jumped through the railing and into the flower bed. Mammy slowly lowered her rheumatism-ridden body on to the porch steps.

"D'clare, Miz Sarah, chilluns ain't what dey wuz when we wuz young."

"We're living in a new era, Mammy."

"You sho' is right. Eben 'ligion is done got new-fangled."

"Well, not exactly. The fundamentals of faith are still the same."

"Don' know 'bout no funnymentals but de preacher say last night he think da mules don' got 'ligion."

"Mules?"

"Yas'm. Dat whut he say. He say eber since Balaam's mule don' whut da Lawd say, mules is had long faces."

"But, Mammy, having a long face doesn't mean you have religion."

"Yas'm, but da preacher say it's de long face dat's got de good ole 'ligion dat Possul Paul preach 'bout."

"Then I must be the biggest sinner in the world because I always try to have a smile."

"No'm, Miz Sarah. Me and da Lawd, we bofe knows yo' heart is a'cryin' a heap a times when yo' face is smilin'."

She was right about that. I wasn't sure I liked been compared to a misunderstood mule, but I knew what she meant.

Billy and the cat tore through the flowers, petals flying everywhere. Mammy and I both jumped up to catch the cat before they did more damage.

"Ain' you sham'd on yo'self actin' like pig chillun." She lifted Billy out of the flowers, "Trompin' on yo gran'ma's putty flowers."

"Well, the cat jumped in them first," Billy complained.

"Does you hafta do whut da cat and da pig chillun does? I gwina tell yo' Ma."

I thought back to how many times I had heard Mammy Sophy say that, long after I was a grown woman. The Mammies were always quick to invoke ultimate authority when they thought it was needed. I picked up Billy and was starting to explain to him about not tearing up the garden, but he gave me a little kiss on the cheek and promised he wouldn't do it again.

"Ma-ma, can I go play on your piano?"

"No, siree, you ain' gwina go bang on Miz Sarah's piano."

"Oh, hush, Mammy. I'm talking to Ma-ma. I just want to play a piece I heard on the radio. I promise I'll play real soft."

What grandmother could refuse? But I reminded him he was supposed to always obey Mammy and not fuss with her. After a few minutes, she brought him back to the porch just as the postman brought the morning mail.

The first letter was from Mary Roach Colburn, a childhood friend from Atlanta. What made it particularly interesting was the ruminations I had been going through about my writing.

> Dear Little Sallie:
>
> I hear that you are writing your memoirs. Are you picturing yourself as others see you, or is it the portrait of a perfect woman? Fearing the latter, I have jotted down my first recollection of you and suggest that you include it in your manuscript, perhaps as a postscript that your descendants may not be discouraged when they fall short of your perfection. Here it is—and be sure that you report it accurately!
>
> Sallie Johnson, as I remember her at age five, was a pretty, bright-eyed, rosy-cheeked, plump little girl. Being full of fun, everybody loved her and she loved to be seen as well as heard. Her sense of humor was wonderful and she

loved to show off. Whenever an opportunity to act appeared, she would be the first one on the stage, but one instance stands out in my mind.

She had just finished her music lesson and I was sitting in the teacher's room waiting for mine. As soon as the teacher turned her back, the little imp walked up to me. I can see her now with her bonnet pushed back on her head, a long-sleeved linen apron tied around her with a sash. White stockings and slippers. Finding me alone, she decided that entertainment was in order. She climbed to the piano stool and commenced with a bang. I never saw such airs and such sounds had never come from that piano. She picked up the teacher's ruler and scraped it up and down the keyboard with a vengeance. Hearing the teacher coming back down the hall, she jumped down and said, "See how well I can play? Would you like me to teach you?"

I did remember the incident and I'm sure that I was a brash little girl. I thought back to my childhood and even with all the difficulties we faced in Atlanta after the war, we faced life with a sense of excitement and assurance. Many of my friends, who had seemed immune to misfortune, now trailed along in deep ruts of so many things gone wrong. Others seemed to have escaped and their lives had remained filled with joy. There were a lot in between who just seemed to plod along, but most were heroes in my eyes, particularly those who had overcome much.

I thought about where I belonged in the scheme of all that I have seen and all that has happened. Of one thing, I am certain: I could not have endured all the things that have happened to me had it not been for the constant reminders of my father: "Sallie, you can do anything!" That sense of confidence, instilled at such an early age, had its limits, as my piano-playing as a child had showed. But on balance, it had led me through a life that I have found eminently satisfying.

A second letter was a remarkable counterpoint to Mary Roach's. It was an invitation to fly to Richmond for a luncheon and play bridge while en route. My first inclination was to refuse. Airplanes were something we enjoyed watching at carnivals, but to get on one and play cards? That seemed a little too extreme. But I thought of my father: "Sallie, you can do anything!" so I believe I will say "Yes."

Changes, changes! What next? From the hoopskirt of our mothers to the trousers of my hostess on an airplane. Everything changes, save life—life with its smiles and tears. We take to the sky in airplanes, we speed across the country in our cars, and the one-horse shay sits idly in the carriage house. Yet how glorious it all is. Even in the dim light of tears there are loving hands to guide. Old Stanton, our gardener for so many years, is right:

> This old world we're living in
> is mighty hard to beat.
> We find a thorn with every rose,
> But ain't the roses sweet?

## *FINIS.*